D0368950

the House of Zondervan

James E. Ruark

ZONDERVAN®

GRAND RAPIDS, MICHIGAN 49530 USA

ZONDERVAN.COM/
AUTHORTRACKER

ZONDERVAN®

The House of Zondervan
Copyright © 1981, 2006 by the Zondervan Corporation

Requests for information should be addressed to:
Zondervan, *Grand Rapids, Michigan 49530*

Library of Congress Cataloging-in-Publication Data

Ruark, James E., 1941–
    The house of Zondervan : celebrating 75 years / James E. Ruark.—[Rev. ed.]
      p. cm.
    Includes bibliographical references and index.
    ISBN-13: 978-0-310-27150-5
    ISBN-10: 0-310-27150-9
    1. Zondervan Corporation—History. 2. Publishers and publishing—Michigan—
History. 3. Christian literature—Publishing—Michigan. I. Title.
    Z473.Z65R8   2006
    070.509774—dc22

                                                    2006011835

This edition printed on acid-free paper.

Interior design by Beth Shagene

Printed in the United States of America

06 07 08 09 10 11 12 • 22 21 20 19 18 17 16 15 14 13 12 11 10 9 8 7 6 5 4 3 2 1

Contents

Foreword

As you read *The House of Zondervan*, you will celebrate a company that has grown, accepted risk, reinvented itself, and lived through difficult days. You may encounter old friends, remember long-forgotten stories, and learn things about Zondervan you never knew. For seventy-five years, Zondervan's mission has been the same, though only recently formulated into these words: "To be the leading Christian communications company meeting the needs of people with resources that glorify Jesus Christ and promote biblical principles."

The House of Zondervan is about the people of Zondervan. First and foremost are Pat and Bernie Zondervan. But the story is also about the many who responded to their leadership and committed their work lives to spreading the gospel via Christian products. Through the years, it has been the people who, every day, ship products out of the warehouse, acquire and edit new content, develop and market new types of products, and find ways to connect authors with readers. In talking with Zondervan retirees as well as those working in the building today, it is clear that the Zondervan team has been, and continues to be, made up of people committed to serving God with their best efforts.

The pages that follow contain much history. Like many companies, growth has come through taking risks and anticipating needs. Committing significant personal and company finances to ensure the completion of the New International Version (NIV) is an example of Zondervan sensing a need and committing the necessary resources. As a result, over the last two decades, the NIV has been, and remains, the Bible translation used by more churches, pastors, and consumers than any other.

Today many major new opportunities for growth and ministry exist. The Internet has opened the door to informing loyal readers of new products in ways never before imagined. Delivery of content via computer and other electronic devices has become the norm and an expectation. The borders of developing and newly developed countries daily present unique and important chances to place Christian products in the hands of millions of people.

We must work diligently to remain relevant in today's culture. In responding to the changes in the English language over the past thirty years, Zondervan launched in the United States the TNIV, Today's New International Version, to reach the eighteen-to-thirty-four-year-old age group. New formats such as short videos and MP3 audio downloads are examples of new products that have been acquired and developed to insure that Zondervan continues to meet the needs of people.

Zondervan is unique in its ability to balance both business and mission. While we view business growth as an opportunity, we look at reaching more people as our responsibility. The combination of the two will carry us forward as we begin to dream about what our organization will look like twenty-five years from now when we celebrate a full century of engaging more people with Jesus.

DOUG LOCKHART
President and CEO
Zondervan
March 2006

Prologue

Before the Dutch came to Western Michigan, there were French traders. And before the French traders, there were Catholic missionaries. And before the Catholic missionaries, there were Ottawa Indians. It is said that Pontiac, the great chief of the Ottawa who conspired against the English in the French and Indian War, held council on the high land overlooking the rapids of a river that wound through Western Michigan toward its mouth at Lake Michigan. Major Indian trails crisscrossed near the rapids. The Ottawa called the place *Owashtanong*, "the Faraway Waters." But the white people who came later gave it the name Grand Rapids.

The Reverend Isaac McCoy was among the first white settlers who came to the area of the rapids—in about 1820. Overlooking the rapids of the Grand River one day in 1825, he wrote that it was "a place of great importance." Why he called it such is uncertain—except that it was beautiful, fertile, inviting, and full of promise. The first permanent settlement began when Louis Campau established a trading post there in 1826. Grand Rapids was incorporated as a village in 1838 and as a city twelve years after that. And by that time the Dutch had arrived.

9

Immigrants from the Netherlands made their first landing on the Lake Michigan shore in 1847. The group, led by Dr. Albertus Van Raalte, called the place Holland. From Holland it was only a short distance to Grand Rapids, and some of the Dutch settlers soon ventured the journey and made their home there. Later came Poles, Scandinavians, Latvians, Lithuanians, blacks, Greeks, and Syrians, among others. But it was the Dutch who exerted the most lasting influence on Grand Rapids' culture, lifestyle, and reputation.

The city's location, well off the main commercial routes and rail lines running between Detroit and Chicago, might have undermined the Reverend Mr. McCoy's prediction, but it did not. Grand Rapids' population eventually grew to 200,000 and became the biggest and most important commercial city in all of Western Michigan. It came to enjoy a varied industry—farming, metal-working, printing and graphic arts, and the manufacture of automobile parts. It was once "the gypsum capital of the world" because of the mining operations that still continue on a small scale. And it is forever nicknamed the Furniture City, even though, as historians point out, "that fame came to rest more on quality than on quantity."[1]

Grand Rapids can also rightfully be called "the religious-book capital of the United States." Five of evangelical Christianity's most respected book publishers are located here, listing as many as four hundred new titles a year. They all have their roots in the Dutch heritage that set the tone for many communities in Western Michigan—Calvinistic, pious, conservative. Grand Rapids became a city of churches—more than five hundred of them at last count. It became the headquarters of the Christian Reformed Church and the home of its two leading educational institutions, Calvin College and Calvin Theological Seminary. And it nurtured three other Protestant colleges, two Protestant seminaries, and a Catholic college.

The Dutch immigrants brought with them traditions of strict observance of the Lord's Day and opposition to such "worldly" practices as dancing, playing cards, and attending movies. More important, they brought an earnest love for the Scriptures and a fondness for theological debate and Bible study. The ministers preached their catechism from the pulpit on Sunday, and the communicants discussed them in the fields or over a pipe of tobacco and a cup of coffee during the week. Thus there was a demand for theological commentaries and reference works. Early on, books were imported from the Netherlands and translated into English—or left in Dutch for the many who preferred to use their native tongue. It seems inevitable that a vigorous religious publishing industry would arise in Grand Rapids.

Louis Kregel began it all when he started selling used books from his home on West Leonard Street in 1909. Under the leadership of his son Robert, the business grew into one of the country's largest dealerships in secondhand religious books. Eventually it began publishing older theological works under the name Kregel Publications. And in time it spawned a competitor: Louis Kregel's nephew, Herman Baker, decided to quit working for his uncle in 1939 and founded the Baker Book House. But that gets ahead of the story. Two other firms were to appear before Baker.

William B. Eerdmans had emigrated from the Netherlands in 1902, intent on entering the ministry. He graduated from Calvin College and completed one year of study at the seminary before going into business selling books with B. Sevensma. The company was called Eerdmans-Sevensma. Sevensma died shortly thereafter, and Eerdmans went into business for himself in 1911; he moved his firm to 208 Pearl Street and named it the William B. Eerdmans Publishing Company. Unlike Kregel, Eerdmans soon built his list as much on new titles as on reprints. Later on, as he expanded his printing facilities, he moved his business to its present location at 255 Jefferson Avenue SE. Both Kregel and Eerdmans prospered as World War I came and went, the Roaring Twenties had their fling, and the country sank into the Great Depression in 1929.

■   ■   ■

Like every other American city, Grand Rapids faced severe unemployment and economic problems as the Depression deepened. The city had maintained a reputation for clean government and clean streets, despite some noteworthy scandals, but seeking solutions to the Depression's ills brought its share of controversy.

The city manager appointed for Grand Rapids just before the Depression hit was George W. Welsh, a future mayor whose stormy political career would span more than a half-century. His major contribution to the city while he was mayor was probably bringing water from Lake Michigan to Grand Rapids through a costly but successful program in the late thirties. It was a somewhat similar plan put forth by City Attorney Lant K. Salsbury in the early 1900s that had precipitated the biggest scandal in Grand Rapids' history. Salsbury's scheme was to issue far more bonds than were needed for financing the water project and to use the excess to fill some pockets. Before the scandal ran its course, it touched the mayor; fourteen aldermen; the city clerk; a state senator; a former prosecutor; leaders in society, church, and business; the three city newspapers; and a few people in New York, Chicago, Milwaukee, Indianapolis, and Omaha.

But that was all in the past and forgotten with the onset of the Depression. Manager Welsh's job in 1929 and the years following was to see that people had something to eat, put business back on its feet, and restore order out of fiscal chaos. Refusing a $12,000 salary and accepting only a dollar a year for the job, Welsh effected economies that turned a city deficit into a surplus of $174,000 in less than a year. A national magazine, *The American City*, praised Grand Rapids a short time later as "a city where everyone has a job." Welsh was invited to various cities, including New York, Cleveland, and Pittsburgh, to tell the Grand Rapids story.

Nevertheless, not everyone back home was pleased with what was happening. It seems that, amid considerable opposition, Welsh got many people fed by multiplying public works projects—a policy encouraged by President Herbert Hoover. Welsh had as many as sixty projects going at the same time. In addition, there was continual haggling in city hall over the "always poor" and the "Depression poor" and who was getting what. Some of the city's policies offended the sensitivities of the Dutch with their Puritan work ethic.

■   ■   ■

Two young men who didn't have to turn to public works, however, were P. J. Zondervan, better known as "Pat," and his younger brother Bernard, whom everyone called "Bernie." Pat had left the family farm in nearby Grandville in 1924 to work for his Uncle Bill Eerdmans—the founder and owner of the William B. Eerdmans Publishing Company. Bernie quit school two years later, having finished eighth grade, and joined Pat at the firm. It seemed to be a satisfactory arrangement. And it was—until one fateful day in the summer of 1931.

Although many people were not enjoying that long, hot summer, a few were. Babe Ruth was hitting homeruns long and often for the New York Yankees and had a little earlier asked for and received a fabulous $80,000 salary. When someone asked him how it felt to be getting a higher salary than President Hoover, Ruth replied, "I had a better year than he did!" Frankie

Frisch of the St. Louis Cardinals and Lefty Grove of the Philadelphia Athletics were leading their teams toward baseball's World Series and were on their way to receiving the Major Leagues' first Most Valuable Player awards. Also that summer an act of Congress made "The Star Spangled Banner"—a common companion to sports events—the country's national anthem.

On the other hand, the University of Michigan, which hadn't sent a football team to the Rose Bowl since 1902, was facing the prospect of another grim season without a championship. One of their new freshman players that fall would be Gerald R. Ford, a talented center from South High School in Grand Rapids.

Grand Rapids was pleased with its new South High School auditorium that summer, but it was even more excited about the new DeVaux automobiles. On January 13, DeVaux-Hall Motor Corporation had wheeled the first of its stylish six-cylinder autos off the assembly line in Grand Rapids, with orders totaling 12,500. The cars sported a price tag of $685 and boasted a top speed of seventy to eighty miles per hour. They were to be used most notably as police cruisers. By summer, however, the firm's plans had begun to sour in the deepening Depression. The company filed for bankruptcy in April 1932 after fourteen months and 5,554 cars.

The book business wasn't good in the summer of 1931 either. Whether it was just the difficulty of trying to turn a profit or whether there were other factors, William B. Eerdmans wasn't happy. His aggressive nephew, Pat Zondervan, was learning the trade well and was pressing Eerdmans to give him a share of the business. Uncle Bill wanted none of that. One day, when his irritation became too great, he told his twenty-two-year-old nephew, "You're fired!" Pat, astonished, immediately left the office, drove over to get his belongings from the Eerdmans home, where he had been living, and went back to the farm.

His mother was surprised to see him. "Why are you home? What does this mean?"

"Ma!" Pat announced. "I just got fired!"

The date was July 31. What happened next led to the founding of a company that would soon begin to make a profound and lasting impact, not only on religious publishing but on the evangelical Christian world as a whole.

This is the story of that enterprise, which Pat and Bernie Zondervan called the Zondervan Publishing House.

I want to be a publisher,
because all they do is laugh and talk all day.
CHRISTOPHER CERF, PUBLISHER'S SON, AGE EIGHT

Dawn at the Farm

It is both ironic and appropriate that the publishing house known as Zondervan should begin on a family farm in Grandville — ironic because neither Pat nor Bernie Zondervan ever felt cut out for farming, and appropriate because the farm held so much of their roots and heritage.

Peter John was born April 2, 1909, in Paterson, New Jersey, a suburb of New York City that still harbors a substantial Dutch community. His brother, Bernard Dick, was born on October 8, 1910, in Harrison, South Dakota, after the family moved to the upper Midwest to take up farming. After that the boys' only sister, Mary Ann, better known as "Bonnie," arrived.

Eventually the children ended up on a farm in Grandville, Michigan, southwest of Grand Rapids, in a then completely rural area. By that time, however, their mother, Petranella, had gone through a divorce and then married a man named Louis Zondervan, who adopted the children so that they would share his surname.

Petranella, an immigrant from the Netherlands, was pleased to be living only a few miles from her brother, William B. Eerdmans. Pat, Bernie, and Bonnie were joined by five more brothers, George, William, Harold, Louis Jr., and Ted.

Somehow Peter came to be known as "Pat," and that's the only name most people ever knew him by. People were as likely to guess that his real name was Patrick. One puzzled bookstore clerk who obviously had never been paid a visit by the brothers wrote to the publishing house in 1945:

Dear Pat and Bernie,

I am not familiar enough with you to know if Pat and Bernie are brothers or if Pat stands for Patricia and you are Mr. and Mrs. I am very interested to find out.

Myra Bemis
The Book Shop
Fullerton, California

For Bernie there was never any confusion. He was named after his mother's father. Dutch names can be fascinating! "Zondervan" is a Dutch expression that means literally "without a from." This name probably dated from the days of the Spanish occupation of the Netherlands when the indigenous Dutch were required to register according to where they lived. The Zondervans evidently identified themselves as "from nowhere." Peter and Bernard not only wore their "out of nowhere" name proudly, but also made it immortal — or at least a household word in many a minister's library and religious institutions around the world.

■ ■ ■

Given the large family and the traditional Dutch love of hearth and hospitality, there was a virtual "open door" policy at the Zondervan farm. Everyone referred to Nellie Zondervan as "Ma." The fellows and girls from the neighborhood and church would often be found at the farm, playing ball in summer and making themselves at home indoors in winter. Ma always had a supply of freshly baked bread, cookies, or other Dutch treats on hand. As her children grew up, the extended family enriched Ma's life. Pat and Bernie's younger brother Bill recalls, "She was a true mother, and she was a true woman of the house. Nothing thrilled her or excited her more than to have all her family — grandchildren and great-grandchildren — come home on holidays."

The home was typically Dutch also in its religious practice. The Bible was read after every meal, and the whole family went to church twice on Sunday. It is no wonder that Pat and Bernie later saw their book enterprise not only as a business but also as a ministry to present and spread the gospel.

It was at the farm as well that the brothers learned to work hard. They got their first taste of selling in driving their dad's horse and wagon into south-west Grand Rapids and peddling farm produce door-to-door. Pat recalled that muskmelons were a special favorite of their customers.

If they didn't care for farming when they grew older, neither did they disparage the Puritan work ethic that had been instilled in them. In later years Louis Zondervan remarked Calvinistically on the way things turned out for his boys Pat and Bernie: "You never know what God will do. He makes one rich, and the other one he keeps poor. That's the way he does it. And these boys succeeded pretty well. I must put it this way: It's God's work and all in his hands. Every way it turned out, God has used them, it's true, but all the same. He was the one who blessed the work, so that's why they got what they got!"

Early on, Pat wanted to be a preacher. Walking behind a plow on the farm didn't suit him; yet it gave him a chance to try out and develop a preaching style. "I wanted to get into the Lord's work," Pat remembered, "and then the only church employment I knew was either as a minister or a missionary. I just wanted to preach."

Perhaps as much for her sake as for Pat's—for who can abide a restless son?—Nellie Zondervan arranged for Pat to live with the Eerdmans family and work for Uncle Bill. This was in 1924, when Pat was fifteen. He had gone as far as the tenth grade in Grand Rapids Christian High School and then tried the Davenport McLaughlin Business Institute briefly. That was the extent of his formal education. But he learned much from his uncle that he could never have learned in school. He also got some advice: William Eerdmans had attended Calvin Seminary for a year, so with some authority he told Pat, "You can have a much wider ministry in selling Christian books than in being the pastor of one church." Pat took the counsel, and his uncle put him to work at once. Even so, Pat did become a gifted lay preacher for the Gideons International by the time he was thirty.

Pat remembered, "I was handyman around the publishing business and around my uncle's house." In the home he helped out as babysitter, auto mechanic, and groundskeeper. At the publishing house, he said, "I began by sweeping floors, then working in the warehouse and shipping. Then I worked in the offices and finally became Eerdmans' first salesman." He was a good salesman. Some of his early selling efforts consisted of pedaling his bicycle around to homes in Grand Rapids to peddle Eerdmans' latest publications.

Then Pat began to sell out of town and gained a passion for travel that he kept for the rest of his life. He dealt with publishers and bookstores, sold books to seminarians, and scouted ministers' libraries for good used books to buy. In this way he gained an appreciation for theological and academic books that figured prominently in his own business later on.

Another invaluable experience for Pat was a trip he took to Europe with his uncle in 1930. Among the publishers and booksellers Pat met in London was Frederick Marshall of the prestigious publishing firm of Marshall, Morgan & Scott. This meeting paved the way to an opportunity for Pat and Bernie to begin dealing in foreign rights some four years later, and foreign rights became another crucial aspect of Zondervan publishing.

■ ■ ■

With all this experience in the publishing world, it didn't take Pat long to decide what to do after he was fired by Bill Eerdmans that day in July 1931. Pat set off the next month for the East Coast by car to see if he could acquire some Christian books that New York publishers couldn't sell because of the Depression doldrums. Among the books he purchased in New York were some "remainders" from Harper Brothers, especially a number of copies of J. Gresham Machen's book *The Virgin Birth*. Harper's price was $5.00 a copy, but Pat bought them for $1.00. Some other titles he bought at ten cents on the dollar.

By the time Pat arrived home, Bernie, who had gone to work for Eerdmans two years after Pat, was ready to join him in the enterprise. Twenty-year-old Bernie and Uncle Bill agreed that they didn't need any family competition. So Bernie left.

Then, later, when Eerdmans heard about Pat's buying the Machen books, he sent a wire to Harper, saying that "these boys don't have the money to pay for the merchandise!"

Too late! The books had already been shipped. Pat and Bernie sold them to seminary students for $1.95 each, and the Harper bill was paid on time.

It was a long time before Uncle Bill forgave Pat for going into competition with him. After all, Pat had learned the publishing business from him! But sometime in the early sixties, when William Eerdmans was in his eighties, he called Pat and said, "Let's have lunch." The two went to the Schnitzelbank, a

German restaurant across from the Eerdmans company, and there they were reconciled.

"Pat," said Uncle Bill, "I want you to know that I don't hold anything against you and I wish you every success in your business." The wish was a little ironic considering that Zondervan Publishing House had been prospering for more than thirty years and had surpassed Eerdmans in annual sales by that time. But the reconciliation was a delight to Pat.

"Believe me, Uncle Bill," Pat replied, "I don't hold anything against you either. If it hadn't been for you, I'd never have gotten started in this business. Thank you for calling this lunch and having this chat."

They parted as equals. Both firms have fared well since uncle and nephews parted ways back in 1931.

■　■　■

It must have become apparent to William Eerdmans, and to everyone else who knew them, that Pat and Bernie had learned the book business well by the time they set out on their own. Pat brought sales experience and the ability to promote products creatively; Bernie had gained a solid knowledge of the financial and production aspects of publishing. They complemented each other perfectly in the partnership they maintained for thirty-five years until Bernie's death in 1966.

The brothers shared many personality traits, even though many who knew them tended to think first of their differences. Perhaps the greatest difference was that Bernie was generally quieter and more reserved. If they were walking down the street and chanced to see one of their employees, Bernie would acknowledge that person with a beaming smile; Pat would as likely wave and call out a greeting. Otherwise, the brothers held in common a strong Calvinistic acceptance of life, a friendly mien, a keen business sense, and a love for work. And true to their religious heritage, they grew up in the Christian Reformed Church, learned and practiced a vital faith, and determined to serve God both in the work of the church and in their vocation.

Their vocation clearly was publishing. "In view of the fact that Bernie and I didn't like farming," Pat once recalled, "and since the only other occupation that either of us knew was book publishing and selling, and since we couldn't get a position with any other Christian publisher, we decided to start our own business. We had both just read a book that told about the beginning of Foyle's Bookshop in London, and that gave us courage to go out on our own, even though we had only $1,500 and were in the heart of the Great Depression." Their friends also gave them encouragement, since they had a lot of faith in the boys. They were young, they were aggressive, and they had nothing to lose.

They received permission from Ma Zondervan to use a spare upstairs bedroom to set up their business. Then they had to settle on a name. They rejected the word *company* as too cold; they wanted the name to have a warm and friendly sound. And since they would be operating out of the farmhouse, they thought *house* would be appropriate. They decided their business should be called "Zondervan Publishing House."

It is interesting that in book publishing, perhaps more than in most other businesses, there is a tradition of naming a firm after its founders. Consider how many prominent publishing firms bear the names of the originators: Scribners; Macmillan; Doubleday; Simon & Schuster; Farrar, Straus & Giroux—the list goes on and on. Perhaps this arises from a regard for books as something more personal than a typical assembly-line item.

Pat and Bernie used the term *publishing* because they resolved to produce their own books as soon as the opportunity arose. But first they had to get established and become known to the book trade.

■   ■   ■

The brothers' plan was to produce catalogs under their own name, listing remaindered stock and whatever other books they could acquire. Then they would call on booksellers and students in the East, South, and Midwest. (Neither ventured across the Rockies to the West Coast until Pat and Mary made the trip in 1937.) Names from denominational yearbooks and business contacts from previous trips were compiled to form Pat and Bernie's first mailing list of 2,000, and this was used for their publishing premiere—a four-page catalog. Much of their business was conducted by direct mail, using one old typewriter and a battered desk and chair.

Business grew and prospered. During the first few months Pat and Bernie each drew $10.00 a week in salary and paid their mother $7.00 of that, leaving them $3.00 apiece for gas, dating, and other personal expenses. Their total sales that December were $1,800.00.

Brother Bill, who, like Bernie, was named for his grandfather, was only a grade-school student at the time, yet he did as much as he could to help the business. After school he would help pack books into one of the closets that was supposed to hold clothes. Bill recalls getting paid $1.50 for eight hours of work.

There was also some outside help. Wilma Plas, one of six daughters of a truck farmer in nearby Wyoming, Michigan, attended the same church as Pat and Bernie — Wyoming Park Christian Reformed. While Bernie was still working for William Eerdmans, Wilma was studying at the Davenport Business School and later was a secretary for the Grand Rapids Credit Men, neither place being very far from the publishing company. They often rode together on the "interurban," the electric train line that ran between Holland and Grand Rapids and connected a number of other towns and cities in West Michigan. They started dating while they were in their teens.

During the earliest days of the business at the farm, Wilma often came to help by stuffing envelopes and licking stamps. "I can still see that crowded bedroom and the stairway filled with books so that we could hardly move in the house," she recalled. "No one used the front entrance, as that was filled with books, and on the farm everybody came through the back door anyway. Finally every available bit of space was crowded with books, boxes, and shipping material." The chicken coop and other space in the farm buildings had long since become stuffed with merchandise.

Until finally Ma Zondervan had to call a halt.

"When the living room began to fill up and there was no room for the rest of the children to play," Wilma continued, "Ma Zondervan said, 'This is enough! It's time to go out and have a sale and get rid of all these books!'"

And that's just what Pat and Bernie did.

2

Some have wondered how Zondervan could develop in so few years
from a hand-to-mouth enterprise to the stately book concern of today.
Well, the push and pluck, the fine helpers, and above all
the excellent business methods explain the mystery.
J. THEODORE MUELLER, AUTHOR, 1945

Publish or Perish

Moving the fledgling book business out from the secure shelter of the farmhouse in February 1932 involved much change and risk. Some months of struggle lay ahead, and at times Pat and Bernie feared they would not survive.

They were able to rent a storefront from Steel Brothers Fuel Company at 543 Eastern Avenue SE to hold the big sale their mother had suggested. They had thought that after using the store for two weeks they would return to a strictly mail-order way of handling business, but the idea of having a store as well as a mail-order business appealed to them. They arranged to rent the quarters for $10.00 a month in summer and $20.00 in winter. Later that year they were able to rent part of a loft next door, popularly called "The Haybarn," and this second-story room served well for storing and packing books. The name apparently stems from earlier years when the fuel company kept hay for the horses that were used to haul coal.

Soon Pat and Bernie had to make several more crucial decisions affecting their long-range plans.

It was clear that they would have to hire some help. Brother Bill was still in school and couldn't come to work in the city. They hired Jim Vroon, Wilma

Plas's brother-in-law, who worked briefly as a part-time general handyman. But he did not enjoy working indoors. Their first full-time employee was John Fiet, a man about their age who had been painting houses but wasn't enjoying his work. In fact, on the day Pat and Bernie hired him, Fiet was cutting wood. "When we hired John," Pat recalled, "we paid him nine dollars a week, which was just a dollar less than what Bernie and I were making then."

John obviously liked the book business. Later he became office manager, and then, after World War II, he became a traveling salesman, covering the eastern states. He stayed with Zondervan for nearly forty-two years, retiring at the end of 1973. He established a pattern of longevity that has been typical at Zondervan. In the next few years seven persons came to work for Zondervan, employees who, as the company approached its fiftieth anniversary back in 1980, contributed 277 years to the company, an average of 39½ years each. Those seven other "founding" employees were Gertrude TerKeurst, secretary to Pat and secretary of the corporation; Willis Cook, retail store manager; Sophie Pollie, who went on to work in the Family Bookstores office; John Idema, Gordon Feenstra, and John Ryskamp in the production department; and Jim Schimmel, shipping manager (who went on to set the record: 48 years as a Zondervan employee).

Another decision for Pat and Bernie involved what to publish. It was one thing to sell titles already in print, such as Machen's book *The Virgin Birth*; it was another to put your own name on a book and thereby give it a more personal stamp of approval. A book is not just a product of manufacturing; it is forged in individual creativity. And publishing is more than printing. The selection of a few titles from among hundreds or thousands of manuscripts received each year reflects a publisher's commitment to certain goals, ideals, and values. This is nowhere more evident than in Christian publishing. It was natural for Pat and Bernie to want to publish their own books, not merely sell those published by other firms.

■　　■　　■

The first book chosen to bear the Zondervan imprint was a work by Abraham Kuyper called *Women of the Bible*. Dr. Kuyper was a familiar name among the Dutch families of Grand Rapids, for he had been prime minister of the Netherlands, a theologian, a pastor, and an editor. Eerdmans had published several of his books in English, so Pat and Bernie knew there would be a good market for this one. It was in the public domain—no longer protected by copyright—and they were free to publish it as they chose.

The brothers paid Henry Zylstra, then a student at Calvin College, $50 to translate the book from the original Dutch. It was a fair price for those Depression times. "He was pleased, and we were pleased," Pat reflected. (Zylstra later became an English professor at the college.)

Pat and Bernie did two things with the book that showed good merchandising skill. Pat added questions to each chapter to enhance its study value and sales appeal. In addition, they published it as two books rather than one, which helped to keep both their cost and the sale price down.

Women of the Old Testament appeared in 1933. The brothers dedicated it "to our loving MOTHER from whom we received an early training to follow in the footsteps of our Savior." Since they did not own a press, they paid to have it printed elsewhere.

The second book, *Women of the New Testament,* was published a year later. A revealing word about Pat's lingering dream was printed on the title page: "The Scripture selections and questions for discussion have been added by 'the Preacher.'" This book was dedicated to "M., W. and M." In a later printing the initials were changed to the names they stood for, three important women in their lives—Mary, Wilma, and Mary Ann.

Two of these women have already been introduced: Mary Ann Zondervan, who was the sister known as "Bonnie," and Wilma Plas. Bernie and Wilma were engaged in 1932 and married the following June. "Bernie didn't have any money," Wilma recalled, "so he couldn't afford to give me my engagement ring until later." He got the money by selling his cornet, which he had played in his church band until the group disbanded. Wilma's savings were used to purchase some furniture and home necessities. It was only a few days after she withdrew her savings that the banks closed. She and Bernie felt the Lord had guided them in their decision and were very thankful.

Wilma was the first of Charles Plas's six daughters to marry, and because Plas had no sons, Bernie became like a son to him. At one point Plas wanted to buy into the business, but the brothers were determined to remain sole partners. They did accept a loan from him to see them through this struggling time, however, and it was repaid on schedule. Pat and Bernie never had any trouble getting loans when they were needed, because their credit was always good with friends, relatives, and the bank.

The third woman was Mary Swier, the daughter of Walter and Suzanne Swier of Grand Rapids. Pat and Mary were married on May 21, 1934.

The Zondervan brothers had made it a practice to have their business trips accomplish as much as possible. Typically they would buy some used books from a minister's library to take home for reprinting and then sell other books out of the trunk of the car farther along the way. So it's not too difficult to imagine that Pat and Mary's honeymoon was more than a honeymoon. They drove over to LaCrosse, Wisconsin, where a firm that was going out of business had some good used printing equipment for sale. They returned to Grand Rapids with happy memories and an agreement to buy a large hand-fed printing press, a small press, type fonts and an Intertype machine, a hand-fed folder, a cutter, and a stitcher.

There was no room at the store for a print shop, so Pat and Bernie rented a room behind the Oakdale Fuel Company across the street and down a block at 614 Eastern. A crowded 50-by-50-foot room contained all their printing and binding equipment and the seven people required to operate it. The first person they hired to run the print shop was John Stellema. "Stelly" worked at Zondervan a few years, left for a while, and then returned to remain a part of the printing operation until his retirement in 1975.

■   ■   ■

Because Zondervan Publishing House was still struggling to become known, it was exciting for Pat and Bernie to be paid a visit by Samuel Zwemer one day in 1934. A native of Michigan and a graduate of Hope College in Holland, Michigan, Zwemer was regarded as "the Apostle to Islam" because of his missionary ministry in the Middle East. More recently he had been teaching at Princeton Theological Seminary. He was concerned about growing liberalism and talked with Pat and Bernie about their publishing his books. It proved to be a good move for everyone involved: for Zwemer, because his books would reach the evangelical community through an evangelical publisher; for Zondervan, because a well-known Christian leader had chosen to identify himself with them. His first Zondervan book was *Thinking Missions with Christ*, which was published in 1934 and went into two more printings in 1935. Among the books that followed were *Taking Hold of God* (1936) and *The Cross Above the Crescent: The Validity, Necessity, and Urgency of Missions to Moslems* (1941).

Like Kuyper, a number of their first authors reflected the ethnic and ecclesiastical environment of the Zondervans. C. Kuipers wrote two books for the company in 1934 that warrant mention: *Deep Snow: An Indian Story* had seven wood-cut type illustrations and apparently was the first Zondervan book with artwork; *Chant in the Storm* used photographs.

Also in 1934, Pat and Bernie published their first multivolume academic title, *Gray and Adams Commentary*. This had previously been published as the *Biblical Museum* and the *Biblical Encyclopedia* and was in the public domain. Zondervan reprinted this five-volume set in 1950.

Until the early forties, all of Zondervan's books had very plain covers or dust jackets consisting of colored paper with ordinary type. After an artist was hired and a color press was purchased, the books took on a more colorful exterior.

By June 1935 the brothers had purchased and moved into a large building a few blocks away at 815 Franklin Street SE. Here they had their store and headquarters, while their print shop remained at 614 Eastern. The publication list began to grow rapidly.

■ ■ ■

From the start Pat and Bernie were committed to evangelical Christianity and conservative theological beliefs such as the inerrancy of Scripture and the deity of Christ. But the writers of their books, many of them ministers, crossed all denominational lines, and evangelical beliefs on secondary issues can vary widely. A striking contrast lay in the various views of eschatology. *The Lamb, the Woman, and the Dragon* by Albertus Pieters of Western Theological Seminary was an exposition of the Book of Revelation from an amillennial viewpoint. On the other hand, Drure F. Stamps, a Southern Baptist missionary to China, offered a postmillennial view in *The Mystery of God's Wrath*. One of the first premillennial titles was *Premillennialism or Amillennialism?* by Charles L. Feinberg; it was issued in 1936 with a foreword by Lewis Sperry Chafer.

The eschatological diversity was curtailed before long. Pat had come to premillennial persuasion, and Bernie, though still an amillennialist, was more open on the subject than most of his Christian Reformed friends. For their own peace of mind and for the sake of their customers, Pat recalls, "We had to make a decision. Bernie and I discussed this thoroughly and decided that the publishing house position would be the premillennial viewpoint."

This commitment was reflected in many books on biblical prophecy and the second coming of Christ that appeared on Zondervan's list in the next few decades. To many evangelicals, "Zondervan" was virtually synonymous with "premillennialism." Things did change eventually; in the seventies the company began to produce books that expressed other views, such as *The New Layman's Bible Commentary,* published in 1979, which takes an amillennial position.

One book on Zondervan's list in the mid-thirties defies theological classification. In 1928 Pilgrim Press, a small denominational house in Boston, published an English edition of a book by Karl Barth called *The Word of God and the Word of Man.* The book comprises sermons preached by the Swiss theologian between 1916 and 1923. Barth's *Commentary on Romans,* which signaled his break with the old liberalism and introduced his neo-orthodox views, had been published in Europe in 1919. So his theological reputation was established and had already had time to reach across the Atlantic by the time Zondervan bought the rights for Pilgrim's book in 1935. The sermons themselves read well in a fine translation by Douglas Horton, who was an evangelical minister in Massachusetts; for the most part they do not deal with fine points of theology. And as Pat said, "It was a good title and a good book."

If Barth's book made a contribution, perhaps it is best expressed in a statement made about Barth himself in 1962 in another Zondervan book, *The Moderns: Molders of Contemporary Theology* by William C. Fletcher:

> There is no doubt that Barth's theology has turned the tide of the older liberalism. In spite of its weakness in its doctrine of Scripture, it has succeeded in turning thousands of people back to the Scriptures and back to the churches. And whatever one's doctrine, if he is receptive to the Holy Spirit as he reads the Scriptures and as people who truly know the Lord witness to him, then the Lord Jesus Christ is standing at the door and knocking.[2]

That Zondervan published Barth at all was an indication of the theological climate in America at that time. Pat later admitted that he probably wouldn't have been able to publish the book in the more conservative mid-seventies. But again, times change. Evangelical culture had come full circle by the early 2000s, when Zondervan began publishing titles on the "emergent church" and a broader diversity within evangelicalism was not only accepted but expected.

■ ■ ■

Pat and Bernie published their first major catalog in 1936, and it featured books such as *The Power of the Blood of Jesus* by Andrew Murray, 50 cents; *In His Steps* by Charles M. Sheldon, 50 cents; *The Certainty of the Gospel* by William Childs Robinson, $1.00; *The Vision of Christ* by W. Graham Scroggie, $1.50; and the *Jamieson, Fausset and Brown Commentary on the Whole Bible*, $4.95.

Why $4.95? There are interesting stories about that book and that price. The commentary had been published in several volumes in the nineteenth century by George H. Doran Company and then went out of print. Eerdmans obtained the old, worn plates and published the commentary, which ran about 1,300 pages and was difficult to read.

One day in the early thirties when he was staying at the Palmer House in Chicago during a sales trip, Pat met Clarence Ditmar, a Doran salesman. Ditmar said, "You fellows are looking for things to publish. Why don't you publish the *Jamieson, Fausset and Brown Commentary* in one volume?"

"Well," Pat replied, "Eerdmans is publishing that."

"Yes, but it's in such small print and the print is so worn that people aren't satisfied with purchasing it."

"How do we go about doing this and getting the rights?" Pat asked.

"What you want to do is get an old copy where the print is clear and recognizable and then have it reproduced by photo offset. You'll sweep the country with it." The commentary was already in the public domain, Ditmar added, pointing out that it was first published in 1871.

Photo offset was a new process at the time. It involved making negatives by photographing the copy, then from the negatives making plates that transfer the inked image to a rubber blanket, which in turn makes an ink impression on the paper. This produces a sharper image than the older letterpress process in which the plate is pressed directly against the paper.

Ditmar gave Pat the name of the Polygraphic Corporation of America in New York City. Pat bought an old set of the commentary with clear type and took it to Polygraphic on his next sales trip to the East Coast. He arranged for a printing of 5,000 copies of a single-volume edition at a cost of $5,000 — a big investment for Zondervan, but a bargain at a dollar per copy—to be repaid over several months. The retail price was $4.95, and the printing sold out quickly.

The price tag apparently appealed to customers, but one rival publisher was indignant. Will Barbour of Fleming H. Revell met Pat a short time after the commentary was published and fumed, "No! This is a prestige business, and the price should be five dollars, not four ninety-five!" This was the same person who thought Pat and Bernie had a lot of nerve to start a new religious publishing house in the midst of the Depression when established publishers were finding business extremely slow. But a nickel made the difference: one could keep his prestige for $5.00 and go broke, or offer a large book at a price that sounded much lower—and prosper.

Later, in 1961, Zondervan had the commentary reset in larger, more modern typeface in the Netherlands, and this added nearly four hundred pages to the volume. It remains one of the strong backlist reference titles for Zondervan, and its price today, in 2006, is not $30.00, but $29.99. (In the early nineties, Zondervan changed its partial dollar prices from $0.95 to $0.99, which still seemed less than a full dollar, but allowed $0.04 more profit per book.)

Several of the books in the 1936 catalog came from Great Britain. Frederick Marshall of Marshall, Morgan & Scott came to the United States in 1934 to find a distributor for his "Shilling Series." When Eerdmans turned him down, Marshall remembered having met Pat in London when Pat was traveling with Uncle Bill four years earlier. Marshall and Pat saw eye to eye and closed the deal.

The "Shilling Series" included classic titles by well-known devotional writers such as Andrew Murray, but Marshall also gave Pat a new manuscript to read. Its author, J. Edwin Orr, was unpublished at the time. The intriguing manuscript—*Can God?*—told how Orr had started an evangelistic world tour with nine cents in his pocket and how the Lord had marvelously supplied his needs during those Depression days. Marshall published the book in hardcover and sold it in Great Britain for a shilling—twenty-five cents in U.S. currency at the time. The book and several like it that followed made evangelist Orr famous throughout the British Commonwealth and the United States.

Pat and Bernie imported the "Shilling Series" in quantities of 50,000 and sold them for fifty cents each—a bargain price, considering that Zondervan had to pay freight and duty and give dealers their regular discount.

Pat and Bernie were not yet ready to go around the world like Orr, but they traveled frequently—often for long distances. In the early years they took turns, for the trips often lasted from four to six weeks. The publishing house had become well known so quickly and the brothers were still so young that booksellers sometimes didn't realize they were dealing with the founders. It was not uncommon for Pat or Bernie to be asked, "Did your grandfather start this business?"

On one trip to the Carolinas in the mid-thirties, Pat was confronted by a friend, John Hill, who told him, "What you fellows need is a good editor."

"Fine," Pat replied. "Do you have anyone in mind?"

Hill recommended Philip Roberts, an Englishman who had formerly worked for the Fleming H. Revell Company. Pat and Bernie hired him. Roberts' health was deteriorating, and he died in 1939. But during his brief time there he nevertheless fulfilled a growing need at the publishing house. Pat and Bernie, after all, were businessmen; as their publication list and stable of authors grew, so did the importance of the editorial function. Editing can involve many things—helping to acquire new manuscripts and authors, analyzing the content of manuscripts, checking over the accepted manuscripts for grammatical and stylistic perfection, preparing them for typesetting, and influencing the final design of the books. Every writer, no matter how skilled, needs an editor.

Pat would never forget one trip in 1932. He was on his way to New York, but he had gone as far as Lansing, some seventy miles from Grand Rapids, when his car was demolished by a streetcar. Using most of his travel money, he bought a new car and headed for Pittsburgh. The roads at that time, of course, were a far cry from the interstate highways that crisscross America today. Not only that, but, as Pat told the story, "back in the thirties you could drive only twenty or twenty-five miles per hour in a brand new car. So that is what I had to do."

Later that day, when Pat was well into Ohio, he noticed he was being followed by another car. "I suppose," Pat relates, "that the driver, seeing me in a new car from Michigan, assumed I had a lot of money. Actually I had spent all but six dollars on the new car, but of course the fellow didn't know that. I couldn't speed up, because my car was new, so there I was, edging across Ohio with this car right behind me. He tried to stop me several times, but I just kept going. Finally he pulled alongside and waved a gun. I pulled over!"

The man jumped into Pat's car and pointed the gun at him.

"I was so scared!" Pat admits—probably one of the few times in his life that he was worried about anything. "I couldn't stop shaking. I had only the six dollars in my wallet. The fellow took that, but wouldn't believe my story about the accident. He tore apart everything I had. Finally he took some new shirts I had and left me all alone—still shaking!"

Unwilling to turn back even after this second misfortune, Pat resumed his journey and reported the holdup to the police at the first town he came to. They didn't believe his story. Neither did the attendant at the toll bridge farther down the road; but he eventually let Pat go through without paying. Late that night Pat pulled up at the Pittsburgh YMCA to spend the night—with empty pockets and a nearly empty gas tank.

Because he had quite a few publishing contacts by this time, Pat was able to get help to complete his trip without further incident.

3

My Book and Heart
Must never part.
THE NEW ENGLAND PRIMER, 1691

A Ministry of Books

When Pat and Bernie were traveling in the early years, Mary and Wilma usually accompanied them. This enabled the women to learn a great deal about the book trade, the people involved in it, and the kinds of books Pat and Bernie were interested in publishing. More than once, Wilma helped Bernie sort through old books stored in dingy basements to find a particular title wanted for reprinting. The wives' traveling tapered off as children were added to the families. Over the course of several years, Pat and Mary adopted four children—Robert, Patricia Lucille, William, and Mary Beth.

After Bernard D. Zondervan Jr. was born to Bernie and Wilma in 1935, he sometimes stayed with Wilma's parents so that she could travel with her husband. Wilma recalls one six-week trip when Bernie Jr., aged two and a half, went with them. The youngster was such a good traveler that his father didn't have to change his itinerary at all. With the birth of Joanne Mae, however, Wilma stopped traveling until the children grew up.

In time, Bernie's traveling diminished also. The brothers agreed that, with Bernie having more and more production and financial details to tend to in the office, Pat should make most of the long trips. It was important, nevertheless, for Bernie to keep in touch with dealers and the book-buying public, so he continued to make frequent trips around Michigan and into nearby states.

Bernie tended to be more fiscally oriented in the business, whereas Pat gave his attention to promotion and sales. Since Pat was on the road much more than Bernie, he eventually became known as "Mr. Outside" and Bernie "Mr. Inside"—nicknames possibly inspired by the Army football team's great running backs of the mid-forties, Glenn Davis and Felix "Doc" Blanchard.

Yet Pat didn't neglect his employees in Grand Rapids. Zondervan workers well remember that both Pat and Bernie made it a habit, whenever they were in town, to drop in at the print shop once a day. They seldom came at the same time. Bernie liked to have breakfast with his family. Pat, on the other hand, enjoyed being at work earlier than most. Until his retirement, it was not uncommon to find Pat at work in his office by 5:30 in the morning.

■   ■   ■

The differences in the brothers' personalities affected not only their roles in the business but their other Christian ministries as well.

Bernie's Christian service, as could be expected, tended to be centered in and near Grand Rapids. Shortly after they were married, he and Wilma joined the Burton Heights Christian Reformed Church, where Bernie soon became an active leader, with a special interest in young people. He helped to establish a youth group that included not only members of his own church but also students from Grand Rapids Christian High School, Calvin College, and other churches. Many of these young people ultimately responded to his challenge and God's call to enter the pastoral ministry or missions.

At different times Bernie also served his church as Sunday school superintendent, deacon, and elder. He liked getting others working in the church community and had the ability to organize people for a task. His approach was low-key but warm. He served on a committee that spearheaded neighborhood evangelism and helped to organize weekly Bible study classes. One of these developed into a community church that has since affiliated with the

Orthodox Presbyterian Church. He was often called on to speak to the group. He also spoke frequently at the local jail.

He was an effective fund-raiser for his church, religious institutions, and missions organizations. A favorite nondenominational mission that he supported in various ways for many years was the Chinese Native Evangelistic Crusade. In addition, he shared with Pat a keen interest in the Reformed Bible Institute, founded in Grand Rapids in 1939, renamed the Reformed Bible College in 1970, and then renamed again just this year as Kuyper College.

While Pat became known worldwide as a lay preacher, Bernie showed a measure of the same gift of speaking. It was customary for a number of years for Bernie to deliver one of the meditations on the Seven Words from the Cross at the Comstock Park Community Church on Good Friday.

But the ministry in which both Pat and Bernie flowered in the speaking gifts was that of the Gideons International. The Gideons are an association of businessmen whose chief aim is to put Bibles in hotel rooms; beside hospital beds; in prison cells; and in the hands of school children and college students, nurses, and servicemen. Today the Gideons distribute 63 million Bibles or New Testaments every year—that means they give away two Bibles every second of every day—and they serve in 180 countries. It is a custom that Gideons speak in behalf of their ministry in churches. They also evangelize.

The story of the Zondervans and the Gideons begins with Pat in April 1938. But it is connected with an incident that occurred the previous January.

Pat was calling on Charles F. Trumbull, editor of *The Sunday School Times*, to promote the new Zondervan titles. Dr. Trumbull in characteristic fashion asked Pat about his own spiritual condition.

"It was then that I realized that I had been operating from my head but not from my heart," Pat said. "At that time I first became a genuine believer and put my faith and trust in Jesus Christ. I determined to tell others as I had been told. I will never forget the verses that Dr. Trumbull shared with me; they have been very dear to me all these years: 'For by grace are ye saved through faith; and that not of yourselves: it is the gift of God: not of works, lest any man should boast'" (Ephesians 2:8–9 KJV).

Three months later, with the fire of evangelism still stirring in his heart, Pat signed up as a Gideon at the urging of a longtime friend, C. P. VanGenderen of Clifton, New Jersey. His first Gideon meeting was the annual picnic of the

Grand Rapids Camp that he and Mary attended at Johnson Park, near the city. Because he and Bernie did so many things together, Pat persuaded his brother to join. Both became active in Gideon leadership.

Pat's first public speaking engagement was at the local jail. Invitations to speak in churches followed in increasing number. "I began to develop an ability to communicate with people with a word regarding the value and blessings of the Bible, God's holy Word," Pat recalled. "What I generally use in my preaching is not necessarily an expository type of message, but I believe strongly in a good outline with illustrations with which one can communicate the gospel truth and at the same time attract people and keep their interest."

Pat was elected president of the Grand Rapids Camp one year after he joined. At one point the brothers served together as officers, Pat as president and Bernie as vice president. In July 1940, during Pat's three years as president, Grand Rapids hosted the Gideons' international convention. At that time the Gideons began their distinctive ministry of distributing New Testaments to people in the armed forces. There was special significance in Pat and Bernie's giving New Testaments to young men in their employ who were called into the service one by one in the next few years.

Bernie's Gideon ministry widened, but he once declined the presidency of the state Gideons in Michigan because he felt it would take too much time away from his church and the publishing operations in Grand Rapids. Nevertheless, he edited the Gideon state magazine, *The Michigideon*, for many years.

By contrast, Pat gave to the Gideons International the energy, dedication, and leadership that Bernie reserved primarily for his local congregation and his denomination. At the time of his death, Pat was one of only two people in the Gideons' history to have held every elective office at the international level. In July 1950 he was elected a trustee and sat on the international cabinet. Two years later he was elected vice president, and in 1956 he began three one-year terms as the international president. He was treasurer from 1972 to 1975, and chaplain from 1975 to 1978. During the years 1950 to 1978 he also served on various international committees. Pat spoke at Gideon conventions in every state of the Union and in seventy countries, always traveling at his personal expense.

No speaking assignment gave Pat more pleasure than his annual invitation from the First Baptist Church of Dallas, Texas, and its pastor, W. A. Criswell. For more than thirty years Pat presented a "Gideon message" on the second Sunday in January to the famous congregation of some 20,000 members. Traditionally Pat and Dr. Criswell had a meal together on the preceding Saturday evening. The fellowship they shared at those times was especially memorable in 1980, as Dr. Criswell suffered a heart attack shortly after the dinner.

Zondervan published its first book with Dr. Criswell, *These Issues We Must Face*, in 1953. Many collections of sermons followed. It was not unusual for Pat to bring Dr. Criswell's latest manuscript with him on his return from the First Baptist Church of Dallas. By the time that Rev. W. A. Criswell died in 2001, at the age of ninety-two, Zondervan had published eleven of his books.

And this brings us back to publishing, which, in the midst of all his ministries, was still Pat's chief concern.

■ ■ ■

At the time the Gideon ministry began for the Zondervans, the publishing house was enjoying steady growth. The store at 815 Franklin and the print shop at 614 Eastern were operating at capacity, and the number of Zondervan employees had been gradually growing. Stuart Anderson joined the firm as a salesman in 1938 and was shouldering some of the burden of travel that previously had fallen wholly to Pat and Bernie. In 1937 Pat and Mary made their first trip to the West Coast, and as that territory became a regular part of the publisher's sales planning, Zondervan's influence continued to spread.

A giant step forward had taken place with the opening of a second Zondervan store. For many years the Methodist Publishing House had operated a bookstore at the Winona Lake Bible Conference, a summer mecca for Bible teachers and devotional speakers in north central Indiana that had become widely associated with Billy Sunday some years earlier. But the Winona Lake Bible Assembly, the board that operated the store, had become increasingly dissatisfied with its selection of book stock, finding that fewer and fewer books reflected their evangelical views. In 1937 the assembly terminated its contract with the Methodists. William Eerdmans, who served on the board, was offered the contract and declined it. Pat and Bernie accepted it and took over operation of the store. It was a big decision for the brothers, because all their enterprise until then was located in Grand Rapids. But they borrowed $1,500 and were able to stock the store afresh. Zondervan Publishing House now had a two-store operation, hardly envisioning that it would someday grow to sixty stores and then, during the 1990s, become a major corporation of 320 stores that is no longer connected with the publisher.

The first manager for Pat and Bernie at Winona Lake was Harriet Fisher, better known as "Aunt Hattie." She was followed by James Meyer, who had been Zondervan's first full-time store manager back in Grand Rapids. Then in the forties, a young man named Willis Cook became manager; this was the beginning of a long career for Willis in the retail book business.

The Winona Lake store benefited Zondervan not only as a highly successful retail operation but also because it was a good place to meet and enlist prospective authors—the Bible Conference speakers. It was there that the Zondervans first met such prominent Christians as Eugenia Price and Clyde Narramore.

In the late thirties, Zondervan Publishing House was branching out in another way as well. Pat and Bernie were getting their first taste of a phenomenon that all publishers hope for: the bestseller. It was a modest bestseller, like so many of Zondervan's "firsts"—but it was real and it was exciting. And indelibly tinged with sadness.

John and Betty Stam were a young missionary couple, graduates of Moody Bible Institute, serving in eastern China under the China Inland Mission. On December 6, 1934, they were taken captive by Communist guerrillas and held for ransom. Two days later the Reds' hatred for Christianity spilled over, and the Stams were beheaded on a little hill outside the village of Miaosheo. The savage murders shocked the evangelical world.

Lee S. Huizenga, a medical missionary in China, quickly pieced together the story of the Stams' ministry and martyrdom and the dramatic rescue of their infant daughter, Helen, who was to become known far and wide as "the miracle baby." He presented the manuscript to Zondervan, since he knew Pat and Bernie, and they published *John and Betty Stam: Martyrs* in November 1935, less than a year after the tragedy had taken place.

The preface to the book was written by Jacob Stam, John's brother, and the introduction by Will H. Houghton, president of Moody Bible Institute. The paperback book had a first printing of 5,000 copies—even though most new Zondervan publications at that time had printings of a thousand, or sometimes two. They were soon sold out, and in February 1936, 10,000 more copies were printed. Another 5,000 followed in May 1937.

Huizenga had dedicated the book "To Christian young people in all English-speaking countries of the world." And it reached many. The martyrdom of John and Betty Stam inspired countless young people to give their lives to Christian service, and it renewed the vision of many older Christians for missions and evangelism.

■ ■ ■

One of the young people whose lives were changed was John W. Peterson. John was sixteen, growing up on a Kansas farm in a Christian family. He had professed a personal faith in Christ but was questioning whether he could ever be used by the Holy Spirit the way men he had read about, such as D. L. Moody and Charles Finney, had been.

> The book … God used to bring the entire issue into sharp focus, was *John and Betty Stam: Martyrs,* by Lee Huizenga. It happened to be published by the Zondervan Publishing House in Grand Rapids, but I did not take any particular notice of that on the Saturday morning when I picked up the little book and began to glance over its pages. In a few minutes I was totally absorbed in that tragic, triumphant story. …
>
> As I turned the last page of that book, something broke inside me. How could it be, Lord, that this bright, promising young couple should be cut down at the very outset of their ministry? Why? To what purpose? Was this what commitment was all about—to come to the end of oneself and lay one's life on the line for Christ, regardless of the consequences? …
>
> I began to weep in anguish as I prayed: Surely, Lord, You wouldn't ask that of me—that I go to China and die for You? I could do so much more for You here … it can't be that You want me to put myself so completely into your hands! …
>
> Hours passed, but I was unconscious of time. My tears had long since dried, for I was beginning to understand that if I wanted God to use my life (and I did), it was necessary for my life to be under His Lordship, His control, free of the pitfalls of blind chance and personal ambition. …
>
> At length the last wall of my resistance crumbled, and I promised Him: Here I am, Lord. I don't know what You want of me, but even if it's China and martyrdom, I'm willing.

Toward evening an inexpressible joy and peace filled my heart.... When I finally tore myself away and went downstairs, the day had passed and evening had come. The family had long since finished dinner, but mother had kept some food warm for me. In her face I saw the understanding that something of unusual importance had kept me closeted all day in my room. She must have sensed that I had gone through a spiritual battle and that the Lord had won.[3]

Peterson became active with two brothers in radio broadcasting and a guitar-strumming gospel trio. By the time he graduated from high school in 1939, he was making serious attempts at writing gospel music.

In time, his hopes for a career in music would be fulfilled. He would become an important composer of religious music, and he would have a monumental influence on an entire generation. His career also would become intertwined with the publisher of that life-changing book about John and Betty Stam.

But war clouds were gathering in Europe and the Far East. They burst open when Germany invaded Poland on September 1, 1939. It was the beginning of World War II. After the Japanese attacked the United States naval base at Pearl Harbor on December 7, 1941, things would never be the same. John Peterson had to set aside his dreams temporarily to serve his country in the armed forces.

And so did many young men at Zondervan Publishing House. The world crisis quickly began to make its effects felt on the book world in Grand Rapids.

4

Winning a War

Zondervan Publishing House was making some great changes at the time World War II was spreading through Europe and the Pacific Islands. It was a time of beginnings, and it was a time of contradictions. The war provided timely subjects for new books but hindered publishing operations and distribution; a dozen or more employees left to fight for Uncle Sam, yet two editors arrived on the scene who were to play key roles at Zondervan for many years.

The first of the two new editors was Herbert Lockyer, a British Bible conference speaker who was hired as editor-in-chief of Zondervan's monthly magazine, *The Christian Digest*. The other was Ted W. Engstrom, a young graduate of Taylor University who joined the staff as the book editor to succeed the late Phil Roberts.

The Christian Digest originated in Omaha, Nebraska, in the middle thirties with the purpose of reprinting, often in condensed form, outstanding articles from religious periodicals under the slogan "The Best in Current Christian Literature." Members of the Zondervan family purchased the magazine in 1939, brought it to Grand Rapids, and cast about for a staff. When Dr. Lockyer became editor-in-chief in April 1940 at the age of fifty-three, he was already well-known in the United States for his speaking and writing. When he retired as the *Digest* editor at the end of 1944, one could hardly imagine that his most lasting contributions to Zondervan were still to come. And it was not as an editor but as a writer that he made his biggest mark in the publishing world.

The Christian Digest saw its best days during World War II, when its sales, largely through bookstores, grew to more than 40,000 copies a month. A popular monthly feature of the magazine was Engstrom's "Adventures of a Christian Soldier." After the war, the magazine became increasingly less self-supporting and perhaps drained away too much energy from its editors, who had other things to tend to—such as books. The *Digest* was discontinued in January 1956.

Ted Engstrom exemplified Zondervan's growing need for additional leadership in book publishing, for when he was hired in October 1940, it was not only as *Digest* managing editor under Lockyer but also as book editor, advertising manager, and production manager.

As a journalism major in college, Ted had written to a number of religious publishing houses, seeking an editorial position. The Great Depression was nearing an end, the book business was not moving ahead very rapidly for the most part, and many of his letters of application went unacknowledged. One day, however, as he was working in public relations for a university, a letter came from Zondervan asking if he would be willing to evaluate some manuscripts. Pat and Bernie had filed his letter and followed up on it after Phil Roberts died. The manuscripts were sent. Ted reviewed them, felt that none was worthy of publication, and told the publishers so. Within days he received an invitation to come for an interview. The brothers knew the manuscripts were not valuable or ready for publication, but they wanted to see how Ted assessed them.

In Ted's first meeting with Pat and Bernie, they gathered around an old pot-bellied stove in the basement of the retail bookstore on Franklin Street. This was the "conference room." Every other part of the building was so crowded that when they wanted to get away for an interview or to talk business, they went to the basement, which was nicely warmed by the coal-burning stove in winter and had a damp coolness in summer.

After they met that Saturday morning, Ted was invited to join the staff as editor at a salary of $30 a week. Being newly married and eager to enter the religious publishing field, Ted would have accepted the job at half that rate!

Ted stayed until 1951, with a brief interruption for service in the army. Joining the army in mid-1943, Engstrom never saw the battlefront because of a jeep accident on Easter morning 1944 in California in which he suffered a leg injury.

■　■　■

Engstrom made a valuable innovation as editor in founding the *Zondervan Book News*. For thirty-three years this flyer, which was issued monthly or bimonthly, announced new titles, acquainted readers with authors, eventually served also the music-publishing division, and provided a kind of running commentary on events and developments in the publishing operation. Many stories of Zondervan's fifty years would likely remain untold forever were it not for this publication.

The first issue, in October 1941, announced the credo that expressed what the firm would seek to follow in decades to come:

> The policy of Zondervan Publishing House is to publish only those books which rank, in our opinion, as the finest and best in their particular field. Every book which we publish has our hearty endorsement and approval. We have pledged ourselves to publish only the soundest of fundamental, evangelical literature. We have the reputation of printing our books in a beautiful and attractive form.

Engstrom succeeded Lockyer as editor-in-chief of the *Digest* while continuing to wear his other hats, and he also took time to write. One of his best works was *Bible Stories for Boys and Girls*, a hefty volume that exploded into the 1948 Christmas market and sold 6,000 copies in one month.

But that was after the war. Engstrom was on the scene for significant changes that had taken place earlier. In fact, from the time he joined the staff, the publishing house was changing.

Pat and Bernie purchased a new building in 1940 and moved their printing operation into it that same year. In September 1941 the rest of the business moved into the two-story brick building at 847 Ottawa Avenue NW. The 18,000 square feet of space served five main divisions: offices, warehouse, shipping room, printing department, and retail store. The *Book News* reported:

It is ideally laid out for the Zondervan organization. It has meant increased efficiency and splendid working conditions for each department. The building is constructed so that five more stories may be added if and when necessary. If the business continues to grow as it has in the last ten years, it will not be long before it will be necessary to add more space!

Before remodeling began at Ottawa Avenue, the office desks, print shop, and bindery were all in the vast, open ground-floor area. One wall telephone served the company, and this was located at the top of the stairs. The shipping department and the warehouse were on the second floor.

The building's location offered some benefits also. It was common during good weather for some of the employees to play softball during lunch hour on nearby Belknap Hill.

In 1942 Zondervan began holding weekly chapel services, and this practice continues to this day. (Since the mid-nineties, one Wednesday a month has been given over to an employee informational meeting rather than a chapel service.) The chapel speakers are usually local ministers, but authors are often invited to speak when they are planning to visit the publishing house.

One of Willis Cook's jobs when he was hired in 1942 was to sort the mail each day. Cook would stack personal correspondence in one pile at a long

Try Again?

One of an editor's responsibilities is to send manuscripts deemed unsuitable for publication back to their authors. Among the manuscripts Ted Engstrom returned in the summer of 1942 was a full-length novel by a farmer's son in Montana. In his letter of rejection Ted wrote:

> I don't know how old you are, Gerard. I take you to be a rather young man. I'm sorry to say that your manuscript is not quite mature enough for publication.... Perhaps some day you will like to try again.

Gerard Terpstra, then sixteen, never did try again. But he did join Zondervan Publishing House as a textbook editor in 1971 and remained there until his retirement in 1989.

table and checks and orders in another. Then Pat and Bernie would sit at the table and decide which letters had to be handled by whom. Typically Bernie might ask, "Pat, do you know anything about this one?" and Pat would reply, "Yes, I met this man on my last trip. I'll take care of that."

Cook was a general handyman who made himself indispensable in one way, and that was in stocking the warehouse. Books were kept in large, deep wooden cases, and Cook knew exactly where he had placed every title and new printing. Anyone else might look hard and long for a particular book and perhaps never find it. So whenever Pat and Bernie needed a book, they had to send Willis to fetch it. This sometimes proved exasperating, but as long as Willis was around, no time was lost.

One portion of the building's main floor that was sectioned off from the rest served to house the new store at the corner of Ottawa and Mason. The store at Franklin Avenue had been closed when those premises were vacated by the company. Even at this time a retail store did not figure strongly in Pat and Bernie's long-range plans; it provided a means of serving the city, but Zondervan was doing bigger volume in faraway places at this time.

Time changes plans even when the vision remains unchanged. The company eventually outgrew the Ottawa Avenue building, which did not grow in size after all. But there was adequate room for the approximately fifty employees who occupied it in the fall of 1941, with the country on the brink of war.

■ ■ ■

The German U-boats prowling the Atlantic had already had some effect on Zondervan's distribution. When a shipment of books was ordered from England, Pat and Bernie could never be certain whether it would come through or end up in the watery depths. Sometimes only a few copies of strong titles would be included. In October 1942, for example, one shipment contained as many as 2,500 copies of 25-cent booklets, but only ten of *Spurgeon's Lectures to My Students*, which sold at that time in two volumes for $1.75. Another shipment—thirteen titles and a total of 3,651 cloth books—was heralded in the January–February 1944 issue of *Book News* under the heading "A Shipment Hitler Didn't Get."

The legwork in sales during the war years was carried out by Stuart Anderson, who was traveling 22,000 to 25,000 miles a year to cover the vast territory of East, South, and upper Midwest, and by Pat and Bernie's occasional trips. For example, Pat spent about six weeks in the spring of 1942 visiting cities as far apart as Toronto, Boston, Richmond, and Oklahoma City. Bernie traveled to the West Coast that fall.

In 1943 Zondervan urged dealers to place Christmas orders early because of the limits imposed on printing quantities by paper rationing. Other rationing played a part also. *Business Week* noted that "the rationing of gasoline is merely a mild forerunner of controls on rail and highway transport which will inevitably include priorities on freight space and ratings." As the *Book News* reported it: "Then there is the shipping problem which will get worse before it gets better. And the demand which will get better before it gets worse." Whether because of manpower shortages or excessive returns or a combination of both, the brothers had already instituted that summer a temporary "no returns" policy on books.

Numerous employees were called to serve their country in uniform. Bill Zondervan spent four and a half years in the army air corps and attained the rank of captain. Others who served were William Roode, Fred LeFebre, Leonard Snoek, Don and Harold Plummer, Marion Laude, Earl Doornbos, Melvin Haggai, John Fiet, John Idema, John Ryskamp, and Jim Schimmel. A future executive who was not yet connected with Zondervan at the time was in basic training with Schimmel: Peter Kladder Jr. Both Louis Jr. and Harold Zondervan saw military duty. Bernie had a high draft number and did not get called. Pat received an induction notice and was prepared to serve in the navy; he was given a farewell dinner by employees before a deferment was granted at the last minute. He and Bernie then served as inspectors in a local war plant.

If operation of the publishing house was affected by the war, so also was the publication list. In early 1941 Zondervan published the book *Dictators Cannot Win* by Sam L. Noel. Its subtitle described it as "A Study of Dictators, Their Methods of Ruling the People, Their Failures and Final Overthrow." The book ends with a fairly eloquent call to the United States to join the struggle directly: "We are not neutral in spirit yet we try to be in the letter."

A number of titles on patriotic themes came from the pen of a young writer who, at age thirty, had earned an LL.D. degree and was predicted by some to become "the William Jennings Bryan of his generation." Dan Gilbert was associate editor of *National Republic* magazine in Washington, D.C. Before the war Zondervan published his *Crucifying Christ in Our Colleges* and *The*

Fifth Column in Our Schools. His wartime titles often combined premillennial eschatology and current events, notably in assigning a role to Japan "plainly and unmistakably" in Revelation 9 and 16. The books included *The Yellow Peril (Japan) and Bible Prophecy*; *The Red Terror (Russia) and Bible Prophecy*; *Who Is the Coming World Dictator?*; *Emperor Hirohito of Japan Unveiled in the Light of Prophecy*; and *Who Will Be Elected President in 1944?* Lest we relegate Gilbert solely to the nonfiction list, it should be noted that in 1942 his novel newly published by Zondervan, *Conquest after Battle*, was being read serially over WMBI by the station's director, Wendell P. Loveless.

Less speculative subjects than prophecy abounded. Wartime introduced Zondervan readers to two prolific writers, cast from similar molds, who would remain on the list for many years: Basil Miller and Ken Anderson.

Basil Miller was a former pastor, founder of *The Sunday School Digest*, and then a California rancher who at the height of his career was writing a million words a year in books and magazine articles. His already impressive list of biographies included Martin Luther, David Livingstone, and Charles G. Finney when he published two wartime biographies that caused a publishing sensation. *Martin Niemoeller: Hero of the Concentration Camp* appeared in 1942 while the German pastor was still confined in Dachau. Miller noted in the book that the pastor's transfer from Sachsenhausen to Dachau "greatly improved his health." Niemoeller survived and toured the United States after the war.

The other book was *Generalissimo and Madame Chiang Kai-shek.* These Chinese leaders were at the height of their popularity in 1943, and the *Book News* stated that the book produced more prepublication orders than any previous Zondervan title, although it did not report the number.

Miller was also writing much juvenile fiction. The "Ken" and "Patty Lou" and "Koko" dog Series remained on the list well into the fifties. Biographies for juveniles came along eventually, notable in the "Ten Famous Series": *Ten Boys and Girls Who Became Famous Missionaries*, *Ten Slave Boys and Girls Who Became Famous*, *Ten Famous Girls of the Bible*, to name only a few. Some 940,000 copies of Basil Miller books were in print by mid-1951, and just how far past a million the total eventually climbed is unknown. He had published at least 136 books by 1955, and his final count probably topped 150.

Miller outpublished—but probably not by much—another popular writer named Ken Anderson. This young pastor, who would also make a name in gospel films, published, like Miller, a great deal of juvenile fiction, including the "Winky," "Tom Huntner," and "Austin Boys" series. But he became equally known for adult fiction, such as *The Doctor's Return*. Anderson's most notable contribution to the "war list" was *Shadows under the Midnight Sun*, a stirring novel about Nazi-occupied Norway. His fame as a juvenile writer prevailed, however, and in 1956, on the occasion of Zondervan's silver anniversary, Anderson was honored as its Young People's Author of the Quarter Century. Anderson's final book with Zondervan was called *Bold as a Lamb*, published in 1991. It was the stirring biography of the persecuted Chinese house-church leader Pastor Samuel Lamb, who had spent many years in Chinese prisons as a result of his activities.

■　■　■

But Zondervan was publishing more than war stories and juveniles. Reference books remained strong, undaunted by the problems created by the war. The *Jamieson, Fausset and Brown Commentary on the Whole Bible* (at $4.95) and interlinear Greek and Hebrew Testaments were meeting good sales response. Textbooks included *A Conservative Introduction to the New Testament* by S. A. Cartledge; *Psychology for Christian Teachers* by Alfred L. Murray; and the very first classroom text that Zondervan published (in 1940), *Principles of Teaching for Christian Teachers* by C. B. Eavey.

There were a number of other authors introduced to the Zondervan list who were to become well known early in their careers. Zondervan published two books by Carl F. H. Henry during the war: *The Pacific Garden Mission: A Doorway to Heaven* and *Successful Church Publicity*. These hardly presaged the great theological works that eventually came from Dr. Henry's pen, but the *Book News* prophetically stated that "we feel Dr. Carl Henry has a brilliant future before him."

At about the same time Zondervan published *Simple Sermons on the Second Coming*, the first of a vast series by W. Herschel Ford that has continued to serve fellow Southern Baptist preachers for nearly six decades. Although Zondervan no longer has any of Ford's books on its list, other publishers have kept reprints of the Simple Sermons series in print.

Another author who, like Ford, would become both prolific and durable on Zondervan's list was M. R. DeHaan, physician-turned-preacher and the speaker of the Radio Bible Class, which he founded in Grand Rapids in 1938.

His first book, *Chemistry of the Blood,* was issued in 1943; his twenty-fifth and last, *Portraits of Christ in Genesis,* was published a few months after his death on December 13, 1965. Some of his books, such as *The Tabernacle,* sold as many as 12,000 copies in the first month of publication. *The Romance of Redemption* had a first printing of 25,000 copies in 1958.

Perhaps the most interesting story relating to the DeHaan titles concerns the first book. Pat Zondervan told the tale: "Roman Catholic Bishop Fulton J. Sheen, well known for his writing and television program, visited the publishing house in 1972 with the local bishop, Joseph Breitenbeck. While Bob DeVries [then director of publications] was showing them some of our books, Bishop Sheen pulled one off the shelf—*Chemistry of the Blood*—and said, 'Bishop, this book contains a chapter on a subject I've never read about apart from the Bible.' Asked which chapter, the archbishop responded, 'It's the one Dr. DeHaan calls "The Chemistry of Tears."'"

Not long after that, when Pat and Mary were on a flight from Dallas to Chicago, a flight attendant began to chat with them. "She seemed to have a problem," Pat related, "and I asked whether she ever attended church. She said she did and was Catholic. I told her about Bishop Sheen's visit and what he had said. I asked her if she would like a copy of the book and, if so, would she read that chapter? She said she would. She gave me her address, I sent her a copy, and about two weeks later she wrote me a letter, which I still have, expressing her gratitude for my having sent that book to her and indicating that the reading of that chapter had changed her life completely."

That story is but one example of the ministry the books have had. In many ways Zondervan's commitment to meet the spiritual needs of Christians and non-Christians alike was continually being fulfilled.

Nor has the Zondervan ministry been limited to books. Other ministries have played a part as far back as the war years. It was during this time that Pat and Bernie began to publish and distribute gospel music that would pave the way for a major division of the Zondervan organization. More of the music story is told in other chapters, but its beginning is part of this era.

Gospel songs and choruses—experience-centered, evangelical, and light-hearted—were the current fad among Christian young people at the time World War II began. Then Christian service centers, established to meet the social and spiritual needs of people in uniform, began to use them in large numbers. Zondervan published several collections under the imprint

"Zondervan Music Publishers," including *Treasures New and Old*, compiled by Paul and Frances White, known as "The Musical Whites"; *Cloud Club Choruses*, compiled by Robert C. Savage and Cecil A. Dye; and *I Sing of Thee* by Charles F. Weigle, who was also the author of some Zondervan books.

But it was Alfred B. Smith and his Singspiration company that made Zondervan a major player in the music business until the eighties. Smith, a songwriter working for WMBI, Moody Bible Institute's radio station in Chicago, began to publish chorus books in the late thirties.

In May 1941, a then-unheralded evangelist from Wheaton College named Billy Graham was holding a series of meetings in Moline, Michigan, twenty miles south of Grand Rapids. He had brought Al Smith along as his song leader. Smith had just published the first in his series of *Singspiration* chorus books but was lacking a distributor who could get them into the stores. Bernie Zondervan drove down to Moline to meet Graham and of course met Al at the same time. Al had heard of the Zondervans and at that first meeting issued an invitation to them to distribute his songbooks. The first collection called *Singspiration* created a sensation in the music world, and it was soon followed by the first of Smith's *Favorites* songbooks. Pat and Bernie's relationship with Smith developed, and their role in Singspiration gradually grew until Zondervan bought the company in 1961. But that's another story. In the meantime, when the war finally ended, Zondervan and the world were on the threshold of a new era.

The transition for the publishing house came slowly, because war heroes and experiences remained good subject matter for books for several more years. Mel Larson, already well known for his biography of Gil Dodds, the "Flying Parson," gained additional fame with the biography *British Field Marshal Bernard L. Montgomery: Man of Prayer*. A lesser-known book about a lesser-known and less controversial personality was *A Very Present Help: A Tribute to the Faithfulness of God* by Lt. Gen. Sir William Dobbie, the defender of Malta. This book was published in cooperation with Marshall, Morgan & Scott, the great British firm that has provided so many books for Zondervan's list. Both Larson's and Dobbie's books benefited in sales from the authors' personal speaking tours in the United States.

Perhaps Zondervan's final acknowledgment of the war was the book it began distributing in this country in 1947 for Evangelical Publishers of Toronto, Canada. The 172-page, illustrated account of concentration camp experiences by the daughter of a Dutch watchmaker relied mainly on her church speaking engagements for sales. The pallid title was *A Prisoner—and Yet*. It remained for another publisher and another book, with a more intriguing title—*The Hiding Place*—to win bestsellerdom some twenty-four years later for Corrie Ten Boom.

So an era ended. And although no single event separated that era from the one to follow, there was a kind of demarcation when Zondervan purchased another building in downtown Grand Rapids and proudly announced in the January 1947 *Book News* that the firm would soon be moving into a new and larger home. It signaled a change for Zondervan even though the move was never made.

I'm not happy when I'm writing,
but I'm more unhappy when I'm not.
FANNIE HURST

5

An Era of Competition

In the spring of 1946 the brothers bought the old Shank Building on LaGrave Avenue in downtown Grand Rapids with the intention of refurbishing it as soon as the economy rebounded from the post-war doldrums. The *Zondervan Book News* announced with great fanfare in January 1947 that the firm would soon be moving into the five-story, 60,000-square-foot building in the heart of Grand Rapids, at 19–25 LaGrave Avenue.

The address has an unfamiliar ring to even the longest-lived employees: it never became the home of Zondervan. Even as late as 1951, Pat and Bernie still intended to make the building their base of operations. The twentieth-anniversary magazine optimistically stated, "Dates and plans for moving are not complete at this time, but the large building stands squarely in the center of the expansion plans for the Zondervan Publishing House."

In reality, the building turned out to be too small. Some of the space was used for storage, but the rest of the operations were to stay at 847 Ottawa Avenue SE, for a few more years.

Only one book seems to bear the LaGrave Avenue address: *Movies and Morals,* an analysis of one hundred Hollywood films, by Herbert J. Miles.

Zondervan was indeed expanding after the war. The firm published 58 new titles (36 in cloth and 22 in paper) during 1944; in 1946 the number skyrocketed to 154, an average of three new titles a week. Moreover, in 1946 some 350,000 new books came off the presses, along with 250,000 booklets and one million reprints. At this time about 10 percent of the printing was done on Zondervan presses, and the rest was farmed out. Some 365 authors were receiving royalty checks twice a year.

The postal delivery on Monday, December 11, 1945, brought a then-record 1,045 pieces of first-class mail to Zondervan, an impressive figure by any account. When the city was nearly paralyzed in December 1946 by a coal strike that all but shut down the railroads, an embargo was imposed on parcel-post shipments out of Grand Rapids. Many businesses in town were trying to get their orders out, and on December 5, the day before the embargo went into effect, some forty-five tons of packages passed through the city's post office—ten tons of it coming from Zondervan! The post office reported in 1951 that Zondervan was one of the five biggest companies in Grand Rapids in terms of amount of mail it received.

As business volume grew, so did the work force. Zondervan had more than ninety employees in 1947. George Benes and Robert MacKay joined as artists in 1946. The sales force grew to four. Stuart Anderson had retired by the end of the war and was replaced by John Fiet, who moved from his position as office manager to take over the Eastern territory. Al Ramquist, who made his home in Kansas City, Missouri, joined the staff in the spring of 1945 to cover the West and the Southwest. By 1947 Lawrence ("Larky") Carlson, in the lower Midwest and Southeast, and Pat and Bernie's brother Bill, serving the upper Midwest, were added to the sales force.

Ramquist was the victim of two auto accidents—neither his fault—in the space of a month in early 1948. First, his car was sideswiped by a truck in Texas; then it was demolished when struck by a drunken driver in Oklahoma. Al was not injured.

Further misfortune befell Ramquist in May 1952 when he suffered a heart attack while calling on a bookstore in Oakland, California. He was strong enough in June to take a train home, and by September he was on the road again.

The sales force continued to see change. Lloyd Van Horn, a navy veteran from the Pacific Northwest, took over Carlson's territory in the fall of 1949 and remained a Zondervan sales representative in the Southeast until his retirement in December 1980. Willis Cook made a couple of long sales trips each year while fulfilling other duties for Zondervan. In the meantime, Bill Zondervan had left to join the Moody Press sales staff, only to return in February 1955 to take over Zondervan's Western area for Ramquist, who had resigned to take a position with his hometown Nazarene Publishing House.

There was also a change in the publishing end of Zondervan. Ted Engstrom resigned in 1951 to become executive director of Youth for Christ, a young organization already active in seventy-six countries. In no small way, he had been well prepared for his new challenge because of his diverse roles in eleven years at Zondervan: head of the editorial, advertising, promotion, and production departments and for a time editor-in-chief of *Christian Digest*.

Engstrom left big shoes to fill, and they were ably filled by a young University of Michigan graduate who had become Engstrom's assistant during 1951. When Ted moved to Wheaton, Illinois, in October, T. Alton Bryant moved into his position at Zondervan. "Al," as he was familiarly known to all during his more than twenty-five years with the publishing house, quickly proved himself to be as energetic as his predecessor. He also showed the same flare for compilations; several dozen books bore his name, including anthologies of poetry, children's stories, and sermon outlines. His first book was published soon after he became editor—*Stories to Tell Boys and Girls*. In 1956 Bryant published his best-known work, a collection of daily devotions called *Climbing the Heights*, a book that sold more than 350,000 copies before it went out of print in 1984. He also compiled *The Compact Bible Dictionary*, a condensation of the *Zondervan Pictorial Bible Dictionary*; this was published in 1967, is still in print, and has sold more than a million copies. He left Zondervan and became senior editor at Word Books in 1977, where he stayed until he retired and once again made his home in Grand Rapids.

Al became the mainstay of the Zondervan editorial department, however, at a time when the publishing house was turning out books at a prodigious rate. The list was spurred in no small way by a series of manuscript contests that began with the announcement of the $10,000 First International

Christian Fiction Contest in 1947. Soon there were contests for biography and missionary manuscripts, textbooks, and juvenile fiction. But it was the dream of writing the Great American Christian Novel and winning the $5,000 first prize that lured writers by the hundreds and brought Zondervan widespread attention.

Many of the contest winners were experienced writers, some of them winning more than once. Some of the books published during Zondervan's "golden age of fiction," however, fell short in the qualities that make fiction great, such as technique, characterization, structure, and imagery. Surely more than a few manuscripts submitted for the contests were dusty, half-written works that could better have been left dormant, for bestsellers are built on something more substantial than dreams and inadequate writing skills. Zondervan's editorial staff was wise to declare the third fiction competition "no contest" when all the manuscripts failed to meet their expectations.

But some writers gained the sought-for fame and glory. First prize in the first fiction contest was awarded to Guy Howard for his novel *Give Me Thy Vineyard*. This story set in the Ozarks was described in one Zondervan ad as "the ruggedly human, yet sensitively spiritual story of Hiram, a hunted outlaw, and Rosie, his sweetheart, who lived and loved among the mountains, where life is swift and love costly." The *St. Louis Post-Dispatch* called the book "a dramatic, compelling, and fascinating story." The *Cleveland News* said it was "dramatic and exciting."

Howard, who was self-described as "the Walkin' Preacher of the Ozarks," came to Grand Rapids to receive his $5,000 first prize on publication day, September 20, 1949. On the same day he autographed books at a party at the new Herpolsheimer's Department Store that had just recently opened downtown at Division and Fulton Streets.

The 25,000-copy first printing of the book was sold out quickly, with sales mounting to as many as 3,000 copies a week. Publishers in Norway and Sweden purchased rights for the book. A $15,000 advertising budget was scheduled, but the final promotion cost actually turned out to be $17,506.12.

■ ■ ■

The second-place winner of that first contest proved to be as important to Zondervan as Guy Howard. *Until the Day Break* was a novel by Sallie Lee Bell, a Louisiana homemaker who was to churn out title after title of romantic fiction in the tradition of Grace Livingston Hill and Harlequin romances.

Until the Day Break had a biblical setting that wove in figures like John the Baptist and Herodias. It also had a record-setting first printing of 75,000 copies. Apparently on the strength of that first novel, Zondervan made a pledge to publish anything Sallie Lee Bell wrote. Pat and Bernie made good on the promise even after her creative powers had waned and the glitter had diminished in the marketplace for Christian romances. Altogether Zondervan published thirty-seven of her books. They were revived in the early seventies in the Hearth Books paperback series, but all are now long out of print.

One of the unusual stories arising out of the contests involves Sallie Lee Bell herself. Unknown to Zondervan, Mrs. Bell gave some of her prize money to Josephine C. Bulifant, a missionary in Nigeria under the Sudan Interior Mission whom she had been helping to support financially for a number of years. The connection between the two became known only after Miss Bulifant was awarded second prize in the Biography and Missionary Manuscript Contest for her book *Forty Years in the African Bush*. Miss Bulifant in turn used her prize money of $350 to build a "Zondervan Cottage" at an orphanage she helped operate for her mission.

Another prize winner commands attention as one who made the fiction contest truly international. The $4,000 first prize in the second fiction contest was awarded for *Thine Is the Kingdom*, a story moving "from the gloomy environs of bureaucratic Moscow to the tranquility which pervades the Canadian woodland in summer." "The reader," the *Zondervan Book News* for September 1951 proclaimed, "feels shudders of fear at the horror of a possible Communistic regime in America." The author was James H. Hunter, editor of the *Evangelical Christian*, a magazine published by Evangelical Publishers of Toronto. Hunter had already published the novels *The Mystery of Mar Saba* and *Banners of Blood*. *Thine Is the Kingdom* sold out its first printing of 15,000 in six weeks and was quickly enlisted by a British publisher. Hunter later published *How Sleep the Brave* and was named Zondervan's Author of the Quarter Century.

A local contest winner was Dena Korfker, who placed third in the first juvenile-fiction contest with *Ankie Comes to America*, the story of an immigrant Dutch girl. The Grand Rapids educator had already written the nonfiction bestsellers *Can You Tell Me?* and *My Bible ABC Book*. She was honored as Zondervan's Children's Author of the Quarter Century in 1956, yet her grandest work, the 512-page, illustrated *My Picture Story Bible*, was not published until 1960.

In all, Zondervan sponsored a couple of dozen of the contests and awarded an estimated $50,000 in manuscript and promotional prizes in the years 1947–1958. Toward the end, the contests weakened in prestige and writer appeal, but the program overall proved to be well worth its cost to the publisher in sales, publicity, and author recognition.

If the contest did little to add to the world's immortal fiction, it is some consolation that what Zondervan published was frequently better than the Christian fiction being published by others at that time. Good Christian fiction was scarce in the evangelical world, and even now, with Christian fiction regularly appearing on the *New York Times* bestseller lists, enduring literary-quality Christian fiction is still scarce.

And there is something else about fiction. For a Christian publisher, fiction may have an evangelistic dimension that is not inherently incompatible with it, even though it often expresses itself naively and weakens the literary quality of a work. But one personal testimony—from a former Zondervan pressman, James B. Phillips—illustrates the power of fiction. The *Book News* published this testimony in 1960:

> *Thine Is the Kingdom* by James H. Hunter was one of the first messengers the Lord used in showing me my need of Jesus Christ as my personal Savior. In 1954 a faithful Christian allowed me to read the book.... The comparisons of communism and Christianity interwoven through the book fascinated me so that I read the book without stopping. Upon finishing the story I had a great desire to know the Savior. Not long after, I found Him whom to know is life eternal.
>
> In 1958 *Thine Is the Kingdom* again crossed my path. This time I was an employee of the Zondervan Publishing House. To my surprise I discovered that this book was a Zondervan publication. Now the Lord has given me the privilege of helping to publish the very book that had been such a blessing to me years before.

■ ■ ■

Another aspect of the contests that had a positive impact for a long time was the textbook competitions. The twofold objective was to improve the quality and quantity of titles and to increase Zondervan's share of the market among Christian colleges and Bible institutes. Even though the firm's publishing backbone and backlist strength lay in academic reference works from the beginning, there was much room for growth in current textbooks for classroom use. The contest apparently succeeded. Both new and established authors contributed to the lists, and some of the textbook winners even remain in print today. A two-time winner was Merrill F. Unger, who was named Zondervan's Theological Author of the Quarter Century.

Simultaneously with the contests Zondervan launched a number of major reprint projects that involved a considerable financial investment and made a substantial contribution to theological libraries. In true Zondervan spirit, no project seemed too great to undertake if the product was worth it. The multimillion-dollar program was a significant publishing achievement by any standard.

Many of the larger projects operated on a subscription basis, a plan by which readers could automatically receive a volume each month. This early direct-mail program proved to be an efficient way to spread out costs to both the publisher and the consumer over a manageable period of time.

The first project was a $100,000 program to publish J. P. Lange's *Commentary on the Holy Scriptures*. The first of the twenty-four volumes came off the press in December 1949 and sold for $3.95. The price for the set when it was completed was $89.90. Lange's *Commentary* remained on Zondervan's list until late 1982, in twelve double volumes totaling 14,134 pages, and the set still commanded at that time the highest price tag on the list: $239.

Other multivolume projects that followed Lange's included these:

- Bishop J. C. Ryle's *Expository Thoughts on the Four Gospels*, 4 volumes, 1950.
- Spurgeon's *Treasury of the New Testament*, 4 volumes, and *The Treasury of David*, 6 volumes, 1951.
- *Spurgeon's Sermons Memorial Library*, 20 volumes, 1952–53.
- W. G. T. Shedd's *Dogmatic Theology*, 3 volumes, 1953.
- *Ellicott's Commentary on the Whole Bible*, 8 volumes, 1954. This set sold for $34.95 in 1954; a set of four double volumes was issued by Zondervan in 1981 for $99.95.

- *The Layman's Handy Commentary on the New Testament*, 18 volumes, 1957–58. This was Ellicott's commentary published in smaller books.
- *The Life of the Lord Jesus Christ* by J. P. Lange, 4 volumes, 1958.
- *Fairbairn's Imperial Standard Bible Encyclopedia*, 6 volumes, 1957–58.
- *The Works of John Wesley*, 14 volumes, 1958–59.

The most ambitious project of them all, however, was the $500,000 reprinting of the Charles Simeon classic, *Horae Homileticae*, which Zondervan issued in twenty-one volumes under the title *Expository Outlines of the Whole Bible*. It was possible for a preacher using this work to organize sermons from every single chapter of Scripture. A volume was to be issued every other month beginning in November 1953, according to an announcement made the previous February. As it turned out, the set began appearing monthly in 1955. But the delay apparently didn't cause the sales to suffer, nor did it dampen the enthusiasm of virtually every evangelical leader in the country, who greeted it with hearty endorsements when it finally made its debut.

■ ■ ■

Two other academic developments of this time are noteworthy even though they were short-lived and in some measure unsuccessful. Zondervan arranged in 1956 to publish *The Evangelical Commentary*, a planned forty-volume series directed by an editorial board of scholars in the Wesleyan and Holiness tradition. This was heralded as "the first new series of evangelical commentaries in over 100 years" exhibiting "the combination of sound scholarship and spiritual insight for which the commentary of Adam Clarke is justly famous."

The project was plagued with problems from the start. Editor George A. Turner of Asbury Theological Seminary had to deal with a disparate group of thirty writers who possessed an uneven quality of scholarship at best. Though a number of the writers, such as Merrill C. Tenney, W. E. Sangster, and Harold B. Kuhn, had tall stature in the evangelical community, others did not. Surprisingly, the man chosen to write the volume on Matthew was Basil Miller—a man who had written dozens of juvenile novels. Unknown to his young-adult fans, he was "Dr." Miller. He held seven earned degrees, including a Ph.D. and an S.T.D. His commentary showed good exposition and style but was weak on exegesis and had to be gracefully abandoned by the editorial board.

That was unfortunate. With an eye on the rival *New International Commentary on the New Testament*, which was being published by Eerdmans, the board had hoped to produce the commentaries on Matthew and Mark first. As Ralph Earle, the writer for Mark, wrote to Pat Zondervan in early 1956: "It seems particularly fortunate that our first volumes are to be on Mark and Matthew, since those volumes have not yet appeared in *NICNT*. You ought to have the whole market — Calvinistic as well as Arminian — for these, and thus get a good start with the set."

Earle's *Evangelical Commentary on Mark* did appear in early 1957 and received good reviews. Next came the volume on Acts, co-authored by Earle and Charles W. Carter, and this commentary remained on the Zondervan list until it was declared out of print in 1981. But Zondervan's hopes for a significant inroad into the Wesleyan-Methodist-Holiness market for the first time waned as the project faltered. In 1962 the publishing house sold the rights for the remaining manuscripts to the Evangelical Bible Commentary Committee.

Ironically, the series was similar in concept — without the Wesleyan orientation — to another multivolume commentary begun in the mid-seventies and not fully completed until 1992: *The Expositor's Bible Commentary*. The beginning of this twelve-volume project was blessed with strong leadership — under Frank E. Gaebelein — strong scholarship, and the use of the New International Version of the Bible. It succeeded where the earlier project had failed. It was so successful that later on Zondervan published a two-volume abridged edition, better suited for laypeople by leaving out much of the technical material that appeals more to critical scholars and seminary students. Moreover, in December 2005, the first volume of the *EBC Revised Edition* (vol. 13, Hebrews to Revelation) was published.

Another well-publicized academic development in 1956 was the appointment of Walter R. Martin as head of a new "Cult Apologetics Division" at Zondervan. Martin had gained a well-deserved reputation as an authority on offshoots of Christianity such as the Jehovah's Witnesses and Mormonism. When he began to publish with Zondervan, he also began to conduct popular "cult seminars" around the country.

In December 1956, *Time* magazine devoted an article to Martin's irenic study of the Seventh-day Adventists. The article, coupled with his subsequent book *The Truth About Seventh-day Adventists*, sparked considerable debate among Evangelicals. Yet many of them, following Martin's lead, were ready to accept the Adventists as basically "theologically acceptable," and the book received higher praise than Zondervan had expected.

Despite this happy development, dealings between Martin and his publishers were becoming strained as the writer invested more and more of his time and resources in magazine publishing and research projects. Although his most significant work, *The Kingdom and the Cults*, was published by Zondervan as late as 1965, Martin had let pass opportunities to produce some promised textbooks on contemporary theology that Zondervan very much wanted to

Contest Winners

There is an interesting story behind many books that see their way into print. Many of the books on the Zondervan list stood out as winners among the thousands of manuscripts entered in the writing contests of 1947–58. More than 200 manuscripts were submitted in the first fiction contest. Some 150 were entered in the fifth fiction competition ten years later; these manuscripts came from thirty-six states, Canada, and three other countries.

Some of the winners enjoyed only fleeting fame. But some of the books remained on Zondervan's list for many years, especially in the textbook line. The following partial list covers just some of the winners in just some of the categories; the dates indicate when a contest began and when the winners were announced.

$10,000 First International Fiction Contest (1947–49)
   First: *Give Me Thy Vineyard* by Guy Howard
   Second: *Until the Day Break* by Sallie Lee Bell
   Third: *The Light in My Window* by Francena Arnold

$2,000 First Christian Textbook Contest (1949–50)
   First: *An Introductory Guide to the Old Testament* by Merrill F. Unger
      of Dallas Theological Seminary
   Second: *Principles of Personality Building for Christian Parents* by
      C. B. Eavey, formerly of Wheaton College

publish. Through no fault of Zondervan's, the Cult Apologetics Division had a short life; yet what Zondervan was able to publish on the cults during that time was well worthwhile.

Although the formation of this new division had been designed as one of the events commemorating Zondervan's twenty-fifth anniversary, it was not the most important achievement as preparations for a celebration week of October 1–6 went forward. Actually some notable works had been published that stood quite far apart from the contests or the reprint projects; some of them involved prominent names that may still be familiar to some Zondervan

$5,000 Second International Christian Fiction Contest (1950–52)

First: *Thine Is the Kingdom* by James H. Hunter
Second: *Hidden Valley* by Douglas C. Percy
Third: *Of Men and Angels* by Lon Woodrum

$1,000 First Juvenile Christian Fiction Contest (1951–52)

First: *Indian Drums and Broken Arrows* by Craig Massey
Second: *The Wolf Dog* by Ken Anderson

$5,000 Third International Christian Fiction Contest (1952–53)

Six months after the deadline passed, Zondervan declared this competition "no contest" with the following statement: "This decision, difficult as it was to reach, was considered the only fair conclusion, inasmuch as declaring one of these average manuscripts a prize winner would have been unfair to prize winners in previous and future contests."

$2,000 Second Christian Textbook Contest (1952–54)

First: *Archaeology and the Old Testament* by Merrill F. Unger
Second: *Bible Doctrines: Beliefs That Matter* by Mark G. Cambron
of Tennessee Temple Bible College

$5,000 Fourth International Christian Fiction Contest (1953–55)

First: *Eternity in Their Heart* by Lon Woodrum
Second: *Each Day Is New* by Orville Steggerda

readers today. Some important organizational developments relating to Bibles, music, and personnel had also been occurring. And once more the company changed its street address.

As the quarter-century mark approached, several new chapters were being written in the story of Zondervan.

It would be easy now to relax, sit back, and enjoy success,
but here it is more than a business — it is a ministry!
And a ministry must continue on — and ever increase.

A QUARTER CENTURY OF PROGRESS,
ZONDERVAN ANNIVERSARY BOOK, 1956

6

The Silver Anniversary

As Zondervan celebrated its twenty-fifth anniversary, there were signs that it was changing from a small company doing big things to a big company doing greater things. In the years immediately before and after that special occasion, the firm was not only growing but also becoming more sophisticated.

From the time that Pat and Bernie had decided not to move into the LaGrave Avenue building, they had felt the pressure of cramped quarters. Finally, in 1954 the company began moving into a new home, one floor at a time, at the five-story Grand Rapids Storage Company building at 1415 Lake Drive SE, in the Eastown section of the city. The building was eventually taken over entirely by Zondervan and was the firm's headquarters for the next thirty-eight years, until January 1992.

But the move was difficult. Pat and Bernie's plans for remodeling were estimated to cost about $60,000. It turned out to be more than double that amount, and that put them in a financial bind. Some people to whom they owed money had to wait almost a year for full payment, but the brothers were able to meet every obligation with interest. At that difficult time Pat made a special commitment to God and managed to keep it until he retired. As a result, he has paid out of his own pocket all his expenses incurred since that time in his worldwide Gideon ministry.

The former furniture warehouse had little aesthetic value even after the refurbishing to adapt it to publishing operations. Additional remodeling continued through the years, though traces of the warehouse, such as the freight elevator, remained. The bindery personnel had to endure working in the dungeonlike basement for some twenty years. But the building was "home," and for a while it was adequate for the needs of the company.

The facade of the building was not substantially altered until the seventies. The face-lifting it received then was representative of broader changes occurring in the neighborhood. Eastown, a couple of miles southwest of downtown Grand Rapids, is an older community that had been declining for some time until new life was infused commercially and residentially in the late sixties and seventies, spurred in part by social action projects by students from nearby Aquinas College. Zondervan's decision in the seventies to stay in the Lake Drive building was a far-reaching force for good also. Throughout the seventies and eighties Zondervan's headquarters stood astride the intersection of Robinson Road and Lake Drive as a symbol of encouragement, progress, and hope.

Nevertheless, one environmental change was viewed by Zondervan with dismay. At the time the firm purchased the building, it had its eye on the triangular site of a service station that stood between the building and the intersection. When the service station closed down, Zondervan stalled at paying the price asked for the land. The site seemed too small for any other commercial use, so Zondervan decided to wait for the price to come down.

Zondervan was outfoxed by a little white-haired old man with a goatee and a white suit. One day in the late sixties, before Zondervan realized what was happening, the "Kentucky Colonel" franchised a local entrepreneur to open a fast-food chicken restaurant on the site. It was one of Zondervan's unhappiest days. And for many years to come, the unpleasant smell of grease wafted through the second-floor offices whenever anyone opened a window during cooking hours.

But in 1954, that event still lay many years in the future. Zondervan moved into the Lake Drive building at a time when the company's business and inventory were increasing dramatically. One hundred thirteen new titles were issued in 1954, and among the new books sold were more than 2,500 sets of the eight-volume *Ellicott's Commentary*. During 1955, a total of a million books passed through the shipping department. Some of them came from Van Kampen Press in Illinois, which Zondervan purchased that summer. With the books came some notable authors: Bob Jones, Charles Ludwig, J. Vernon McGee, and Jack Wyrtzen.

The Van Kampen transaction was small compared with acquisitions that came later. Zondervan's strong list, with a good balance between popular books selling in high volume and a steady backlist of classic reprints, has enabled the firm to make some major acquisitions right up to the present. The financial decision making that was necessary to undertake these later ventures has depended in no small way on a different kind of "acquisition" in 1956. This was not a publishing company, but a person.

▪ ▪ ▪

When Harold Carlson, who had been heading the accounting department for some time, resigned, someone recommended to Pat and Bernie that they consider Peter Kladder Jr. to replace him. They invited him to dinner and offered him the position of treasurer, and when he had had time to think and pray about it, he accepted.

Kladder was born and reared in Grand Rapids in a family of eight children. He was educated in accounting and business administration in the city and then took a job with General Motors Acceptance Corporation. After three years in the army, including one year in Europe in World War II, he returned to GMAC. But some time later, when that company wanted him to head up their Battle Creek office, he declined, preferring to stay in Grand Rapids. It was about that time that he received the offer to join Zondervan Publishing House.

The treasurer's financial background played an important role in Zondervan's growth in other ways besides acquisitions. For many years Zondervan had operated a division called "Glad Tidings Books and Bibles." This was a service organization to distribute greeting cards, vacation Bible school materials, and novelties and jewelry by mail order. These products were not being produced by Zondervan itself, and they had not been profitable for some time. At Kladder's instigation the Glad Tidings operations were discontinued.

Kladder's role grew as the company grew. He was made vice president of operations in 1962, and in 1970 he was appointed the president of the newly reorganized corporation. The changes that were made under his leadership during the seventies were many and far-reaching. And by that time the firm was far different from what it was when he came in 1956.

An organizational change that preceded Kladder's coming by several months was in music publishing. Zondervan and Singspiration had been enjoying a gradually deepening relationship, and in February 1954, Zondervan became not only the exclusive distributor but also the producer for Al Smith's music. Then, when Smith began talking about turning this work over to a music publisher in Wheaton, Illinois, Pat and Bernie decided it was time to go into music publishing on their own again. In late 1955 they incorporated Zondervan Music Publishers—taking the same name they had used in printing some gospel chorus books on a small scale in the thirties and forties. They hired as their music director Robert J. Hughes, who had been associated with the Salvation Army in Canada.

In music, as in all their other publishing endeavors, Pat and Bernie believed they could produce quality materials at a reasonable price. The first major objective of Zondervan Music Publishers was to provide a new hymnal for use in evangelical churches. Before that could come to fruition, however, Al Smith's plans in Wheaton fell through, and he returned to Zondervan. As he turned increasingly to Pat and Bernie for help, a partnership developed in 1957, and at the end of 1961 Smith sold to them his remaining interest in Singspiration.

■   ■   ■

One of the things Al Smith had going for him in 1956 was his music mastermind, John W. Peterson, the man whose life was changed by reading *John and Betty Stam: Martyrs* at age sixteen.

In the late forties, as a student at Moody Bible Institute, he published some choruses that became well known, sometimes through a Jack Wyrtzen rally or a Billy Graham crusade—"He Owns the Cattle on a Thousand Hills" and "Jesus Is a Friend of Sinners," for example. One of his songs was inspired by his wartime experiences in flying the "hump"—the air route over the Himalayas to bring war supplies into China. The song "It Took a Miracle" catapulted him to national attention in 1948 when evangelist Percy B. Crawford published it and used it on his radio broadcast *The Young People's Church of the Air.* Peterson joined Singspiration in 1955 and the next year was working on his first cantata, which won for him a permanent place in religious music history for its innovative form. He became a partner with Smith and the Zondervan brothers in 1957, though he had met Pat and Bernie only the year before. Peterson describes the occasion of their meeting:

> I had corresponded with the Zondervan brothers, but the opportunity to meet them in person did not come until they invited me to Grand Rapids for the silver anniversary of the founding of the Zondervan Publishing House. Driving toward Grand Rapids, I felt a mixture of anticipation and apprehension. Pat and Bernie had the reputation of being superefficient businessmen who worked hard, kept a short rein on their commercial interests, and rarely made a wrong move. Perhaps I feared that they would be cold-hearted and "all business."
>
> But when I walked down the hallway toward Pat's office and he came out to greet me with a big smile and a hearty "John, it's a delight to meet you!" I knew my fears had been groundless. Bernie proved to have the same warmth, the same great heart, the same deep love of music. I had found two priceless men who would be my friends throughout eternity.[4]

The silver anniversary was nearing, and of course there were other things on the Zondervans' mind in addition to music. It was a big year in book publishing, with some important names highlighting Zondervan's list.

All of these prominent authors were a little too new to Zondervan's list to be honored in the quarter-century awards, but they were all to make a lasting place in religious publishing. And none had a greater impact than Eugenia Price.

By the age of twenty-two, Eugenia had become the author of her own "soap opera" on NBC radio, *In the Care of Aggie Horn.* Later she wrote scripts for *Joyce Jordan, M.D.* In 1944 she opened her own production office in Chicago, writing and producing programs for networks.

In 1949 "Genie," as she was known to her friends, became, in her own words, "a transformed pagan who took God at His word." At the age of thirty-three she became a believer in Jesus Christ and suddenly had, in her words, "something about which to write!" A year after her conversion she began writing, directing, and producing the top-rated dramatic radio series from Chicago, *Unshackled,* stories from the Pacific Garden Mission.

How Zondervan came to publish Genie's first book in 1953 can best be told in her own words, as she related the experience in *The Life of Faith*, a British magazine, in 1962:

> My dream of writing books was still only a dream, then somewhat pushed in the background by the activity of my new life in Christ, in the year 1952. I was busy writing and directing *Unshackled* and speaking more and more frequently. The summer of that year I happened to be speaking at the Bible Conference in Winona Lake, Indiana. In the hotel dining room, Mr. Bernie Zondervan of the Zondervan Publishing House [which ran the conference bookstore] approached me pleasantly and said something like this: "Genie, when you're ready to write that first book, we want to publish it for you!"
>
> I laughed. But I thanked him and thought no more about it until several friends urged me to publish in book form some columns I had been doing for a small Christian publication. These were merely my way of clarifying for myself some of the discoveries I was making in the way I enjoy most—by writing them down. When Mr. Zondervan approached me again, some months later, I mentioned these short pieces to him.
>
> They resulted in my first book, finished when I was three years old in Christ, titled—*Discoveries: Made From Living My New Life.*

Sales were good, but it was Genie's second book that made her a nationally acclaimed writer and spurred *Discoveries* into two more printings in the next two years. In mid-1955 *Discoveries* was also published in a deluxe edition that featured a new jacket and "headbands" (headbands are the colorful strip of cloth applied where the spine meets the top edge of the pages—an attractive binding feature customary on Zondervan cloth books today but rare at that time).

Genie's second book, *My Burden Is Light*, was published by Fleming H. Revell, who had requested the autobiographical work. Although Genie returned to Revell two years later with a sequel, *Early Will I Seek Thee*, all the rest of her religious nonfiction has been published by Zondervan.

In the meantime Genie had left the popular *Unshackled* program after handling it alone for five years, and she began a radio interview program, *A Visit With Genie*. And from her pen came a steady stream of books.

Her second title for Zondervan was *Never a Dull Moment*, a book for teenagers. Within a month and a half of its publication in mid-1955 there were

37,000 copies in print in simultaneous cloth and paperback editions. Genie and Zondervan were on their way! By the time Zondervan held its silver anniversary celebration, *Never a Dull Moment* had 100,000 copies in print, and *Discoveries*, 50,000. Eventually the figures for Genie came to be counted in millions rather than thousands, with upwards of 12 million copies of her books in print, including both fiction and nonfiction.

Having her origins in the nonreligious media, Genie Price brought a sophistication and professionalism to Zondervan that eventually influenced the rest of the Christian publishing world too. She expected, merited, and received national attention and promotion for her books, and to some degree she taught Zondervan how to achieve it. She gave to Zondervan fully as much value as she received, and no other author appeared so often and so consistently on Zondervan's list over the course of its second quarter-century.

Zondervan reissued two titles in 1979 to commemorate her silver anniversary as a Christian writer—*Discoveries* and *Beloved World: The Story of God and People*—and a new title, *Leave Your Self Alone*, which went through many printings. In the article quoted previously from *The Life of Faith*, Genie called *Beloved World* "the book which has changed my own life so deeply."

> I wrote through the entire Bible, from Genesis to Revelation, attempting to tie up the altogether amazing story of God's love for His beloved world. I will never be the same again.
>
> I write books for two principle reasons: (1) I love to write! (2) I am a thoroughly *convinced* follower of Jesus Christ, and I find it impossible to keep the Good News that God *is* discoverable in Him to myself!

There is an interesting and little-known tie-in between Genie and one of Zondervan's other prominent writers of 1956: Billy Graham.

Zondervan had published several smaller books by Graham, but in February 1956 brought out a longer volume, *The Seven Deadly Sins*. It sold well, but not as spectacularly as Zondervan had hoped. In fact, with one exception, Zondervan was never to publish the evangelist's biggest and most durable books. For twenty years he published with a general publisher in New York, even though, by his own admission later, the publisher had never taken the personal interest in him or shared the sense of ministry that others did. It is worth noting, however, that one of his books published in New York, *Angels: God's Secret Agents*, sold more copies in 1975 — 810,000 — than any other cloth book of any kind published that year, according to the trade journal *Publishers Weekly*.

The Zondervans tried to get bestsellers from Graham. During the sixties they were eager to publish a book by Graham for teenagers and commissioned as ghost writers two persons well equipped for the role, since they were published authors in their own right. Their names? Eugenia Price and Joyce Blackburn, the author of the well-known "Suki" books for juveniles. The book was never finished because Graham had other commitments that kept him from providing the raw material for the writers. But some of the material later emerged in Zondervan's big Graham book, *The Jesus Generation*.

If any book had the makings of a bestseller, it was *The Jesus Generation*. This was so for several reasons: it was Graham's first youth book in fifteen years. It was being published in late 1971 while the nation and the world were riding the crest of the Jesus Movement that had already helped to create a publishing phenomenon in Hal Lindsey's *Late Great Planet Earth*. Moreover, Zondervan was pulling out all the stops with a 250,000 first printing in cloth and paperback editions and a vigorous national promotional campaign, aided by the evangelist's crusades and telecasts.

The manuscript went to typesetting in August on an accelerated schedule. By October 4, there were 111,000 copies on back order, and Zondervan ordered another 250,000 books printed. The first quarter-million were sold out by publication day, November 10. But momentum never developed beyond that initial push, and returns to Zondervan ran very high after a few months. Some 80,000 books were still in inventory five or six years later, and the Zondervan Family Bookstores had trouble even giving them away, which they literally tried to do. Of course, the book was closely tied in with the Jesus Movement. This mighty stirring of the Holy Spirit among young adults, especially in the counterculture, had peaked by the time *The Jesus Generation* was released, and many of the youth affected by the movement had begun to be absorbed into the organized evangelical community. And, though it was a bestseller, the book perhaps fell victim to some extent to the distorted picture of reality painted by the phenomenal and unexpected sales of *The Late Great Planet Earth*.

Just As He Is

More than twenty-five years would pass before Zondervan and Graham were to have their greatest joint success with the release of Billy Graham's autobiography, *Just As I Am: The Autobiography of Billy Graham,* copublished with HarperCollins in 1997. With a million-copy first printing, the book debuted at #11 on the general religious nonfiction list at *Publishers Weekly* but soon rose to the top. As *PW* put it, "Considering that this is the first time this world figure has looked back on his remarkable life and career [in print], it's no surprise that the book is hitting national charts." Graham was interviewed on numerous network TV talk shows in the ensuing weeks.

Another important author in that silver anniversary year was Clyde M. Narramore. His first book, *Life and Love*, published that spring, was described by Zondervan as "the first really authoritative work on the subject of sex from a Christian point of view." It was different. Zondervan had published several books on sexuality over the years, mostly by preachers. Typical among them were two by Oscar Lowry, an evangelist and a professor at Moody Bible Institute, in 1938 and 1940: *A Virtuous Woman* and *The Way of a Man With a Maid.* These books were quite frank for that era; they sold very well. Narramore dealt with subjects, like homosexuality, that were usually taboo in Christian publications. Yet even *Life and Love* was fairly mild compared with some very explicit books that Zondervan has published since the late sixties, such as Herbert J. Miles's *Sexual Happiness in Marriage,* Tim and Beverly LaHaye's multimillion-seller *The Act of Marriage,* and Ed Wheat's *Love Life for Every Married Couple.*

Narramore was not a preacher, but a psychologist. Through his writing, radio broadcasts, and the Narramore Christian Foundation, he made psychology widely "respectable" to evangelical laypeople as well as clergy. Many other books by Narramore have come from Zondervan presses, and all have enjoyed a long life.

■　■　■

To the names of Pat and Bernie, Peter Kladder, Eugenia Price, Billy Graham, and Clyde Narramore could be added a number of others that were important in Zondervan's twenty-fifth anniversary year. Two belonged to persons who were working behind the scenes in one of Zondervan's newest interests: Bible translations. It is regrettable that the names of these two persons remain unfamiliar to this day to thousands who have read and been blessed by the fruit of their labor, *The Berkeley Version in Modern English* and *The Amplified Bible*. For few people have shown more dedication to their work than Gerrit Verkuyl and Frances Siewert.

The Berkeley Version, though not published in its entirety until 1959, was the most lasting achievement of the projects commemorating Zondervan's twenty-fifth anniversary. But since these projects were still in progress at the time of Zondervan's celebration, let us leave the fascinating stories of the Berkeley and the Amplified versions to another chapter.

Headlines in Grand Rapids newspapers were heralding events other than Bible publishing. In January 1956 they reported the killing of five Protestant missionaries by Auca Indians in Ecuador. Their martyrdom struck the world with the same profound impact as the deaths of John and Betty Stam thirty years earlier and the killing of Wycliffe translator Chester A. Bitterman by terrorists in Colombia later on, in March 1981.

A disastrous event occurred in the Grand Rapids area in the spring of that year. On Tuesday, April 3, a devastating tornado struck the west and southwest suburbs of the city. The twister swept through Hudsonville, claiming thirteen lives, and demolished dozens of homes and stores that lay in its tortuous path through Walker and Standale. The newscasts about it prompted many phone calls to the Zondervan offices from bookstores around the country, but, as the *Book News* reported the next month, "To our knowledge, no employee of the publishing house was directly affected by the tornado, although friends and loved ones of employees incurred severe damage.... The publishing house itself was several miles east of the path of the tornado."

Three years before, in June 1953, a series of tornados ravaged portions of Ohio and Eastern Michigan, including the city of Flint, taking 142 lives. Six lives were lost and eighty persons were injured near Grand Rapids on Palm Sunday, April 11, 1965. Again, on May 13, 1980, a tornado struck the heart of Kalamazoo, doing severe damage and taking five lives. But seldom have such severe storms struck so near to Grand Rapids, which lies some miles to the north of Michigan's "tornado alley," as happened in 1956. The usually confident Dutch demeanor was shaken. The twister of 1956 will never be forgotten.

In the first two weeks of July 1956, the shipping and production departments of the publishing house closed down for two weeks while the employees went on vacation. The two-week shutdown remained a standard practice for the production department (though not shipping) for thirty years, until the printing presses and bindery were shut down for good in 1987.

■ ■ ■

The time was moving quickly toward Zondervan's celebration week, October 1–6, and when the time arrived, Zondervan celebrated in style. Much of the attention of the rest of Grand Rapids was focused on what was going on too.

During celebration week there were special luncheons and evening meetings, an open house, and a special edition of the weekly Zondervan chapel service on Friday morning. At that service Al Smith and Helen McAlerney Barth, one of Zondervan's most outstanding recording artists, sang a duet, "Precious Hiding Place."

The climax of the week was the banquet held at the Pantlind Hotel on Friday night. More than 150 authors, editors, dealers, suppliers, city officials, pastors, and friends of Zondervan attended. Former editor Ted W. Engstrom served as toastmaster. Gerrit Gritter, a Grand Rapids commissioner, spoke for the city. R. Gordon Mitchell, then president of the Christian Booksellers Association and owner of the Home Evangel Book Store in Toronto, Canada, brought greetings. The Reverend Mr. F. J. Huegel, veteran missionary and professor at Mexico Bible Seminary, was the main speaker.

A number of employees were honored for longtime service, including John Fiet and Neal Nederveld, more than twenty years, and Millie Gritter, John Idema, Gerard Meyer, William Roode, John Ryskamp, Jim Schimmel, Gert TerKeurst, Harry VanDyk, fifteen years or more.

The highlight of the evening was the presentation of author awards by Pat and Bernie to James H. Hunter, Author of the Quarter Century; Merrill F. Unger (theology); F. J. Huegel (devotional writing); Ken Anderson (young people's books); and Dena Korfker (children's books). *Spurgeon's Morning and Evening,* a devotional classic, was named "the Publication of the Quarter Century."

Perhaps the significance of the event is best summed up in the statement that Pat and Bernie cosigned, for it holds true as a testimony today, another quarter-century later:

> Our hearts are humbled as we see how God has so abundantly blessed during these twenty-five years. It is only by His grace and the wonderful cooperation of a consecrated staff that so much could be accomplished. God promised, "Call unto me, and I will answer thee, and show thee great and mighty things, which thou knowest not" (Jeremiah 33:3 KJV). How He has carried out this promise has been a vital experience for us.... Anew we pledge to Him—and to you, our friends—our deep desire to glorify Him through every avenue of this business enterprise which bears our name and which is dedicated to Him, whose we are and whom we serve.

P. J. Zondervan caresses a Bible
as he holds it. It is an old friend.
Times Union and Journal,
Jacksonville, Florida, January 20, 1979

7

Sharing God's Word

Bible publishing had always been prominent in the minds of Pat and Bernie because they considered God's Word the most important book of all. From time to time they had taken on the distribution of different editions of the King James Version, such as the Newberry Bible in 1951, which used marginal references to focus on the semantic distinctions in the original languages.

But with the publication of the Revised Standard Version in 1950 by the National Council of Churches, a generation of Bible translation began that brought forth many attempts to give new, meaningful, and contemporary expression to the truths of God's Word. When Zondervan celebrated its silver anniversary in 1956, its role in Bible translation was just beginning. Translation work was soon to give Zondervan a role as a major Bible publisher.

Early in 1956 Franklin Logsdon, a pastor in nearby Holland, Michigan —and later pastor of Moody Church in Chicago—paid a visit to his friends Pat and Bernie. He brought with him a copy of what was then being called

"The Amplified Gospel of John," which he had obtained from a friend in California. The distinction of this edition was its use of several English words or phrases to illuminate the Greek language where an exact word equivalent was not available. The English text was "amplified" to include various meanings of the Greek.

Logsdon advised them, "You ought to make arrangements with the people of the Lockman Foundation in California to publish and distribute this."

"Frank," Pat replied, "we don't publish little items like that." But Logsdon insisted that they look into it, so Pat agreed to talk with F. Dewey Lockman in La Habra if he had the opportunity on his forthcoming trip to the West Coast.

Pat was planning to fly to Los Angeles and then on to Japan for a Gideon conference. Because of a series of delays, he had to stay overnight in Los Angeles; so he gave Lockman a call. Lockman arranged to have him picked up at the airport.

"We have a Prophet's Room in our home," Lockman said, "and you can stay here overnight. We'll converse in the morning." Probably few of the occupants of that room ever suited its name quite as well as Pat, considering what was about to happen.

The next morning Pat and Lockman met in the office, one of the rooms in Lockman's spacious home. The elderly gentleman opened a desk drawer and pulled out a set of proofs of the entire New Testament of the Amplified Scriptures. "This is what we've done," he said, "and we're looking for a publisher." What Pat saw was no "little item": it amounted to a thousand pages!

Pat was immediately interested and the two agreed to discuss the project further. Lockman invited Pat to come to Palm Springs a few weeks later when his board was to meet to complete its work on the project. At that meeting Pat met the translators and the woman who was to become the single most important person in the entire Amplified Bible project—Frances Siewert, the editorial director. It had been her responsibility to render the translators' amplifications in final form and type the entire manuscript. Altogether some 12,000 hours of work were invested in the New Testament by Mrs. Siewert and the translators.

Actually, Frances Siewert's role has been somewhat obscured in the publication of this work. She initiated the project, drawing on various existing translations and her own biblical studies. She held B.Lit., B.D., and M.A.

degrees at the time and was working on a doctorate, which she later completed. When Lockman published "The Amplified Gospel of John" in 1954, it bore Mrs. Siewert's name as the author and was more precisely called "The Self-explaining Gospel (the Holy Glad Tidings) of John." But Lockman did not wish to use her name when the project was given over to Zondervan.

At the end of a week of discussions, it was agreed that Zondervan would repay the foundation for its financial investment and publish the New Testament on a royalty basis. When Pat returned home, he and Bernie tried to figure out how to accomplish the mammoth task. A thousand-page New Testament was an awesome project! At one point Lockman, unhappy with the Zondervans' delay, threatened to take the proofs to another publisher: the foundation had invested too many years in the work to let the proofs lie idle.

Zondervan finally arranged with World Publishing Company in Cleveland for a first printing of 10,000 copies. World had thin "Bible paper" in stock and the technology needed for the job. Pat and Bernie had no way of knowing whether people would be interested in this unusual edition of Scripture.

■ ▒ ▒

The Amplified New Testament was published in May 1958 in a compact hardcover edition with 1,024 pages and a price of $3.95. The response was sensational! It was promoted as "the understandable new translation ... that explains itself," and words of praise for the concept poured in from evangelical leaders. The first printing sold out in just over a month, but World couldn't put it back on press until September, since its presses were scheduled months ahead of time. Nevertheless, there were three printings of 25,000 copies each that fall. During one two-and-a-half-month period in 1959, a quarter-million copies were produced, the largest print-paper-and-bind order placed by Zondervan to that date. Banners at the Christian Booksellers Association convention, held in Grand Rapids in August 1959, proclaimed 385,000 copies in print, and the figure climbed to a half-million by March 1960. Still in print, the Amplified Bible has sold more than 3.5 million copies.

Zondervan was making publishing history with a new version of Scripture at a time when other publishers, religious or general, could only dream of such a performance for any book.

The Lockman Foundation was not interested in producing a companion Old Testament, but of course Zondervan was. Pat and Bernie were given permission to use the name "Amplified" and to publish both testaments under one cover. They convened a group of scholars to work under the direction of Mrs. Siewert.

The Old Testament was initially published in two volumes to match the New in size and format. Part II (Job to Malachi) was actually printed first. It came off press in February 1962 with an initial printing of 100,000. Sales were good, but not as strong as Zondervan had expected, since the New Testament by that time had 750,000 copies in print. The cause was traced to the fact that the Old Testament jacket was the same blue color as that of the New; it apparently was confusing the buyer, who thought, *I've already bought that.* The problem was solved by changing the color to brown in later printings. Sales improved. The incident is worth mentioning, because it was a rare occasion when Pat and Bernie didn't make the right decision in merchandising a product; their record was amazing, the envy of many a book publisher.

Part I (Genesis to Esther) was published in September 1964.

To publish the whole Amplified Bible under one cover, Zondervan awarded a million-dollar contract to World. It was Zondervan's biggest contract to that date and one of World's largest also. The whole Bible appeared in September 1965. Just a few weeks earlier, Zondervan had marked the sale of the millionth copy of the *Amplified New Testament.*

It is worth noting that the publication of the *Amplified New Testament* marked the end of an era — an era of low-budget struggle for Zondervan. This publication generated the capital needed to develop bookstores, undertake some ambitious long-range publishing projects, and add some fringe benefits for employees, such as group insurance.

■   ▓   ▓

Zondervan was in the middle of another exciting adventure in Bible publishing as the *Amplified New Testament* was coming into print. The Berkeley Version was nearing completion.

The Berkeley Bible was born when a Presbyterian minister about to retire at the age of sixty-five decided he had not yet finished his life's work. Indeed, Gerrit Verkuyl's vision for a new English translation of the Bible had been haunting him since college days. Alice K. Montin tells the story:

> In his undergraduate days at Park College [Missouri], Verkuyl studied Greek with a professor who inspired him to compare the King James Version,

and the Dutch Bible he had known as a child, with the Greek version. He was amazed to learn that the Dutch was more faithful to the Greek than was the English.

He developed a great desire to retranslate the Bible from Greek even though it seemed far beyond the realm of possibility. What business did a farmer's son from Holland have even to think of such a thing, when he did not know well either the language he wanted to translate into, or the languages in which the Bible had been written? . . .

At night and in every spare moment he taught himself English by means of a Dutch-English dictionary and a New Testament that had parallel columns of Dutch and English.[5]

Eventually Verkuyl joined the staff of the Board of Christian Education of the Presbyterian Church, U.S.A., in Chicago, and served that church for more than thirty years, teaching and traveling widely. He enjoyed his work thoroughly but never abandoned his desire to translate the Bible. Finally in 1936 he began to translate the New Testament, working mostly in the early morning before going to his office. The next year he moved to Berkeley, California, and in 1939 he retired from the Board of Christian Education.

Verkuyl published the *Berkeley Version of the New Testament*—named for his adopted home city—in 1945. About 40,000 copies had been sold by 1950 when Verkuyl's publisher, Gillick Press, sold the rights to Zondervan. Pat and Bernie gathered a group of nineteen Hebrew scholars, from several denominations, to work with Verkuyl in preparing the Old Testament translation. Their aim was to work from the Hebrew, and they had the opportunity also to make use of relevant Dead Sea Scrolls discovered in 1947.

In June 1956 the translation committee held one of its meetings at Calvin College in Grand Rapids. The *Book News*, reporting on that session, defined the translators' task this way:

... to provide concerned Christians with a sound, fundamental, new translation from the original manuscripts—a translation that is reliable, documented, up to date, timely, and most of all true to the Word. This translation in modern English will clear up in the minds of many Bible lovers passages hitherto somewhat obscure because of archaic words and phrases no longer meaningful to this generation.

The first copies of *The Berkeley Version of the Bible in Modern English* came off the press on April 10, 1959. Gerrit Verkuyl was eighty-six years old. The version was met with enthusiastic response. Even though its impact on the Christian community was eclipsed to some extent by the emergence of *The Amplified New Testament* eleven months earlier, the Berkeley sold very well. Three printings by July brought the total of copies in print to 50,000, and the version enjoyed strong and steady sales for many years.

In 1971 the version was given a new name, for the old had become a victim of current events. The university in the city for which the version was named—Berkeley, California—had become a center of student revolt and the Free Speech Movement in the mid to late sixties, and the name *Berkeley* was a byword for antiestablishment protests. Zondervan gave the Berkeley Version the new name *The Modern Language Bible*.

■　■　■

With the publication of the Amplified and the Berkeley versions, Pat and Bernie sought other opportunities to publish in the Bible field. In the fall of

Helping Others

A handwritten letter about *Hurlbut's Story of the Bible* came to Zondervan during the Vietnam War from the daughter of the famous missionaries Jonathan and Rosalind Goforth, who was herself a missionary:

Dear Mr. Bryant:

I have been a long time in finishing my Old Testament stories. Here is a list of the ones I would like your permission to use for printing in the Vietnamese language. I have quoted parts from the following stories from Hurlbut's Story of the Bible:

[She lists the titles of 17 stories.]

Please excuse my poor writing—I am almost blind. This will probably be my last publication for the poor suffering ones in V.N. We make no money on it. It is for distribution among troops of all nationalities, prisoners of war, orphans + others.

I will be so grateful for your permission and so will the desperately needy millions of V.N.

Sincerely, Ruth Goforth Jeffrey

1961 they issued *Norlie's Simplified New Testament*, a version well suited for young people and family use, prepared by Olaf M. Norlie, a Lutheran professor in Minnesota. The first printing of 35,000 copies sold out quickly. This was followed by an illustrated *Children's Simplified New Testament*. Although Norlie's did not remain on Zondervan's list as long as other Bibles, it made a good contribution and filled a need that existed at the time.

Zondervan learned that when Holt, Rinehart, the prominent New York publisher, took over the John C. Winston Company of Philadelphia, it did not want to keep Winston's line of Bibles and religious books. So in 1962 Zondervan began publication of the popular *Christian Workers' New Testament*; the next year it purchased other products in Winston's line, including *The Marked Reference Bible* and several significant reference books, the classic *Cruden's Complete Concordance*, *Irwin's Bible Commentary*, *Peloubet's Bible Dictionary*, and *Smith's Bible Dictionary*, all of which remained in print for many years. *Cruden's* is still in print. Another Winston title was *Hurlbut's Story of the Bible*, which won recognition in *Time* magazine in March 1968 as one of the bestselling religious books of all time.

■　■　■

Other important events in Bible publishing were still in Zondervan's future, namely, the acquisition of the Harper Brothers' Bible Division and the publication of the New International Version. But we should turn our attention now to the corporation developments and book publishing that were taking place in the late fifties and early sixties. A number of important things occurred in 1958.

One of Zondervan's new authors that year was Rosalind Rinker. "Ros" had spent several years in China as a writer-missionary associated with Mrs. Charles E. Cowman, and after that served eleven years as a staff member of InterVarsity Christian Fellowship in the United States. In January 1958, she became Genie Price's associate and partner and came to the attention of Zondervan. Genie wrote the introduction for Ros's first Zondervan book, *The Years that Count*. It was the first of many books that Ros published with Zondervan, of which the most significant was *Prayer—Conversing with God*. In this book and others, she developed the concept of "conversational prayer," a kind of group participation in prayer that was greatly valued, especially in

Bible study and sharing groups. She held a wide ministry of conducting prayer workshops.

The year 1958 also brought publication of the first of the books that are known as the "All Series." In 1956 Harper & Row published a book by Edith Deen called *All the Women of the Bible*. This book attracted much attention and led Pat Zondervan to propose to Herbert Lockyer that he consider preparing a book on the men in the Bible. Lockyer was then seventy years old. He had assisted Zondervan as an editorial consultant for many years after leaving the *Christian Digest* in 1944 and had published a number of books with them during that time. But he had never undertaken a manuscript of this size; Pat and Bernie envisioned that it could run to as many as a thousand pages of type. As he had done many times before, Lockyer wrote this entire manuscript in a scrawled long-hand.

Pat wrote prophetically to Lockyer in England in February 1957, "It's good to learn about the splendid progress you are making on the monumental task of preparing the manuscript on all the men of the Bible. You are making history, brother, in putting that together."

The manuscript was completed in April 1957. Production of the book took a long time, partly because corrections and proofs had to be sent to and from England. Zondervan was able to keep the length to 384 pages by using a large trim size, with two columns of type on a page rather than the conventional single column. The large trim size is often used for reference books and commentaries, and for many years it was commonly referred to in Zondervan's editorial department as "the All size."

All the Men of the Bible was finally published in September 1958. There had already been considerable discussion at Zondervan about whether to plan for an extensive series of books of this kind and what subjects to include; Pat and Bernie were by no means certain *All the Men* would sell well. But it did. It went into two more printings within six months.

The publishing house had received a manuscript on prayer from Lockyer back in 1955. Lockyer was calling it *Great Prayers of the Bible*, but Zondervan was revising the format and preparing to publish it as *1000 Sermon Outlines and Illustrations on Prayer*. Then when *All the Men* began to take shape, the manuscript was changed again and Lockyer was asked to expand it so that it could become *All the Prayers of the Bible*. It was published in October 1959 as the second "All" book.

While *All the Men* was still in progress, Lockyer had also proposed two other volumes that were rejected, *All the Fruits and Flowers of the Bible* and *All the Birds and Beasts of the Bible*. In fact, he was proposing so many titles that it was almost too much for Zondervan to handle; Pat and Bernie had to remind Lockyer to choose his subjects carefully and take the time to do the job well. Lockyer repeatedly asked Pat and Bernie to let him do a book on the kings and queens of the Bible, but they resisted because they believed subjects such as parables and miracles would make a more significant contribution. They wisely did not grant his request until the series was more established.

There were sixteen titles in the "All Series," with more than three million copies in print altogether. Ten of those sixteen are still in print. The final volume of the series, published in 1977, was *All About Bible Study*, which is undoubtedly the last book manuscript written in long-hand ever accepted for publication by Zondervan.

The "All Series" by Herbert Lockyer

1. *All the Men of the Bible* (1958)
2. *All the Prayers of the Bible* (1959)
3. *All the Miracles of the Bible* (1961)
4. *All the Kings and Queens of Bible* (1961)
5. *All the Promises of the Bible* (1962)
6. *All the Parables of the Bible* (1963)
7. *All the Doctrines of the Bible* (1964)
8. *All the Books and Chapters of the Bible* (1966)
9. *All the Women of the Bible* (1967)
10. *All the Holy Days and Holidays* (1968)
11. *All the Trades and Occupations of the Bible* (1969)
12. *All the Children of the Bible* (1970)
13. *All the Apostles of the Bible* (1972)
14. *All the Messianic Prophecies of the Bible* (1973)
15. *All the Divine Names and Titles of the Bible* (1975)
16. *All About Bible Study* (1977)

Lockyer never really retired from writing. He continued to write at his home in Colorado. He wrote a host of books for other publishers, including more volumes of the "All Series," including such titles as *All the Music of the Bible*, *All God's Comfort*, *All about the Second Coming*, and *All the Teachings of the Bible*. The final work he wrote for Zondervan was a daily devotional based on the New International Version of the Bible, *Light to Live By*, published in 1979, at which time he held the distinction of being Zondervan's oldest living author. He died in November 1984 at the age of ninety-eight.

■   ■   ■

There is a footnote to the "All Series" story that reveals an interesting sidelight about publishing. In October 1958, a month after Zondervan issued *All the Men of the Bible*, Eerdmans decided to publish a manuscript on angels that had lain all but forgotten in their files for ten years. Their title was *All the Angels of the Bible*. Lockyer had submitted it to Eerdmans after Zondervan turned it down in 1948. This was neither the first time nor the last that a manuscript rejected by Zondervan found a publisher elsewhere, although the time span in this case may have set some kind of record.

When editors see a book announced on someone else's list that their publishing house rejected, there is always a twinge of doubt: did we make a mistake? But the doubt is fleeting. The truth is, there were sound reasons for rejecting it, and there is seldom any regret. There are some outstanding examples in the general book trade of manuscripts that were rejected by several publishers before being accepted and published and becoming bestsellers, but very few. Among them are *The Caine Mutiny* by Herman Wouk, which an editor at Simon & Schuster snubbed as a story about "a crazy captain and a ship's mutiny"; *The Day Lincoln Was Shot* by Jim Bishop, which Bennett Cerf, the cofounder of Random House, rejected with the comment, "Jim, every kid knows your story; they even know who did it";[6] and *Jonathan Livingston Seagull* by Richard Bach, which bounced around a half-dozen or so children's departments until it was finally accepted and published as a book for *adults*. The fact is, many a bestseller might well have flopped if one of the rejecting publishers had actually published it. Not only are bestsellers made up of the right author with the right idea at the right time, but they also have to be published by the right publisher.

Even fewer titles of this kind would probably be discovered among Christian publishers. One noteworthy example for Zondervan, however, is *The Living Bible*. Kenneth Taylor had offered to Zondervan some of his paraphrased epistles of the New Testament during the sixties; but Zondervan had misgivings about the concept—and understandably, since Zondervan had invested much time and money enabling groups of scholars to prepare the translations for the Amplified and Berkeley Bibles. *The Living Bible* sold about 5 million copies in 1972, the year it was published by Tyndale; *Publishers Weekly* cited it as the bestselling hardcover book of any kind sold in 1972 and 1973.

There is another footnote to the Lockyer story. Although Dr. Lockyer was Zondervan's oldest living author, another writer can lay claim to having published a book at a hoarier age. In 1965 Zondervan published *The Jew Returns to Israel*, and it enjoyed a second printing that same year. The author, an overseer in the Christian Catholic Church in Zion, Illinois, was the Reverend Mr. Anton Darms. He was ninety-six years old.

8

How many a man has dated a new era
in his life from the reading of a book.
HENRY DAVID THOREAU,
WALDEN, "READING," 1854

A Handbook to Remember

Pat and Bernie had been co-owners and partners of Zondervan Publishing House from the time it began in the farmhouse in Grandville. They always made important decisions together. When the participation of others was needed for a decision, they operated by consensus. As the staff grew, there was never any hesitation to delegate authority. Zondervan was a smoothly and efficiently run company, as its growing annual sales testified: from the $1,800 sales in December 1931, the business had grown to a quarter of a million dollars annually in 1940 and to more than a million annually in the early fifties.

In 1958 Pat and Bernie decided to incorporate. From then on, until Bernie died in 1966, they served alternate years as president. They had a strong supporting staff, foremost of whom was Peter Kladder, the treasurer.

The editorial committee had traditionally consisted of Pat and Bernie and "the Editor"—Phil Roberts, Ted Engstrom, and then Al Bryant. In the early years, editorial and production meetings were held on a weekday afternoon on the mezzanine at the Pantlind Hotel in downtown Grand Rapids; if there was unfinished business, it was handled on overtime—Saturday mornings.

The editor also had oversight of other departments, including advertising, promotion, and production. This changed in 1958. Ward Oury, a Wheaton College graduate with journalistic and sales experience, was hired as Zondervan's first full-time advertising manager. Oury did not stay long. He was succeeded in 1959 by Gilbert ("Gib") Malcolm, who continued to serve Zondervan in various advertising roles into the 1980s.

Peter deVisser was hired for a new position also, that of director of publications. It was intended that, besides giving oversight to the whole book-publishing operation, deVisser would spearhead Zondervan's plans for developing a more extensive line of classroom textbooks, a goal stimulated by the successful textbook contests a few years earlier.

Pat and Bernie had been hoping for some time that deVisser would join the firm. Peter and Bernie attended the same church, and Bernie told him more than once, "Anytime you want to come to work for us, just say the word." Peter had twenty years' experience in publishing, much of it as general manager of the rival publisher house a short distance away, William B. Eerdmans Publishing Company.

■ ■ ■

DeVisser left Eerdmans in 1956 to satisfy a long-standing desire to have his own publishing firm. With a friend he started Grand Rapids International Publications. He also served for a year as acting managing editor of a new evangelical periodical, begun in 1956, *Christianity Today*. After two years, Peter discovered that there were many aspects of running a business that he didn't enjoy, so he and his friend closed theirs down. DeVisser turned to Zondervan, where, as director of publications, he could do the things he liked to do.

DeVisser fulfilled all of Pat and Bernie's hopes, and more. He was a personable, professional, and skillful executive who shared his employers' vision. His career was tragically cut short by a fatal heart attack on September 3, 1963, but in his five years with Zondervan he completed several important publishing projects and launched others that were finished after his death.

One important project was the one-volume edition of *Matthew Henry's Commentary on the Whole Bible*. The magnificent work of this seventeenth-century British expositor was originally published in six volumes and is rightfully called "the greatest devotional commentary of all time." A. Morgan Derham describes it in *The New International Dictionary of the Christian Church* in these words:

> It set a style in detailed, often highly spiritualized, exposition of Scripture which has shaped evangelical ministry ever since; C. H. Spurgeon acknowledged his debt to Henry; many others have neglected this courtesy. Critical textual problems were not within his purview. Suffice to say that he could write 190 words of comment, including a three-part sermon outline, on Genesis 26:34.[7]

Zondervan's one-volume edition, published in 1962, was edited and abridged by Leslie F. Church; it contains 3 million words on two thousand pages. It has made available to more than a million laypeople and pastors a work that in its six-volume form many of them could not afford, and it is still in print.

Zondervan had long wanted to publish its own Bible dictionary. Most of those in print when deVisser joined Zondervan were quite old, including those later acquired in Winston's religious line. Recent scholarship and archaeological discoveries had created a strong need for a new dictionary, and new developments in graphic arts made possible the extensive use of illustrations and photographs in attractive ways.

Pat and Peter recruited Merrill C. Tenney of Wheaton College as general editor to head a team of sixty-five scholars. The project required an investment of more than $100,000 before the first copy came off the press. *Zondervan's Pictorial Bible Dictionary* was published in February 1963, and the first printing of 35,000 copies sold out quickly. Based on the King James Version, it was for many years one of the leading reference works on Zondervan's list, and there are more than 600,000 copies in print. True to its promise, it contains more than seven hundred photographs, drawings, and charts and forty maps. In 1987, Zondervan revised this classic reference work to make it compatible with the NIV Bible by publishing *The New International Dictionary of the Bible: Pictorial Edition.* That edition has sold more than 160,000 copies.

At the time the original dictionary was published, preparation of *The Zondervan Pictorial Bible Atlas* was already under way. Edited by E. M. Blaiklock, it was published in 1969.

No sooner was the dictionary completed than deVisser put Tenney to work on a multivolume Bible encyclopedia. This was a project of much greater scope and magnitude than the dictionary, and it required nearly twelve years to complete. But its publication in 1975 owed much to the foundations laid in 1963 by deVisser.

DeVisser's influence on the publishing of classroom texts can be assessed in a special sixteen-page edition of the *Book News* devoted to textbooks, commentaries, and reference works in February 1962. Some of the books were backlist items:

- "The Modern Cult Library" by Walter R. Martin
- Four volumes in the All Series by Herbert Lockyer
- Twenty-two volumes, most of them by J. B. Lightfoot, J. A. Alexander, or F. L. Godet, in the "Classic Commentary Library"
- *Matthew Henry's Commentary* in one volume
- *The Jamieson, Fausset and Brown Commentary* in one volume
- *Principles of Biblical Hermeneutics* by J. Edwin Hartill
- *Christianity through the Centuries* by Earle E. Cairns
- *Christian Theology* and *Elemental Theology* by Emery H. Bancroft
- *Principles of Teaching for Christian Teachers* by C. B. Eavey.

With these were several pages of new and forthcoming titles, including the following:

- *Dooyeweerd and the Amsterdam Philosophy* by Ronald H. Nash
- *Adventures in the History of Philosophy* by John F. Gates
- *A Christian View of Being and Knowing* and *A Systematic Theology of the Christian Religion, Vol. 1,* by J. Oliver Buswell Jr.
- *Theology of the Older Testament* by J. Barton Payne
- *Archaeology and the New Testament* by Merrill F. Unger

There was also a page devoted to the writings of J. Sidlow Baxter. Zondervan had begun to publish many of the books of this renowned Bible expositor from Scotland in 1969. Fourteen of Baxter's titles eventually appeared on Zondervan's lists, including the masterful exposition *Explore the Book,* originally published in six volumes and eventually combined into one.

Perhaps Peter deVisser's contribution to Zondervan and to evangelical publishing as a whole is best summed up in the tribute paid to him in the dedication in Walter Martin's *Kingdom of the Cults:* "If you seek his monument, consult the libraries of the informed."

■ ■ ■

One of the most important books that Zondervan has ever published was already a million-copy bestseller when the publishing house obtained the rights to it on June 17, 1960. There is an incredible story behind this book that is one of a kind—*Halley's Bible Handbook.*

Henry H. Halley, a nephew several generations removed from the English scientist who named Halley's Comet, was born in the bluegrass region of Kentucky in 1874. After graduating from college and teaching briefly in Kentucky, he was ordained to the ministry in 1898. Ten years later he was forced by ill health to leave the ministry.

A short time after that Halley was taking a trip from his home in Kalamazoo, Michigan, to California. The long train journey—three days and four nights—was tiresome. An idea entered Halley's mind as he stared out of his coach window at the sagebrush of western Kansas: to relieve the boredom, he would repeat familiar passages of Scripture and meditate on them, passages such as the Twenty-third Psalm and the Beatitudes. *Now I'm all alone, with nothing to interfere with my thoughts,* he mused. *I can make a blessing instead of an irritation out of this trip.*

Before the trip ended he had begun to memorize other passages of Scripture. As time passed he continued to memorize new passages, not only when traveling but whenever he had a few minutes to spend with his New Testament. After several years the daring idea struck him of memorizing the entire Bible. He abridged the Bible to about one-third its size, then began to commit the abridgment to memory.

One day a phone call came from a church not far from Kalamazoo: "Our pastor is sick. We want you to come and preach for us."

Halley agreed. He entered the pulpit determined to speak only words from God—none of his own. Quietly he recited the Sermon on the Mount and other passages from the Gospels. The response was overwhelming. Calls began to come from other churches that heard what he had done. Halley was soon traveling a great deal in a new ministry, which he began to call "Bible Recitals."

Halley moved to Chicago and gradually the part-time real estate business with which he had supported his family faded as he spent more and more time in the recital ministry. Sometimes he would recite Scripture nightly for two or even three weeks in one church.

"The story of the crucifixion, abridged from the four Gospels, was by far the first choice. It took an entire evening to give it," Halley once told a newspaper reporter. The next night he usually gave the biblical account of the resurrection. Repeated requests came also for the Book of Revelation, the creation narrative in Genesis, the books of Job, Ruth, and Ecclesiastes, the story of Pentecost, and Paul's missionary journeys. "The most difficult to recount was the Epistle to the Hebrews," Halley said. "It was the only book I was ever afraid I would forget."[8]

Halley's schedule usually called for his mornings to be spent in the study of archaeological findings and Bible history in the library of whatever town he was visiting. In the afternoons he rested, to protect his naturally weak voice, and reviewed his Bible abridgments. Before reciting a passage, Halley would give his audience a background sketch for it. In one Indiana town, one day in 1924, a stenographer sat in the front row taking shorthand notes of the preliminary remarks, noisily shuffling her notebook pages. Because of this distraction Halley decided to prepare a leaflet for free distribution and eliminate the spoken introductions.

This leaflet of sixteen pages was called "Suggestions for Bible Study," and Halley gave out 10,000 copies the first year. The next year he expanded it to thirty-two pages and distributed another 10,000. From year to year the leaflet grew in size and numbers; when it grew to be about a hundred pages, Halley had to start charging people for it.

■ ■ ■

For twenty years, from 1921 to 1941, Halley maintained the Bible Recitals ministry, supported by freewill offerings, and spoke before an estimated 2 million people. World War II put a stop to the recitals. At home in Chicago, he and his wife, Madge, a school teacher, began to assemble the "leaflet" into a Bible handbook. Its contents were described on the familiar blue and gray jacket that became its trademark as "An Abbreviated Bible Commentary, Amazing Archaeological Discoveries, How We Got the Bible, An Epitome of

Church History, Select Bible Verses." Halley had it printed by Rand McNally & Company in Indiana.

In May 1960, just before Halley granted publication rights to Zondervan, Andrew McNally III, president of Rand McNally, presented Henry and Madge Halley with a specially bound millionth copy.[9] It was in its twenty-second edition, ran to 968 pages, and sold for $3.75. It had been selling more than 60,000 copies a year. It had also been published in Spanish, Chinese, Japanese, and Korean, and in one year alone the Japanese edition sold 20,000 copies. Even so, the twenty-fourth edition, published by Zondervan in July 1965 and based on the King James Version, went beyond anything the company had imagined. According to a news release that September, the first printing of 75,000 copies was "nearly exhausted," and a second printing of 75,000 more copies was in the works.

Halley's Bible Handbook is still one of the "best buys" among religious books in terms of number of pages per dollar. Zondervan also publishes large-print cloth and softcover editions. In addition the book appears in twenty-two languages besides English. It is consistently one of the top-selling volumes on Zondervan's list, and there are now more than 6 million copies in print. That twenty-fourth edition is still in print in standard and large-print editions. But, not counting a golden-anniversary edition, published in 1974, that included a facsimile of the original sixteen-page leaflet, some thirty-six years would pass before the twenty-fifth edition would come into being, with changes reflecting a new readership and a new era.

The handbook is often the first religious book, after the Bible, that a new Christian will buy. It is an indispensable possession for thousands of Bible students. Halley died in 1965 at the age of ninety-one. His legacy is best expressed in the citation of the Gutenberg Award, presented to Halley in 1961 by the Chicago Bible Society: "Throughout the years, *Halley's Bible Handbook,* in one edition after another, has aided the sincere Bible student to find his way more deeply into the blessed and saving knowledge of our Lord and Saviour, Jesus Christ."

■   ■   ■

Henry H. Halley was one of four Zondervan authors featured at the eleventh annual Christian Booksellers Association (CBA) convention held in Chicago in August 1960. The others were Dena Korfker, author of the new bestseller,

My *Picture Story Bible*; Rosalind Rinker, whose book *Prayer—Conversing With God* had just appeared in a new softcover edition; and Eugenia Price, whose latest book, *Strictly Personal* (retitled *What Is God Like?* in 1965), was selling a thousand copies a week and had 40,000 in print since its publication in May.

There were also some unfamiliar faces in the Zondervan sales booth, including the new sales manager, Frank R. Lehmann, and the new representative for the Midwest, Art Miller.

Robert Kregel of Kregel Publications in Grand Rapids was president of the association that year.

CBA was founded in 1950 to serve the growing number of religious bookstores that were springing up around the country and in Canada. The annual summer convention drew hundreds of book dealers to exhibits and programs sponsored by religious book and music publishers and manufacturers of religious supplies, and it became the biggest Christian book event of the year. The event is more of a "selling convention"—in which publishers not only exhibit their merchandise but also receive orders from dealers—than its counterpart in the general book trade, the convention of the American Booksellers Association.

One of the most significant CBA conventions for Zondervan was the tenth, held in Grand Rapids August 17–20, 1959. The convention began with a Sunday afternoon concert by Zondervan recording artists. The *Book News* reported:

> It was the hottest week Grand Rapids had seen in many years, but the air-conditioned facilities of the Civic Auditorium and the Pantlind Hotel provided a comfortable and adequate setting for the greatest attendance and the largest number of exhibits ever at a CBA convention. The total registration was 1,586, of which 698 represented 367 bookstores, 5 from countries outside the U.S. and Canada. There were 125 trade exhibits, all on one floor of the Civic Auditorium, with 498 personnel representing the exhibitors.

In Zondervan's exhibit were sales representatives John Fiet and Lloyd Van Horn, assisted by mail-room supervisor Vernon Mitchell; Peter deVisser; Al Bryant; Charles Van Horn, office manager of the music division; and of course Pat and Bernie. Special guests who greeted the booksellers were authors Genie Price and Ros Rinker, the convention's devotional speakers, and tenor Ralph

Nielsen, a Zondervan recording artist well known on the *Temple Time* radio broadcast that originated in Grand Rapids.

On Friday, the last day of the convention, more than three hundred conventioneers toured the Zondervan offices and plant on Lake Drive and, along with the employees, were served lunch in the general-office area. Each visitor received a complimentary copy of *Our Daily Bread*, the new daily devotional book by M. R. DeHaan.

That was the only time the CBA convention met in Grand Rapids.

Today the organization, based in Colorado Springs, serves some 2,300 bookstores in the United States and another 1,000 in fifty countries worldwide. It works with more than 600 publishers and manufacturers, and its annual convention (now called the International Christian Retailers Show) attracts thousands of people each year. Zondervan has played a leading role in its growth all the way.

But the story of Zondervan in CBA is more than books and Bibles. In the early sixties, as we have seen, Zondervan was attracting attention with new versions of Scripture, a growing textbook program, *Halley's Bible Handbook,* and the writings of Eugenia Price. But two other interests of the Zondervan company were becoming prominent in its growth—music publishing and retail stores. These are the focus of the next chapter.

I have no song to sing
But that of Christ my King;
To Him my praise I'll bring
 forevermore.
His love beyond degree,
His death that ransomed me,
Now and eternally,
 I'll sing it o'er.
JOHN W. PETERSON, 1954

9

A Song to Sing

Although Zondervan is not now a player in the Christian music business, it was once a widely recognized and influential force.

Zondervan's music publishing division beat an unsteady tempo on its way to developing into the distinctive and widely known part of the corporation that it eventually became. Long before Zondervan and Singspiration merged, the two names were often spoken together. Many people in the industry still hold the mistaken belief that Zondervan founded Singspiration. In reality, the story of Zondervan music until the early sixties must be viewed as something like three melodies in counterpoint, gradually converging into a chorus sung in unison: Zondervan as an independent music publisher; Singspiration as a publisher whose products were distributed by Zondervan; and the distribution of audio recordings, an operation kept separate from that of printed music.

The beginnings of both Zondervan Music Publishers and Singspiration in the late thirties have already been described. Zondervan began distributing songbooks for Singspiration's founder and guiding genius, Alfred B. Smith, in 1941, but continued to produce a few songbooks of its own. The two publishers had similar tastes and interests in music, focusing on gospel choruses and hymns and vocal selections that would serve smaller churches with nonprofessional, volunteer musicians. Pat and Bernie considered music important to their company, even though it was not until about 1952 that it began to get a good amount of promotion. The *Book News* began to devote full pages to music at that time and changed its name to the *Book and Record News*.

Nevertheless, Zondervan was already producing some materials that achieved both distinction and success during the decade of the forties. In 1944, Zondervan took over publication of the songbook *Word of Life Melodies*, compiled by Norman J. Clayton, who is perhaps best known for his popular hymn "Now I Belong to Jesus." The next year Zondervan issued *Word of Life Melodies No. 2*. By late 1945, there were 100,000 copies of the first of these songbooks in print, and 75,000 of the second. Another publication that year was *Sing above the Clouds* by "Merv" Rosell. Also, the song "God Bless Our Boys" by Louis Paul Lehman Jr. was so popular that it was published in separate leaflet form.

At the same time, Al Smith was publishing the *Handy Hymnal*, more volumes in the *Favorites* and *Singspiration* series that launched his fame, and the book *Action Songs for Boys and Girls*. This last, published in 1944, is believed by some at Zondervan to have been the biggest-selling Singspiration publication of all time; hundreds of thousands of copies were sold. The action choruses took their name from the hand motions described with the music; these proved popular with Sunday school and vacation Bible school teachers, and many of today's Christian leaders grew up on songs like "This Little Light of Mine" and "Fishers of Men." Subsequent *Action* books included choruses like "Cheer Up, Ye Saints of God," "Give Me Oil in My Lamp," and "Deep and Wide."

■   ■   ■

Zondervan began distributing phonograph records — 78 rpm — in March 1947. The Singspiration label featured vocalists George Beverly Shea, Rose Arzoomanian, George Edstrom, Al Smith, and organists Herman Voss and Doug Fisher. Zondervan also offered organist Lorin Whitney and the Haven of Rest Quartet on the Sacred Records label, the Biola Student Choir and Male Quartet on Sunshine Hour recordings; the Stamps-Baxter Quartet, and the Old-Fashioned Revival Hour Quartet.

The ministry that developed from the recordings is exemplified by the story of a little girl in Decatur, Illinois. A newspaper wire service carried this story in the summer of 1947:

> The doctors say that four-year-old Carolyn Robb is dying. Before she does, her parents would like to find for her a recording of her favorite song, "Jesus Loves Me."
>
> She is suffering from a cancer at the base of her brain, and frequently she is wracked with pain. Doctors agree that her case is incurable.
>
> Her mother said she has a record player, but she has been unable to find a recording of the song the blue-eyed little girl loves so well.
>
> Her father, a veteran of World War II, has promised her that Christmas will come early this year.
>
> "I wish Santa would hurry up," Carolyn told him. "The doctor's been here so much lately."
>
> "There isn't anything we can do now," Carolyn's mother said, "but trust the Lord that He will find a better place than she has now."

Pat and Bernie sent a copy of the Singspiration record by George Beverly Shea that contained the song. Carolyn died a few weeks later. Although the *Book News* never reported Carolyn's response, we can assume that she found happiness in having a recording of the song she loved so much.

There were several technological developments over the next few years that greatly improved the quality and marketing of recordings. "Unbreakable" varieties of flexible plastics came into use, making records more durable than before. New masters were produced for old recordings by means of electronic filtration that eliminated background noise. For a while all the Singspiration recordings were cut by RCA Victor, a leader in the record industry. Longer-playing records at a speed of 45 rpm began to become popular in 1939. Four years later ten- and twelve-inch records at $33^1/3$ rpm began to appear in great numbers. The development of long-playing records spurred the recording industry as a whole and was the most significant innovation until stereophonic records were introduced in 1957 and compact discs (CDs) in 1988. Singspiration's first "LPs," as the new long-playing records were called, had three songs to a side; later, LPs usually had five or six. The LPs sold for $3.65 including tax; single 78s were $1.10.

In 1952 Zondervan became the exclusive distributor for a number of Singspiration recordings and artists, and two years later it began to produce

Singspiration's printed music. Another event in 1952 was the publication of *Singdex*, a looseleaf registry, updated from time to time, of all the Singspiration records, indexed by title and artist, and all the songs in the Singspiration songbooks. *Singdex* proved to be a valuable aid to both dealers and their customers.

■   ■   ■

By this time the name of John W. Peterson was becoming well known in the field of gospel music. Peterson was working for radio station WMBI in Chicago and getting some songs published here and there after "It Took a Miracle" brought him nationwide attention in 1948. Among the best known were "So Send I You," for which Margaret Clarkson wrote the words; "No One Ever Cared for Me Like Jesus," which became identified with George Beverly Shea at Graham crusades; and "Over the Sunset Mountains," which Peterson recorded with Bill Pearce and Dick Anthony, two musicians associated with him at WMBI. In 1953 he began to produce a series of songbooks for Moody Press with the title *Melody-Aires*, and he also published the first book in a very successful songbook series called *Miracle Melodies*. Yet he did not know where his career was leading him.

Then in 1955 Al Smith came to Chicago and gave him a check for $1,000 in exchange for ten or twelve songs. That was considerably more per song than Peterson had received before. His first sale was a song called "Yet There Is Room." He received $8 for it from R. E. Winsett, a publisher in Dayton, Tennessee, in 1940; the glow of success was dimmed, however, by the fact that Winsett misspelled his name "Patterson." But everyone in gospel music knew how to spell Peterson's name by the time Al Smith came to see him.

Today a composer receives a royalty — a kind of "commission" — on the music he publishes, figured on the number of recordings or printed copies sold. But in those days it was customary for a publisher to buy a song outright from a composer and copyright it in its own name. Peterson, like other Christian composers, accepted this arrangement because most of those who were publishing his works were in a publishing business that had an aspect of ministry.

Smith had published two of Peterson's songs already by the time he came to visit John in Chicago. One was "He Owns the Cattle on a Thousand

Hills." The other, "Jesus Led Me All the Way," illustrates that some songs come into being in unusual ways. Smith, having just led a congregation at Moody in the singing of Fanny Crosby's hymn "All the Way My Saviour Leads Me," suggested to John that he use the last line as a title and write a song to go with it.

While Peterson was struggling to get his career started at Moody, Smith had moved his Singspiration company from Wheaton to Montrose, Pennsylvania, home of the well-known Montrose Bible Conference founded by R. A. Torrey many years before. In 1951 Smith and a friend launched into choral music on a large scale, forming a company called Better Choirs. Five times a year this organization published two magazines that contained arrangements for group singing. *Songster* was for small groups, including quarters and duets; *Chorister* was for the "average choir" to use in Sunday-morning worship. The arrangements included both old hymns and new compositions, and the magazines were well received.

Peterson sent Smith a number of songs as they had agreed. Then Smith returned a couple of months later to ask Peterson to leave WMBI and join the Singspiration enterprise in Montrose. The invitation came as a surprise, and Peterson accepted after some deliberation. Smith was a man of good ideas who was on the cutting edge of the distinctive genre of gospel music; Peterson was pleased to become associated with him.

Another man who was a member of the Singspiration team for a while after Peterson joined was Harold DeCou. John had met the young organist when DeCou was traveling with George Sweeting's gospel team from Moody. (Sweeting later served as president of Moody Bible Institute, from 1971 to 1987.)

■　■　■

One of the first challenges to face Peterson was the need for choral music. This was not a strong feature in his training, but his first efforts were encouraging. The need, as Peterson described it, was for

> choral music with strong evangelical texts, and with attractive and singable arrangements that could be learned quickly and performed capably by even a small group of volunteer singers. Another company had made a beach-head in this area, but it did not begin to meet the demand.[10]

Shortly thereafter, Smith reorganized Better Choirs and moved the new company, and another named Accent, to Minneapolis. Peterson remained in Montrose while writing for Singspiration and editing for Accent.

In 1956 Peterson was in a Better Choirs staff meeting when someone, during a discussion of choral music, suggested, "Along with these things we ought to produce a cantata." Everyone looked at John.

> A cantata? That was the furthest thing from my mind. I had never considered such a project—didn't even know how to begin. What's more, I was then consumed with an ambition to write a Broadway musical, a Christian Broadway musical....
>
> But I thought and prayed about a cantata and finally came up with something based on the old Bliss hymn "Hallelujah! What a Saviour." Frankly, I was feeling my way, but I did have a pattern in mind. I wanted to set forth the resurrection story in a combination of narration and singing. Another thing: I introduced a recurring musical theme which, along with the narration, would give continuity to the work.[11]

It was not the first cantata ever published. Cantatas had evolved from more classical forms of choral writing such as oratorios. Zondervan was selling a cantata published in 1953 by George S. Schuler, one of Peterson's mentors at Moody; it was a work for Easter called *He Lives!*

But Peterson made several innovations that were to give him a permanent place in the history of religious music. Besides the recurring melodic theme and the spoken narrative with music background, he showed a style that was a little more "Broadway" and less formal than that displayed in older cantatas. Also, his cantata was promoted with a combination music book and demo-record (a recording of a performance), a new kind of marketing strategy that worked well and was used by Singspiration for many years after that.

Hallelujah! What a Saviour met with good response. Some time later, Peterson found on his desk an artist's sketch of a new book cover. It was the proposed cover design for a Christmas cantata to be called *Love Transcending*—and his name was on it. His colleagues insisted that he write the work, and this cantata, published in 1957, became Peterson's most famous and most enduring. Cantatas followed in a steady succession after that: *Night of Miracles* in 1958, then *No Greater Love* for Easter, and on and on. There were 2 million copies of Peterson's cantatas in print by 1967, including seven

Christmas cantatas, six for Easter, and some nonseasonal ones identified as "festival cantatas."

Popularity has its pitfalls, however. Peterson once received a letter from a woman after she had read an article about him in a Christian magazine. She wrote,

> I must write you a confession.... In recent years, both on radio and in churches, every time one of your songs or cantatas was played or sung it was announced as John W. Peterson's song or cantata. Literally every piece was prefaced with "John W. Peterson's!" After awhile I felt a resentment build up in me at the mention of anything you had written, because I was convinced there must be some legal clause included in your writings or at least some understanding to the effect that your name must always be mentioned in connection with the use of your works. I felt this was bringing glory, not to the Lord in whose worship they were used, but to the man who composed them.... Then came the ... article. God must surely have sent it, because I cried with remorse for having misjudged such an unselfish, dedicated man of God, and your compositions will have even more meaning to me now!

At the time Peterson began writing cantatas, his path crossed Pat and Bernie Zondervan's for the first time. The course of Singspiration was leading him inexorably toward Zondervan, although it wasn't apparent yet.

In the meantime, Zondervan was producing many records and new songbooks under the direction of Robert Hughes, who had joined the firm in 1955 as the editor of the newly incorporated Zondervan Music Publishers. Another key member of the staff was Charles Van Horn, brother of book salesman Lloyd Van Horn. "Chuck" was hired by Zondervan in 1950 and later served as the office manager of Singspiration until he retired in January 1981.

Many of the songbooks Hughes produced followed the style of Al Smith's, with books for high voice, low voice, and children's choirs, to name a few categories. But one of his and the Zondervan brothers' primary objectives was to publish a new hymnal. *Songs for Worship*, a hymnal with 279 selections, was issued in 1958.

It is noteworthy that by 1958 Zondervan was publishing six songbooks in Spanish, compiled by Robert C. Savage, a missionary to South America. Later on, a full-sized hymnal with 371 selections was published in Spanish as *Himnos de Fe y Alabanza (Hymns of Faith and Praise)*.

Among the many recording artists featured on Zondervan and Singspiration labels were Lee Childs, a mezzo soprano who had performed on Broadway and in a network radio series; Back to the Bible Broadcast singing groups; Wilmos and Gladys Csehy, instrumentalists; Joe Springer and the singing groups of radio station HCJB in Ecuador; baritone Gary Moore; and the Keller-York Evangelistic Team. Zondervan introduced its new Victory label in 1956 with the album "The Holy City" by tenor Ronnie Avalone, whom the press had dubbed "the second Caruso" when he was an opera star.

■　■　■

In 1957 Al Smith formed a partnership in Singspiration with the Zondervan brothers and John Peterson. Peterson was named president of the reorganized company. Some of Smith's staff, such as the young editor Norman Johnson, eventually became important members of the Singspiration team.

Local Talent

In the mid-fifties Zondervan recordings featured a wealth of musical talent from the Grand Rapids area. Several well-known Christian radio programs were originating from the city and stimulated the appearance of these artists on Zondervan's list.

The Radio Bible Class Quartet was heard weekly on the broadcast begun by M. R. DeHaan in 1938. The members of the quartet recording in the fifties were Anthony Haaksma, Gary Bergsma, Simon Oppenhuizen, and Henry Bosch.

Cherrie "Cherry Blossom" Lehman of the *Children's Bible Hour* sang two Stuart Hamblen songs, "Open Up Your Heart" and "The Lord Is Counting on You." Hamblen's first song, "It Is No Secret," was the most popular gospel song of the early fifties and was recorded several times by Singspiration and Zondervan artists.

Another local figure was the Reverend Leonard Greenway. He taught music before entering the ministry in Reformed and Christian Reformed churches, and he regularly played the organ on his weekly radio broadcast. So it was only natural that he perform on a three-manual pipe organ on a couple of Zondervan recordings.

Johnson, like Peterson, grew up in Kansas, and the boys' parents had in fact known each other there. "Norm" did some writing for John as a student at North Park College, and later on they collaborated on some pieces while Norm was with Accent. Norm has been a key member of the Singspiration staff since 1961.

Al Smith finally had to remove himself completely from the Singspiration company he had begun in the late thirties. With this change in late 1961, the company became a three-way partnership between Pat, Bernie, and John Peterson.

Peterson hired Harold DeCou, who for the previous few years had been working for Youth for Christ. In 1963, the Singspiration offices moved to Grand Rapids, since there was no longer any reason to stay in Montrose. With the company now on a solid financial footing, the musicians could do what they most wanted to do—compose, arrange, and publish.

The King's Choraliers, a men's singing group founded and directed by Peter Vanden Bosch, also recorded for Zondervan. Vanden Bosch later served as a vice president with Zondervan in the position of administrator of the two radio stations the company owned for a while. The King's Choraliers were on the program for the CBA convention in Grand Rapids in 1959, along with tenor Ralph Nielsen, soloist on the *Temple Time* broadcast, which is still being broadcast, though it is now called *Words of Hope*.

One recording made in 1954 might stir some nostalgia, even though it did not feature Grand Rapids artists. *Christian Herald* magazine took a survey and published a list of the ten favorite hymns of all time selected by its readers. The list was featured in *Colliers* magazine in its issue of April 16, 1954, and organist Doug Fisher recorded the ten songs for Singspiration. The hymns were —

"In the Garden"	"Sweet Hour of Prayer"
"What a Friend"	"Rock of Ages"
"He Leadeth Me"	"Jesus, Lover of My Soul"
"The Old Rugged Cross"	"Nearer, My God, to Thee"
"I Love to Tell the Story"	"Abide With Me"

At the end of 1964, Singspiration moved into new quarters at 4145 Kalamazoo Avenue SE, in suburban Kentwood. This was Singspiration's home for sixteen years until it moved to a new home across the street from Zondervan's headquarters on Lake Drive in the fall of 1980.

One other development in the music field occurred for Zondervan in 1963. Maurice "Maury" Lehmann, who had been a Zondervan salesman before briefly heading up his own record company, Diadem, became the manager of the Zondervan record division.

■ ■ ■

All that was happening in music in the late fifties and early sixties occurred quite independently of the book and Bible publishing of Zondervan. It seems, moreover, that every part of the Zondervan organization's "family tree" was branching out at this time. We have already traced the developments in Bible publishing and the growth in textbooks. Still another part to experience change was the retail enterprise; Zondervan was starting to have a greater interest and emphasis on the Christian bookstore.

The small retail store that Pat and Bernie opened at 543 Eastern Avenue SE in 1932 was moved to 815 Franklin SE two years later and then to the corner of Ottawa and Mason NW in the early forties. By that time Zondervan had two other related operations. The firm had begun to manage the summer store at Winona Lake Bible Conference in 1937, and it had a mail-order and door-to-door sales enterprise called "Glad Tidings Book and Bible House." Glad Tidings was never really a big part of the company, but it gave Pat and Bernie an opportunity to sell books and supplies in places where there were no stores.

A catalog for Glad Tidings for Fall and Winter 1942 – 43 states:

> It is our purpose and aim to distribute only books with a distinctly evangelical flavor. We feel that ours is a distinct ministry of distributing these good character building and inspirational books, booklets, religious plaques and novelties.... We are glad to offer our customers the privilege of returning any book ordered that proves unsatisfactory provided they return them within ten days after receipt of same. When returning these books, use the new book rate, 3¢ per pound.

Glad Tidings offered an especially valuable service during World War II, when many transportation services and the availability of cars were greatly curtailed. Glad Tidings itself was terminated in the late fifties.

James Meyer was the first retail manager at Ottawa and Mason and was also the manager at Winona Lake. When he left Zondervan in 1945, he was succeeded at the Grand Rapids store by Ray Weiskopf and at Winona by Willis Cook. Weiskopf had worked for Moody Press for more than six years. Besides serving at Winona, Cook was assistant office manager in Zondervan's Ottawa Avenue headquarters and made two long trips each year as a salesman.

(Two other men joined Zondervan at about the same time as Weiskopf, but stayed much longer. Herbert V. Montgomery, who had worked for Standard Oil for twelve years, became office manager; he later served as credit manager and retired in 1975. He began work on August 13, 1945, the same day as Tony Sytsma, who worked in the production department until his retirement in 1976.)

The Grand Rapids store later moved to Monroe Avenue. Weiskopf left Zondervan in 1957, and Willis Cook took over as the store manager. After about a year he moved it to 24 South Division Avenue, and by 1959 the store was located across the street, in larger quarters, at 25 South Division.

Cook was an effective manager, and in the first year of operation at 25 South Division sales increased 60 percent over what they had been the previous year across the street. Yet, though both the Winona and Grand Rapids stores were doing well, Pat, Bernie, and Peter Kladder were not ready to expand the retail business on a large scale.

Then in 1960 Rogers Plaza opened in Wyoming as the first large shopping mall in the Grand Rapids area. Cook would have liked to open a store there but the company did not approve of the plan. However, the next year, when a strip mall called Southland (today named the Wyoming Village) opened near Rogers Plaza, Cook had another opportunity to sell his idea. Not only would the rent be cheaper than at Rogers Plaza, but a street-front store was a more familiar entity to Zondervan. Cook met regularly with Pat and Bernie every other week to discuss the retail business. Cook persisted in pressing for a Southland store, and finally Bernie told him, "If you think you know what you're doing and can handle it, go ahead."

A lease was signed in 1962, and Cook designed a floor plan that remained basic to Zondervan stores for many years. One concern of the Zondervans was that a new store would cause a loss of business at the downtown store. Southland was operating in the black after only eight months; and although sales at the Division Avenue store declined by 14 percent the first year, it regained that ground the next year and continued to grow after that.

■　■　■

Next Zondervan learned that a small Holiness bookstore in downtown Flint, on the other side of the state, was for sale. Cook and Peter Kladder liked what they saw, and it was there that Zondervan opened its fourth store. Stores in an East Lansing, Michigan, shopping center and in Indianapolis soon followed. There was no doubt now that Zondervan Publishing House was ready to expand the retail business in a major way.

But not everyone was ready for Zondervan. Despite Zondervan's very professional approach to business, religious publishing aroused many suspicions among shopping center managers outside the Grand Rapids area. Most cities were not so conservative and rooted in religious tradition as "the religious-book capital of the United States." Managers of these shopping centers feared that business volume would be low because of the religious stock; and since most malls require a percentage of the profits of its lessees, they did not expect a Christian bookstore to last very long. But Zondervan stores dispelled these notions quickly.

As the stores opened, it fell to Cook to train personnel, get a store operating smoothly, and be a troubleshooter for whatever problems arose. Cook was successful in managing the retail operations for several reasons. One was that, as he put it, he adopted Pat and Bernie's "psychology."

"When I first started working for them as a teenager," Cook said, "I became intoxicated with enthusiasm. They would begin a conference by excitedly talking about what great things were happening and how good sales were going to be. Then they would tactfully point out weaknesses in the operations and suggest ways to improve. By the time the discussion was over, I wanted to do my very best for them and believed I could do a good job!"

Cook was also grateful to Peter Kladder, who gave proper guidance to his vision for a network of retail stores. Zondervan was also willing to invest some capital in the early sixties and, as Cook put it, "absorb some failures." Some of the first attempts to establish a store in California in the sixties were unsuccessful.

Cook continued to have a leading responsibility for the retail operations until the late sixties. Then, when Family Bookstores was incorporated as a major division of Zondervan with plans for further expansion, Cook felt he had reached his limits. After two men proved unsuccessful as general manager, Cook recommended that Bill Zondervan, who had been a sales representative for many years, be put in charge of the division. Bernie Zondervan Jr., who was then a company vice president, offered the position to Bill in February 1969. Cook devoted the rest of his working life to the store on South Division.

There has probably never been a better bookseller than Willis Cook. For many of those who had seen him at work over the years, it was not difficult to believe that there was only a handful of people living today who had sold as many religious books on a retail basis as he had.

Two humorous incidents stand out among many that Willis experienced. One of Zondervan's leading titles in the fall of 1964 was a new book by Eugenia Price. Willis had constructed a prominent display in the window of the Division Avenue store. An old gentleman trudging up the sidewalk stopped to look at the display for *God Speaks to Women Today,* and Willis heard him mutter, "It's about time."

Early one morning in September 1980 an electrical fire broke out in a rear storeroom on Division Avenue. There was little fire damage, but smoke and water left the interior looking battered and grim. Willis had the store open for business before the last fire hose had been removed. An elderly woman entered the store, looked around at the smoke-blackened walls and ceiling, and mumbled to her daughter, "This must be the original."

It isn't. But to Willis it is the best.

Rush-hour traffic directed by police at West Fulton Street and Market and Grandville Avenues in Grand Rapids about 1920.
(Courtesy, Public Museum of Grand Rapids)

A tourist information booth and a trolley at Campau Square in downtown Grand Rapids about 1920.
(Courtesy, Public Museum of Grand Rapids)

Bernie (left) and Pat in their first store at 543 Eastern Avenue SE in August 1932.

The Zondervan farmhouse in Grandville where Zondervan Publishing House began.

Bernie pointing to the upstairs bedroom where the publishing business began, as "Ma," Pat, and Louis Zondervan Sr. look on.

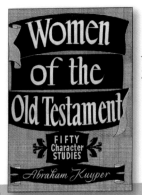

The first book published by Zondervan — and still in print!

1933   1937   1941

Zondervan opens first store outside of Michigan in Winona Lake, Indiana.

The building at 847 Ottawa Avenue NW that in 1941–42 brought Zondervan under one roof for the first time since 1931.

Pat Zondervan and family: Peter John "Pat" Zondervan; P. J. with his wife, Mary Swier Zondervan, and oldest son, Bob; Mary and Pat with three of their four children—Bob, Patty, and Billy—in the late 1940s.

Bernie Zondervan and family:
Bernard Dick "Bernie" Zondervan
Sr.; Bernie and his wife, Wilma Plas
Zondervan, on their 25th wedding
anniversary in 1958; Bernie, Wilma,
and their two children—Joanne Mae
and Bernie Jr.—in the early 1950s.

Pat looking at proofs
from a printing press
in the 1940s.

WE DID OUR BEST!

HE HELPED HANDLE 10 TONS OF
ZONDERVAN PARCELS, THEN PASSED
OUT — AND ALL HE KEEPS ON
MUMBLING IS THAT...

A cartoon by staff artist
George Benes noting
Zondervan's heavy traffic
the day before a parcel post
embargo began in Grand
Rapids in December 1945.

The Zondervan shipping
room in 1941.

One of the weekly chapel services — a Zondervan tradition since early 1942 — with accordionist Tony Sytsma (left) and leader Ted W. Engstrom (right).

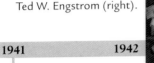

1941   1942

The first annual Christmas banquet, attended by 41 of the 45 members of the Zondervan Publishing House "family."

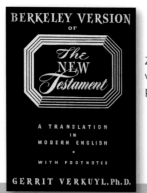

Zondervan's first venture into Bible publishing.

Arlene Stehouwer operating a saddle-stitch machine in the bindery.

Author Dena Korfker (center) of Grand Rapids autographing a copy of one of her books as her sister, Trena Haan, looks on.

Three scenes at the Zondervan plant at 847 Ottawa Avenue NW: Henry Remelts filling an order in the shipping room; print-shop foreman John Weeda instructing Ralph Snippe; driver Jim Schimmel ready to make a delivery of Zondervan books.

A Zondervan storefront on Monroe Avenue in downtown Grand Rapids.

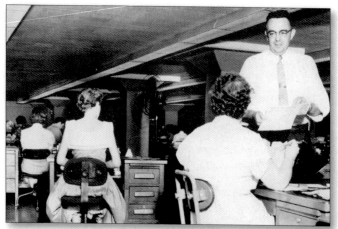

The credit department in 1951, led by Herbert V. Montgomery (right), office manager and credit manager.

Editor Ted W. Engstrom (center) with Bernie (left) and Pat in 1951.

The building at 1415 Lake Drive SE in the Eastown section
of Grand Rapids at the time Zondervan purchased it in 1954
(which Zondervan occupied until 1992).

Bernie (left) and Pat reflecting on some of the noteworthy books
among the 1,600 titles they published during Zondervan's first
twenty-five years.

 Singspiration

John W. Peterson, president of
Singspiration from 1957 to 1971.

The logo for
Singspiration in 1961,
when the music company
became fully owned
by Zondervan, the two
having been connected in
various ways since 1941.

1957   **1959**   **1961**

The Zondervan booth, featuring *The Amplified New Testament*, at
the convention of the Christian Booksellers Association (CBA)
held in Grand Rapids in August 1959.

A classic book published by Zondervan since 1960.

1960

The Zondervan store that opened at the intersection of Division and Weston in downtown Grand Rapids in 1959.

Henry H. Halley holding copies of his original handbook, published in 1924, and the first Zondervan edition.

The Zondervan booth at the CBA convention in 1966, with (from left) future publisher Bob DeVries (at the time with Moody Press) and four Zondervan sales reps: Hugh Johnson (foreground), Bill Zondervan, Lloyd Van Horn, and John Fiet.

The Zondervan booth at the CBA convention in 1960, featuring authors Genie Price (second from left) and Joyce Blackburn (third from left).

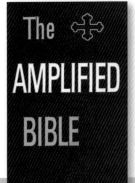

A major component of Zondervan Bible publishing, released in 1966.

One of the prime publications involved in Zondervan's acquisition of the Harper & Row Bible list.

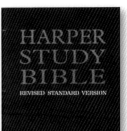

1966

1966

Cofounder B. D. Zondervan Sr. dies at age 55 (1910–1966).

Pat Zondervan (center) with U.S. Senator Mark O. Hatfield of Oregon (left) and Congressman Gerald R. Ford in Grand Rapids in June 1966.

The blockbuster book published in 1970 that was later called "the biggest-selling nonfiction book of the 1970s" by the *New York Times*.

1970

Peter Kladder Jr., a Zondervan executive from 1956 to 1985, serving as president from 1970 to 1984.

Vice President B. D. Zondervan Jr. dies at age 34 (1935–1970).

Zondervan becomes a publicly held company.

Hal Lindsey, author of *The Late Great Planet Earth*.

The New Testament
published in 1973
for what has become
the bestselling Bible
version today.

1973

Zondervan publishes *The
Layman's Parallel Bible*, with
four versions set side-by-side
on a two-page spread — an
achievement of computer
technology.

The key to the city presented to Pat by Patrick Barr (right), Grand Rapids
City Commission president, on "P. J. (Pat) Zondervan Day," December 4, 1973,
with Dick Hatfield of Singspiration (left) as emcee.

A special millionth-copy edition of *The Late Great Planet Earth* presented to author Hal Lindsey (right) by Executive Vice President and Publisher Bob DeVries.

Zondervan purchases the John Rudin Company in 1972 and the next year celebrates the 50th anniversary of *The Book of Life* with a special edition in gold binding.

John Rudin, who began publishing *The Book of Life* in 1923.

Country singer Johnny Cash signing copies
of his autobiography *Man in Black* in 1975.

June Carter Cash at a book signing for *Among My Klediments*,
an autobiographical scrapbook published in 1979.

Pat Zondervan breaking ground for the Kentwood plant on
November 1, 1973, as Kentwood Mayor Peter Lamberts looks on.

The plant at the corner of Broadmoor and 52nd Street SE in Kentwood
that housed much of the Zondervan enterprise from 1974 to 1992.

The Zondervan book editorial
department outside the
Kentwood plant in 1981.

Two views of the high-rise warehouse
in the Kentwood plant: (left) some
conveyors not yet fully installed in 1974;
(right) a computer-guided Racker-
Stacker in a cavernous storage aisle.

The complete *New International Version*, a work of the Committee on Bible Translation and the International Bible Society.

Where Is God
When It Hurts

Philip Yancey

1978

A winner of the Gold Medallion Award in the first year the awards were presented by the Evangelical Christian Publishers Association.

Author Philip Yancey (left) and publisher Bob DeVries displaying the Gold Medallion Award for the Best Inspirational Book of 1977.

The computer department at the Lake Drive building about 1979, with Sue-anne Boylan (who is now senior vice president of information systems) at a keyboard (third from left, in back).

The changing face of Zondervan presented to its customers over the years: 1950s and 1960s (top four lines), 1973, 1990, and 2001.

James G. "Jim" Buick, president from 1984 to 1993.

1984

Billy Graham and Joni Eareckson Tada, both Zondervan authors, on one of the many occasions when they shared the platform at a Graham event.

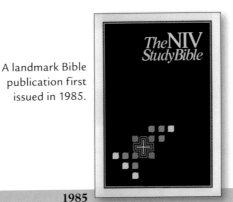

A landmark Bible publication first issued in 1985.

1980s	1985	1986

Zondervan purchases a number of companies and book imprints in the early 1980s — Benson Music, Tapley-Rutter, Chosen Books, *Today's Christian Woman* magazine, Fleming H. Revell Company, B. W. Moore, Marshall Pickering Co. — and sells all but the music before the end of the decade.

An innovative publication (with creative marketing on a semi's side panel) that was part of Zondervan's growing line of Bibles during the 1980s.

HarperCollins*Publishers*

Zondervan is acquired by HarperCollins Publishers, a division of News Corporation.

The NIV Study Bible for Kids

A popular edition of the Bible for younger readers published in 1988.

1988

1992

Zondervan's headquarters at Patterson Avenue and 52nd Street SE in Cascade Township, today (right) and in 1992 (below), when all of Zondervan came under one roof for the first time since 1954.

Zondervan's headquarters at Patterson and 52nd: (above) the "Divine Servant" sculpture (by Max Greiner Jr.) and fountain in the main lobby; (right) Sarah Jongsma of Zonderkidz in a typical office—a modular setup with movable walls in an open-office environment; (below) Bonnie Hines in the massive distribution center.

Bruce Ryskamp, Zondervan executive from 1983 to 2005, serving as president and CEO from 1993 to 2005.

1993   **1995**

The logo of Editorial Vida, purchased by Zondervan in 1995, and two of this division's prominent books: *Everybody's Normal Till You Get to Know Them* by John Ortberg and *Boundaries Face to Face* by Dr. Henry Cloud and Dr. John Townsend.

Terri Blackstock, whose fiction series, Sun Coast Chronicles, sparked a fiction revival for Zondervan in 1995.

1999

zonderkidz
The children's group
of Zondervan

The Zonderkidz logo and a taste of this department's variety: a children's edition of a bestselling book, an edition of the Bible designed for a particular audience, and the lovable Boz the Bear featured in a new series for preschoolers.

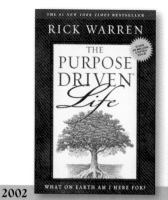

The bestselling hardcover book in history (according to national news magazines) and its author, Rick Warren, senior pastor of Saddleback Church in California.

inspirio™

We have a gift for inspiration.

The Inspirio logo, designed in 1999, and some of the gift products created since the gift division was founded in 1992.

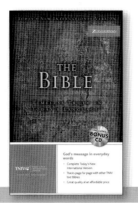

Today's New International Version with the New Testament in 2002 and the complete Bible following in 2005.

Douglas A. "Doug" Lockhart, president and CEO since 2005.

A view of Zondervan's headquarters, with Patterson Avenue in the foreground, after another warehouse-distribution "pod" was added in 2004–5 (upper left).

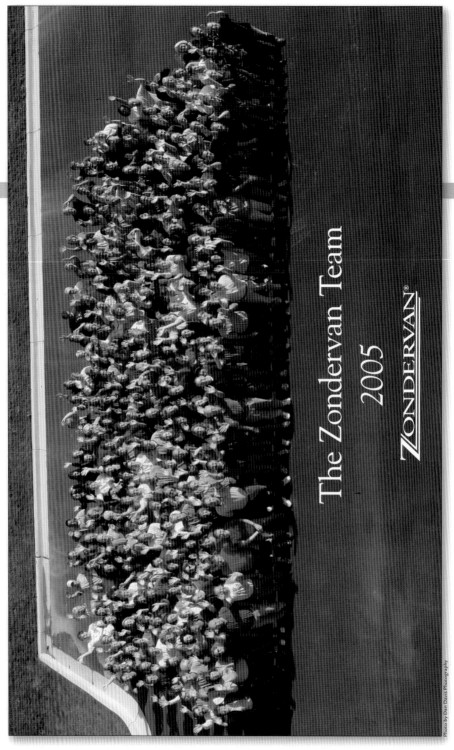

The Zondervan Team
2005
ZONDERVAN®

Photo by Dan Davis Photography

The measure of a life, after all,
is not its duration, but its donation.
PETER MARSHALL,
MR. JONES, MEET THE MASTER

10

In the Shadows

The Zondervan story from the middle sixties through 1970 is one of personalities more than titles and publishing lists. It's not that what was being published was unimportant. Rather, the tragedies of human experience were having the most far-reaching effect on the future of the company, which had grown from a bedroom book depot to a many-faceted enterprise with a worldwide ministry.

The saddening events of those years that cast the longest shadows over the company were the death of Bernard D. Zondervan Sr. on July 3, 1966, and the death of his son, B. D. Zondervan Jr., a company vice president, on January 2, 1970.

Words cannot adequately express what it meant for Pat to lose his brother and partner. They had a rare friendship. The bond they shared as brothers for fifty-five years, and in business for thirty-five, was one of the most admirable and heart-warming of human experiences. We must let Pat's words, simply expressed, reveal his feelings when the bond was broken: "My brother Bernie's death was the greatest blow I've ever suffered. Bernie and I were so close. We seldom made a decision without involving the other. It took me more than two years to recover to the point that I realized I could not continue operating the business alone."

Bernie had always enjoyed excellent health. He and Wilma were traveling extensively in 1964 and 1965. They visited missions and students associated with the Sudan United Mission in Nigeria, West Africa. Then they visited some Christian Reformed missions in Mexico. Upon their return to Grand Rapids, Bernie was making plans to visit HCJB in Quito, Ecuador, when the first signs of illness began to appear.

Bernie was chairman of a fund-raising committee for Calvin College. He was also the planning chairman for the twenty-fifth anniversary banquet of the Reformed Bible Institute—a school that was dear to his heart—on May 13, 1965. He was called on at the last minute to be the speaker when the scheduled speaker had to cancel out. It was about this time that strong signs of illness became apparent. By mid-June Wilma sensed the illness was serious.

An examination by doctors revealed a brain tumor that they deemed inoperable. The news of Bernie's illness spread rapidly, and a great volume of prayer rose in his behalf in churches and in bookstores. On July 24, 1965, while Bernie was in the hospital, the Reverend Edgar H. and Nelle Smith, missionary friends, came to visit him. Smith said, "I believe I have a message from the Lord, Bernie, that I want to share with you." Just then the Reverend Arnold Brink, Bernie's pastor, entered the room and joined the others assembled there—the Smiths, Wilma, her daughter Joanne, Bernie Jr. and his wife, Beverly, and Wilma's brother-in-law, Jim Vroon.

Smith related that he and his wife had been reading together from the devotional book *Daily Light on the Daily Path*. The reading for July 23 included the passage from James 5 regarding the anointing of the sick. Smith said that at first he didn't feel free to put the message into action because the elders had not been called, as the verses command. Nevertheless, he said, the message for July 24 contained this statement concerning Abraham: "He staggered not at the promise of God through unbelief." He was compelled by the Holy Spirit to come to minister to Bernie.

Smith told Bernie, "I'd like to pray with you and with your pastor and anoint you with oil. I have never done this, but I feel constrained to do so because of what I read in the Scriptures today." Bernie agreed, and those assembled in the room held hands and laid hands on Bernie as they prayed.

On the way home, Joanne said to her mother, "I really believe daddy's going to be all right."

"Honey, there's such a burden off my shoulders, I can't believe it," Wilma responded. At Wilma's home, the family prayed together again and believed God for the healing.

The next day, as the family was visiting him, Bernie felt wonderful. After a joyful time of talking together and praising the Lord for his goodness, the family suggested he rest a bit, and they went out into the waiting room. A few minutes later they heard a nurse say, "Mr. Zondervan, what are you doing?"

"I'm simply taking a walk," he said.

"You can't walk out there by yourself," the nurse said.

"Why not? I feel fine."

■ ■ ■

Bernie returned home before the week was over, and his condition improved steadily for a number of months. The September *Book News* informed his friends in the book trade around the country: "Good news! Bernie Zondervan is home from the hospital, is playing some golf, and is his usual exuberant self. He appreciates the thoughtfulness and prayers of his thousands of friends. Continue to remember him, won't you?"

Bernie was unable to maintain a full working schedule, but he spent as much time in the office as his strength permitted. Then his health began to decline again, and he reentered the hospital in April 1966.

Willis Cook recalls his last visit with Bernie at the end of June. As Willis was leaving, Bernie said, "I feel privileged to have accomplished more than most men my age and have been around the world. There's no place I've wanted to visit that I wasn't able to visit. There's only one land I have not yet toured" — and at this point he waggled his finger in a gesture familiar to all who knew him and pointed at Willis — "and you know where that is. I'm going there soon."

Bernie died on Sunday, July 3, 1966, at 11:55 p.m. at the age of fifty-five. He had not suffered pain and he was at peace in his spirit.

Later, Wilma reflected: "Bernie was a man with a very strong character, well disciplined, and a man of tremendous integrity. It seemed to me that he was always happy, and dearly loved people. He showed his love in a very natural and easy way. He was a deeply spiritual man, but did not wear his spirituality on his shirt sleeve. There was nothing superficial as far as his Christianity was concerned.

"I really believe that the Lord put Pat and Bernie together, not only as blood brothers, but as the closest of friends. They were so different and yet in so many ways they were very much alike. They really loved each other deeply."

Shortly before he died, Bernie had pledged funds for an organ for Calvin College's new Knollcrest campus. The gift was to be anonymous, but after Bernie died, the family fulfilled the pledge and dedicated it as a memorial to him.

Bernie's death cast a shadow over the company's thirty-fifth anniversary celebration, which was held at the Sherman House in Chicago in August 1966 during the Christian Booksellers Convention. But the sorrow was mingled with thankfulness and appreciation for the role he had played in Christian publishing.

Pat was grateful that in facing the loss of Bernie, he could turn to Treasurer Peter Kladder and to Bernard D. Zondervan Jr. for support in running the company.

■ ■ ■

Bernie Jr. and his father had been good friends. Bernie affectionately called his son "Lad" or "Laddie." It became a family ritual that they do the dishes together on Sunday afternoons, and during these times they shared some of their deepest discussions. Bernie Jr. enjoyed the opportunity to accompany his father on speaking engagements. As a teenager he often helped around the publishing house. Bernie Sr. delighted in his six-foot-three-inch son's athletic ability. Bernie Jr. was named to the all-city basketball team as a student at Christian High School, and he was a member of Calvin College's championship team in the Michigan Intercollegiate Athletic Association one year.

Bernie Jr. eagerly looked forward to joining Zondervan after he graduated from Calvin, but his father wanted him to gain experience elsewhere, and he saw the wisdom in that. He went to work for the Hekman Biscuit Company in Grand Rapids. But he kept himself constantly informed of what was happening at the publishing house. Then, after five years, when Hekman wanted him to transfer to Chicago at the end of 1961, he decided it was time to join his father and uncle. Pat's son William joined the firm at the same time.

Several organizational changes were made in Zondervan on January 1, 1962. Peter deVisser was appointed vice president of publications and secretary of the company; Peter Kladder, continuing to serve as treasurer, was named vice president of operations and procedures; Bernie Jr. was made assistant controller, eventually (in 1966) becoming vice president of production. C. E. ("Ted") Andrew was named vice president of sales on July 1. Ted had formerly been with A. J. Holman Bible Company and Fleming H. Revell and had also managed a bookstore.

Bernie Jr. was an outstanding administrator and was in line to become president of the corporation. But he had suffered from a lingering malignant melanoma for several years, and it claimed his life on January 2, 1970, at the age of thirty-four.

Later that year another person highly qualified for the position was appointed president of Zondervan: Peter Kladder.

Bernard D. Zondervan Jr. left a widow, Beverly, who had been his high school classmate, and four children: Bernard III, who is now employed in the corporation; Cynthia; Andrew; and Daniel. Beverly later married Dr. William Jensen, a Grand Rapids anesthesiologist and a widower.

Wilma Zondervan married Claude J. Teggelaar in 1975. She was a member of the board of directors of the corporation for a number of years.

Joanne, sister of Bernie Jr., married Reverend Mr. Warren J. Boer, a marriage counselor in Grand Rapids. She became a member of the board of directors and served as corporation secretary.

Pat and Mary's four adopted children did not become as strongly involved in the company as Bernie's children. Robert had a psychiatric practice in Southern California; Patricia Lucille was a homemaker in Southern California; William left Zondervan after Bernie Jr. died and worked in western Florida; and Mary Beth became a counselor with the Bethany Christian Services of Grand Rapids.

■ ■ ▨

There were some other significant personnel changes in the book and Bible publishing in the middle and late sixties.

The sales staff grew in the winter of 1964–65 with the addition of three people, each of whom would someday become sales manager of Zondervan Books and Bibles. John McElwee, new assistant sales manager, had formerly worked for McGraw-Hill and Fortress Press and had also been an interpreter and chaplain's assistant in Japan; he was sales manager from 1967 to 1969.

Ronald N. Haynes, former manager of the Biola Book Room in Los Angeles, became sales representative for the Southwest and Rocky Mountain states; he was named manager of Zondervan's Bible Department in 1970 and in that role expedited the publication of the New International Version of the Bible. He was vice president in charge of sales from 1976 to 1980, when he left Zondervan to begin his own publishing firm.

Paul VanDuinen earned a degree in criminology and then worked for Fortress Press before becoming the Northeast sales representative for Zondervan. In the mid-seventies he went to Word Books but returned to Zondervan in 1980 and became Haynes's successor as sales manager.

The editorial department had begun to grow under Peter deVisser, and that growth continued under Floyd Thatcher, who filled the position of director of publications that was left vacant by deVisser's sudden death.

Thatcher had gained editorial experience with the Cowman Publishing Company in California and before that had been a coffee salesman. He was named director of publications in February 1964. He soon came into conflict with Pat Zondervan, and the three-and-a-half years he spent at Zondervan proved to be uneasy at times. He left in the summer of 1967 and soon after became the executive editor of Word Books in Waco, Texas.

The Ministry of *Streams*

Some books seem to find a special ministry of their own. *Streams in the Desert* has been a long-time favorite of people in the armed forces and also those incarcerated in the nation's prisions. One time an inmate in a southern prison wrote Zondervan to say that some uknown person sent him a copy of Mrs. Cowman's *Streams in the Desert*. It changed his life. "What wisdom! What inspiration! What food for thought!" he wrote. "I'm convinced that if every inmate would faithfully study *Streams in the Desert* and seriously reflect, pray, and turn to God, they would be changed." Another prisoner, from Montana, wrote that through reading *Streams in the Desert*, "I have been encouraged to see our Lord's light even in this dark place ... and to receive my desire to look forward to what each new day holds for me, rather than fear it."

Nevertheless, some important publishing events occurred in which Thatcher played a part. One was the purchase of Cowman Publishing Company by Zondervan on January 1, 1965. Pat told how it came about: "Over the years, as Bernie and I visited the Winona Lake Bible Conference, we often met Mrs. Charles A. Cowman, who spoke at Winona and held a week of meetings sponsored by the Oriental Missionary Society. The OMS had a home there, which she occupied in the summer. We were much interested in the OMS and the Cowman publications, particularly her famous book *Streams in the Desert*. One day, while Bernie and I were in California, we approached the people who were managing Cowman Publishing and made arrangements for its purchase. The ministry of Mrs. Cowman through the books that she has written and compiled has continued worldwide. We later added another selection of materials that she had assembled but had never published, and we published this in a book entitled *Streams in the Desert, Volume 2.*"

There were already an estimated 2 million copies of *Streams in the Desert* in print when Zondervan began publishing the book. Many stories can be told of the book's impact, but one suffices. In the seventies Asian Outreach, a missions organization, began to publish books in the new simplified Chinese script that was instituted by the Chinese Communist government. Paul E. Kauffman, founder and head of Asian Outreach, tells of the publication of *Streams in the Desert* as the first book selected for the new language:

> This daily devotional book, written by a former missionary to China, is the most popular book among the Christian Chinese around the world. We retranslated and published it, in the contemporary language of China, on the occasion of the fiftieth anniversary of its first publication in English.[12]

When the great Chinese leader Chiang Kai-shek died in 1975, four books were buried with him in Taiwan: one was his Bible, and another was a copy of *Streams in the Desert*.

     ■ ■ ■

The acquisition of Cowman Publishing Company brought significant authors and titles to Zondervan's list. One author was Donald E. Demaray, whose *Handbook of the Bible* Zondervan published as *A Layman's Guide to Our Bible*. There were also several books by Dr. Richard C. Halverson, a pastor from

North Dakota, who was appointed Chaplain of the U.S. Senate in January 1981 and served in that position until his death in 1995. His devotional book for men, *A Day at a Time,* appeared in many editions.

Another acquisition in 1964 was the Dunham Publishing Company in Findlay, Ohio. Dunham was a small publishing house with strong ties to Dallas Theological Seminary in Texas. This purchase brought to Zondervan's list many books by the seminary's founder and late president, Lewis Sperry Chafer; by the seminary's president from 1953 to 1986, John F. Walvoord; and by a professor there, J. Dwight Pentecost. Many of these writings deal with eschatological subjects, including Pentecost's magnum opus, *Things to Come.* The books also include Chafer's eight-volume systematic theology.

Two provocative titles published in 1964 were *The Gospel Blimp* by Joseph T. Bayly and *Hellbent for Election* by Phyllis Speshock. The former is a classic tale about evangelism that was later made into a film; the latter is an allegory dealing with Christian relationships. One review of *Hellbent* suggested, "Not everybody will like it, but God forgive publishers as well as ministers who give the people only what they want."

The acquisition of the Harper & Row Bible Department on January 1, 1966, helped to make Zondervan a major Bible publisher in terms of both volume and variety. The transaction, which involved nearly a million dollars, included printing plates, existing inventory, and publishing rights for Bibles and religious books. The Bibles included various editions of the King James Version, the Revised Standard Version, and the Harper Study Bible edited by Harold Lindsell.

Twenty-five of the books were ancient-language textbooks, such as lexicons, analytical concordances, and interlinear texts, originated several decades ago by Samuel Bagster and Sons, of London, England. With a single stroke Zondervan became the proprietor of the largest collection of biblical language aids in the United States and perhaps in the world. Language aids such as *The Englishman's Hebrew and Chaldee Concordance of the Old Testament* and *The Septuagint in Greek and English* were esoteric items that necessarily demand a substantial price because they have a relatively small, though steady, sale. If they and others like them were not available, the evangelical community and our religious culture would have suffered in biblical scholarship and ministry. Over the years many of the Bagster books have been eclipsed or replaced because of more recent scholarship and newer versions of the Bible, but they have left a valuable legacy. They contributed greatly to the burgeoning interest of laypersons in the biblical languages since the seventies, and publication of biblical language resources, especially those linked to the NIV and the TNIV, remains one of Zondervan's most important and lasting contributions to religious book publishing.

In contrast to the scholarly language books, the Harper transaction included another Bagster product, *Daily Light on the Daily Path*. This devotional book, compiled by Jonathan Bagster (Samuel's son) in the 1800s, with Bible verses that center on a different theme for each day, is one of the world's best known and has been published in various versions of the Bible and in many languages. Zondervan published the KJV edition from 1969 to 2000, but in 1981 originated the NIV edition, which has sold half a million copies.

One other biblical publication for Zondervan in the sixties was the development of *The New Testament from 26 Translations*, published in 1967. The concept and impetus for the project originated with Jack Hamm of Dallas, Texas. William H. Rossell, a professor of Old Testament at Southwestern Baptist Theological Seminary in Fort Worth, Texas, was the general editor until his sudden death in July 1965. After that, Curtis Vaughan of the same seminary became general editor of a group of fourteen scholars. Their task was to provide an eclectic edition of the New Testament that would use the King James Version as the basic translation and incorporate for each verse the four or five phrases from among twenty-five other versions that reflect the most significant variations. This book proved useful in Bible study and helped to preserve the most valuable features of some translations that were no longer published or widely known.

At this time the foundations were being laid for the crowning achievement in contemporary Bible translation, the New International Version. But Zondervan was not yet playing a role in the project, nor was the evangelical community at large aware of what was happening. That story was to unfold to the public in the seventies.

■ ■ ■

Zondervan was approaching what might be called "the modern era" of its history. Its evolution as the leading religious book publisher was given an important new impetus by the arrival of the computer age to the sales and shipping departments in 1965. It continued with the appointment of Robert

K. DeVries as director of publications in September 1968 and of Robert G. Bolinder as sales manager in July 1969.

Bolinder rose to the position of senior vice president before leaving to become sales manager of Tyndale House Publishers in 1977. Some people remember that Bob was a distinguished night fighter pilot in Europe during World War II. Around that time, long after the war ended, his plane, the P–61 "Black Widow," became familiar to young craftsmen in a model plane kit available at hobby shops and department stores throughout the country.

DeVries is a graduate of Wheaton College and holds a Th.D. from Dallas Theological Seminary. Before coming to Zondervan, he was manager of the seminary bookstore and was then editor-in-chief of Moody Press for five years. His academic and publishing background enabled him to revitalize Zondervan's textbook program and bring to the growing editorial staff a professionalism and awareness that prepared it to meet the challenge of the seventies.

Yet publishing at Zondervan has never been all textbooks and theology. There has usually been a place for humor. In 1967, Zondervan published the book *Peter Piper, Missionary Parakeet* by Gertrude Warner and Leila W. Anderson. The parakeet accompanied the Reverend Anderson on her travels as an itinerant missionary in rural sections of the eastern United States. The bird's vocabulary of eight hundred words and phrases is listed in the book; some of his favorite lines were "I'm tired of being a Congregationalist," "You look like a Democrat," "Need a tenor? Peter sings," and "I'm a missionary. Where's the money?"

11

The Late Great Seventies

During the same week that men walked on the moon for the first time, Hal Lindsey was addressing the International Convention of the Gideons in Chicago. Lindsey had been given a New Testament by the Gideons when he was a schoolboy, but it had lain barely used and nearly forgotten until he began reading it while he was a tugboat captain on the Mississippi River. God opened his heart, and he became a Christian. He obtained a theological education and later developed a campus ministry. He was invited to address the convention of the Gideons in July 1969, and Pat Zondervan was among the many Gideons from around the world in the audience.

In his testimony Lindsey mentioned that he was on his way to Grand Rapids, Michigan, to deliver a book manuscript to Bob DeVries, the director of publications at Zondervan and a former classmate at Dallas Theological Seminary. The book, which Lindsey wrote with C. C. Carlson, a California homemaker, concerned prophetic events relating to the second coming of Christ. Lindsey, taking his title from a phrase in Revelation 6:2, called his book *Behold a White Horse*.

A short time later the Zondervan editorial committee accepted the manuscript. But the title had to be changed because Zondervan had already accepted a prophetic novel by Joe Musser entitled *Behold a Pale Horse*. Lindsey came up with the intriguing title *The Late Great Planet Earth*, inspired by a non-Zondervan book, *The Late Great State of California*. The title well suited the book in tone and content, since it is a popular, even sensational, treatment of current and anticipated events pertaining to the "last days" of mankind and the Second Coming from a premillennial viewpoint. The book was scheduled for release on May 29, 1970, with a first printing of 10,000 copies, some in cloth and some in softcover.

At that time Zondervan announced a new publication list three times a year, and the sales representatives then took orders from dealers before the new books were even off the press. Other books on the list with *The Late Great Planet Earth* were important to the publisher, including *At Least We Were Married* by Terry Thomas, *A Survey of the New Testament* by Robert H. Gundry, and *Children Are Our Best Friends* by Mark W. Lee. In addition, several recent Zondervan releases were becoming bestsellers and keeping the publisher and dealers busy, especially *Love Is Now* by Peter E. Gillquist, *Purple Violet Squish* by David Wilkerson, and *Black and Free* by Tom Skinner. *The Late Great Planet Earth* was expected to receive a fairly good response, especially among the Jesus People, a growing evangelical subculture that showed a strong interest in biblical prophecy.

Even so, the advance sale of the book was greater than Zondervan had anticipated, and before the first printing was off the press in May another printing was planned, and then another. The CBA convention in August gave the sales further impetus, and by October there were 60,000 copies in print. The book was truly becoming a bestseller, but Zondervan had no way of knowing what the dimensions of its popularity would be. Some other significant books were being published by Zondervan that fall, among them a high school textbook, *Biology: A Search for Order in Complexity*, edited by John N. Moore and Harold Slusher; *A New Face for the Church* by Lawrence O. Richards; *Between Two Worlds: A Congressman's Choice* by U.S. Rep. John B. Anderson of Illinois; and a publication from the Bible Department, *The Layman's Parallel New Testament*.

The numbers for *The Late Great Planet Earth* kept climbing. By New Year's Day 1971, there were 135,000 copies in print. By the next summer the book had begun to receive extensive media attention and there were 400,000 copies in print. In the fall it overshadowed another Zondervan bestseller, *The Jesus Generation* by Billy Graham. It reached the million-copy mark in February 1972 and was selling at the rate of 25,000 copies a week.

The Late Great Planet Earth not only became the No. 1 Nonfiction Bestseller of the Decade, as adjudged by the *New York Times*, but it also helped to change the face of evangelical book publishing. Several social forces combined with the publication of the book to bring about a cultural revolution.

█   █   █

Numbers do not tell the whole story. For the record, the *New York Times* calculated the total sales at 7,286,769 copies by the dawn of 1980. But this figure includes neither all of Zondervan's sales nor the sales in other countries that resulted from the book's being translated into numerous languages. In all there were more than 10 million copies in print. Many of the sales counted by the *New York Times* were those of Bantam Books, a mass-market paperback publisher that issued an edition for the general book trade. Even ten years after the Zondervan edition was originally published, the *New York Times* reported on March 15, 1981, that the Bantam edition was still selling at the rate of 20,000 copies per month. To date, the book is still in print and more than 30 million copies have been sold.

Before Zondervan ever granted these rights to Bantam, there was a chasm between general and evangelical book publishing that was seldom bridged. Trade publishers, even those with religious-book divisions, marketed their books through general stores and distributors and usually disregarded the increasing number of religious bookstores. Leading evangelical books never appeared on bestseller lists of the mass media, because the media also ignored religious stores.

But with the publication of *The Late Great Planet Earth*, an evangelical book became a familiar sight in places where it normally would not have been seen before, including general bookstores, supermarkets, and airport newsstands. The interest of trade publishers grew, and soon more and more books from evangelical publishers began to find a home in the general marketplace and, in some cases, appeared on major bestseller lists. For four years in a row, according to *Publishers Weekly*, the leading nonfiction cloth book in general stores was one either written or published by an evangelical press: *The*

Living Bible by Kenneth Taylor (Tyndale House) in 1972 and 1973; *The Total Woman* by Marabel Morgan (Fleming H. Revell) in 1974; and *Angels: God's Secret Agents* by Billy Graham (Doubleday) in 1975.[13] Several trade houses expanded their religious book divisions or initiated evangelical imprints.

The trade publishers tended to follow the leading of their discovery that "religious books sell" while failing to appreciate the message and spiritual ministry of the evangelical titles appearing on their lists. They were reaping the harvest of a search for values and meaning in life that had its roots in the turbulent unrest of the sixties.

This spiritual search grew out of youth countercultures and campus ferment that followed the assassination of President John F. Kennedy in 1963, agitation for civil rights, and the subsequent escalation of the conflict in Vietnam. The malaise spread to the general public as disillusionment grew over Vietnam, and this was fueled in the early seventies by the Watergate affair.

A revival of interest in religion was sweeping the United States. It found expression in occultism and Eastern mystical religions, but also in the Jesus People, the charismatic movement, and an emphasis on experiential, self-conscious faith. The *New York Times*, reflecting on book publishing in the seventies, commented:

> During the turbulent 1970s, Americans bought more books, in hardcover and soft, than during any preceding decade.... Their selections were as varied as human taste, but the titles that attracted them most often were books that provided entertainment and escape, books that offered religious inspiration and hope, and books concerned with hedonistic impulses.[14]

The top-selling fiction titles of the decade in the general trade were *The Godfather* by Mario Puzo (13,500,000 copies in print), *The Exorcist* by William Blatty, and *Jonathan Livingston Seagull* by Richard Bach. In nonfiction, Lindsey's *Late Great Planet Earth* was followed by *Chariots of the Gods* by Erich Von Däniken, *Your Erroneous Zones* by Wayne W. Dyer, and *The Joy of Sex* by Alex Comfort.

■　■　■

The religious revival influenced evangelical publishers in other ways besides bringing their books into the general marketplace. The publication of mass-market books mushroomed. From 1973 to 1976, for example, more than 50 percent of the Zondervan books sold annually were mass-market paperbacks. After that the percentage declined, partly because of changing preferences among religious-book buyers and partly because of the effects of an inflationary economy that made "quality" or trade paperbacks, with their image of greater durability, a better buy. By the beginning of the eighties, Zondervan's mass-market sales constituted only about 40 percent of the copies sold annually, concentrated in a considerably smaller number of titles than in the mid-seventies.

Another development, establishing a trend that continues to the present, was an increasing openness among Roman Catholics for books of evangelical and Protestant origin. This came about as a result of greater interest in Bible reading engendered by Vatican II and the charismatic movement, and perhaps by the evangelical propensity for publishing books on social issues and family living. A number of evangelical books received wide exposure in Catholic periodicals, book clubs, and bookstores, especially personality books, books dealing with marriage and sexuality, and certain reference works. The philosophical works of Norman Geisler of Dallas Theological Seminary, such as *Philosophy of Religion* and *The Christian Ethic of Love*, have especially appealed to them because of Geisler's Thomistic overtones.

The "honeymoon" between general and evangelical publishing inevitably did not last. In failing to appreciate the unique spiritual qualities of books, trade publishers did not always choose wisely which titles to reprint. What is more, booksellers often failed to understand their product. One anecdote illustrates this well.

Pat and Mary Zondervan were vacationing in Anchorage, Alaska, one summer in the mid-seventies. When their departure was delayed by bad weather, Pat walked into the airport bookstore to see whether it was carrying any Zondervan publications. He saw several, but contrary to what he expected, he didn't see *The Late Great Planet Earth*. He asked the clerk about it.

"We have a few copies over there in the ecology section," she remarked. "By the way, what is there about the book that makes it sell so fast?"

"Well," Pat replied, "that isn't necessarily the place for you to display it. It has to do with prophecies that have come to pass, that are coming to pass, and that will come to pass."

A year or two later Pat was in the Anchorage airport again. As he was passing the bookstore on his way to the gate to catch his plane, he heard someone call his name.

"Mr. Zondervan," the book clerk called, "I just want you to know that we're still selling a lot of copies of *The Late Great Planet Earth*—and it's no longer in the ecology section!"

The glamour of evangelical books faded also as the general public became more aware of what they were buying. True, in 1976 the country had elected a president who described himself unashamedly as a "born-again Christian" and a Gallup poll proclaimed that as many as a fifth of all Americans at that time considered themselves evangelicals. But there was a growing suspicion and then even resentment toward proponents of a faith that still seemed to have some pretty well-defined statements regarding the Bible and Jesus Christ and demanded more than lip service; such a faith could not peacefully coexist indefinitely with the secular humanism that had become increasingly characteristic of American society. This feeling was undoubtedly intensified as evangelicals became greatly involved in politics and in crusading for moral values as the seventies ended.

Yet, although the honeymoon faded and the marriage went through some rocky times, there was never a divorce. As we will see, one day a second honeymoon between Christian books and the general public would occur that could hardly have been imagined in the seventies. And so would a resurgence of evangelical political involvement.

■　■　■

Another part of religious book publishing in the seventies that has borne similar results was the so-called personality book. "Celebrity" and personal-experience books became plentiful as Christian television networks developed and "talk shows" became popular. Zondervan has always been a cautious publisher and promoter in this regard, for the publishing house is concerned that books have other values besides sales potential and attractiveness for multimedia exposure; they must also have distinctive and lasting spiritual value for their readers.

First came *Man in Black,* the autobiography of country-western singer Johnny Cash, in 1975. A paperback edition was issued for the general trade by Warner Books, and total sales in all cloth and softcover editions have reached

750,000 copies. Zondervan followed this with *Among My Klediments*, an autobiographic scrapbook by Johnny's wife, June Carter Cash, and *Disciple in Blue Suede Shoes*, the autobiography of their friend, country singer Carl Perkins.

In 1979 Zondervan published *Terry Bradshaw: Man of Steel*. This autobiography, written with TV sportscaster David Diles, tells of the personal and professional struggles of the star quarterback of the Pittsburgh Steelers. Bradshaw had led his pro football team to three Super Bowl victories in the years before the book was published, and, a few months afterward, the team won a fourth.

But the most outstanding of the personal stories of the seventies was *Joni*. Johnny Cash and Terry Bradshaw had been in the limelight for many years by the time their books were published. Joni Eareckson was just coming into the public eye.

Managing Editor Al Bryant was watching the television show *Today* one morning in 1975 as Barbara Walters interviewed a young woman with quadriplegia who had learned to draw while holding a pen between her teeth. Joni told how she had broken her neck and become paralyzed when she dived into the Chesapeake Bay at the age of seventeen. She also expressed how she was able to rebuild her life and accept her incurable condition because of her faith in Christ.

Bryant, who had watched the show with more than casual interest, mentioned the interview to others at Zondervan, and Joni was contacted about writing an autobiography. Zondervan teamed her with writer Joe Musser, and the book was published in 1976. The dust jacket bore a photograph of her drawing with a pen in her mouth, and the title was simply *Joni*—pronounced "Johnny." The book was an instant success. Within five years it sold more than 2,250,000 copies, including a paperback edition from Bantam. It has sold more than 6 million to date. In 1979 Joni published a second book, *A Step Further*, coauthored by Steve Estes; this biblical and personal study of the problem of suffering sold 1,200,000 copies in its first two years.

Joni won the hearts of millions with her radiant personality and her testimony, expressed in her books, her artwork, and many speaking engagements, including a number of appearances at Billy Graham Crusades. She also enacted her own life story in the dramatic motion picture, *Joni*, released in 1980 by Worldwide Pictures. Today she directs a ministry to the handicapped called Joni and Friends, in California, a ministry that was even featured in an

Joni in Chinese

Dr. Zhang was a thirty-five-year-old orthopedic surgeon in northeastern China when he suffered a spinal cord injury while diving into shallow water. For the first year after his injury, Dr. Zhang wanted only to die, his despair was so great. But a Japanese physical therapist, knowing that the doctor could read English, gave him a copy of *Joni*, and it changed his life. The book filled him with such hope that he decided others in his native country needed to hear Joni's message. In only two and a half months, usually after hours in the hospital with the help of family and friends, he translated the book into Chinese. It was eventually published by the HuaXia Publishing Company in Beijing. Dr. Zhang, through this experience, was eventually able to open a thirty-bed rehabilitation center in AnShan, China, to help others with spinal injuries.

article in *Time* magazine in 1980. She continues to mature as an artist and continues to write at a prodigious pace. She has nearly a dozen Zondervan books in print.

Joni holds a special place in the hearts of Zondervan employees also. Few of the weekly chapel services that Zondervan has conducted since 1942 have matched those occasions when Joni was the speaker. The services at the Kentwood plant, which Zondervan opened in 1974, are usually held in conventional surroundings in the second-floor lunchroom. When Joni spoke, however, a vast area was cleared in the ground-floor bindery amid the machinery and stacks of books in various stages of production. Her audience, swelled by visitors, far outnumbered the chairs, so people sat on skids and cartons and wherever else they could make room. And some stood. As one Zondervan ad for her books says, "You will never forget Joni."

■ ■ ■

But spectacular books such as *The Late Great Planet Earth* and *Joni* represent only a small part of Zondervan publishing in the seventies. The greater part of the list consisted of the kinds of books that had always been Zondervan's strength: books on theology and doctrine, reference books and classroom texts, inspirational reading, Bible study guides, and books on current issues.

The changing scene of the American church and society made books on social subjects important and plentiful. Popular psychology, single lifestyles, family living, and sexuality all captured the attention of general and religious publishers alike. In addition, there were new forces at work in the church for evangelicals to write about, including church renewal, sharing groups, charismatics, and cults—trends that continued into the eighties and nineties. Just a few of Zondervan's significant titles dealing with these subjects in the seventies are—

- *The Act of Marriage* by Tim and Beverly LaHaye, which has more than two and a quarter million copies in print, and *How to Win Over Depression* by Tim LaHaye
- *The Art of Understanding Yourself* and other books by Cecil G. Osborne
- *But I Didn't Want a Divorce* by André Bustanoby
- *You're Someone Special* and other books by Bruce Narramore
- *Where Is God When It Hurts* by Philip Yancey
- *Brethren, Hang Loose* by Robert C. Girard
- *Let's Quit Fighting Over the Holy Spirit* by Peter E. Gillquist
- *The Charismatics: A Doctrinal Perspective* by John MacArthur Jr.
- *Youth, Brainwashing and the Extremist Cults* by Ronald Enroth
- *Armageddon, Oil and the Middle East Crisis* by John F. Walvoord and his son, John E. Walvoord

At this time Zondervan also launched the "Woman's Workshop Series" of inductive studies on Bible books and biblical topics, including Proverbs, James, the attributes of God, Bible marriages, and faith.

One Zondervan book even helped to spark controversy on a major theological issue that was at the center of a debate among Evangelicals at that time. *The Battle for the Bible* by Harold Lindsell, then editor of *Christianity Today*, took issue with a number of denominations, persons, and institutions prominent on the American church scene. The book, published in 1976, prompted response in the form of other books from other publishers. Zondervan published a sequel, *The Bible in the Balance*, in 1979 and also issued academic titles that reflected the publisher's commitment to the inerrancy of Scripture. These books included several prepared by the International

Council on Biblical Inerrancy such as *The Foundation of Biblical Authority*, edited by James Montgomery Boice.

In 1978 Zondervan began copublishing books for teenagers with Campus Life, the publishing arm of Youth for Christ International. This helped to fill a need that Zondervan was not meeting strongly at the time, although it had a considerable list for youth leaders. The Campus Life books were well received and included *The Trouble With Parents* and *After You Graduate* among a half-dozen titles. The writers and compilers of these books were staff members of Youth for Christ; the executive editor of Campus Life Books was, at that time, Philip Yancey.

Children's books had never constituted a large part of the list, but two series launched in the late seventies met with a good response. One was the Pathfinder line of fiction and nonfiction adventure stories for late elementary age; the other was two colorfully illustrated sets of four books each in the Learning to Read From the Bible series created by Gilbert V. Beers.

■　■　■

A book published in 1970 serves to demonstrate that not every bestseller is an overnight success like *The Late Great Planet Earth* or *The Act of Marriage*. Many books have been written on the Twenty-third Psalm, and *A Shepherd Looks at Psalm 23* came to be published chiefly because the author, W. Phillip Keller, was himself a shepherd who brought unique insights to the reader's understanding of Scripture. It was three or four years before this inspirational book began to receive the widespread attention it merited. Since then, it has achieved the status of a Christian classic and has more than 1.8 million copies in print.

Zondervan Publishing House gave a passing nod to one other phenomenon of the seventies, the "instant book." An instant book is a paperback that is produced in a fraction of the usual time schedule of six to nine months, usually because of its timely relationship to a recent news event. In 1974 the first copies of Hal Lindsey's third Zondervan book, *The Liberation of Planet Earth*, came off the press just seven weeks and two days after the manuscript was ready for typesetting. That was a fast pace, but not an instant book.

In 1976 Zondervan was offered a manuscript by U.S. Senator Jesse Helms of North Carolina. Because the book was to be used in congressional campaigns, it had to be produced on an accelerated schedule. The manuscript, a political manifesto, was reviewed over the Labor Day weekend and approved by the editorial committee the day after the holiday. The entire production process, from editing to binding, was compressed into ten working days, which included shuttling proofs back and forth between Grand Rapids and Washington, D.C. On the tenth day, 50,000 copies of *When Free Men Shall Stand* were ready to be shipped, with another 50,000 off the press two days later. And this was before the days of personal computers, digital technology, and email.

The rapid growth of evangelical publishing as a whole in the seventies tended to find many books appearing in the marketplace that perhaps should not have been published. Publication lists grew longer, and the number of evangelical publishers themselves increased substantially. Zondervan resisted the trend toward longer lists, however. Over the first four decades of its history, it steadily increased the number of new titles published annually. Its lists grew from 58 in 1944 to 76 in 1951, then to 113 in 1954 and 141 in 1960. The production leveled off at about 120 new titles a year during the sixties, then dropped to a rate of 75 to 80 in the early seventies and into the eighties. By the late eighties, however, the list was growing quickly again, and eventually leveled off at 140 to 150 titles a year, where it remains today.

The reduced output at that time served to keep the quality of Zondervan books high. In both 1977 and 1979 Zondervan was named *Eternity* magazine's Publisher of the Year. The honor was conferred on the publisher who had the most titles among the top twenty-five selected by a nationwide panel of

"He Restoreth My Soul"

Zondervan received a letter in 1972 from a reader of *A Shepherd Looks at Psalm 23*:

> The book has wrought a near miracle in my life, and just when I desperately needed it.... Our church librarian ... had read it and said excitedly, "This you must read." She just didn't know what she was doing, but God did....
>
> The entire book is tremendous, but the passage I am now absorbing most gratefully is the fifth chapter, "He restoreth my soul." It gave me answers I needed.

consultants. Both popular and academic books were featured among the chosen books, along with the New International Version of the Bible. Zondervan also received frequent mention in *Christianity Today*'s prestigious annual selection of the twenty-five best new books.

The decision as to what academic books Zondervan would publish generally rested with the Textbook Committee, a panel that included both members of the Zondervan staff and outside specialists in different fields, and the General Editorial Committee, which was comprised of members of Zondervan's editorial, sales, marketing, and promotion departments and then-President Peter Kladder.

■   ■   ■

Although thousands of unsolicited manuscripts pass through the editorial department each year, typically only five or six eventually see their way into print. Discovering the rare book that meets this happy fate is an enjoyable and rewarding part of publishing. An example is the historical novel *Coronation of Glory: The Story of Lady Jane Grey*. This was the first book written by Deborah Meroff, a librarian in Maine. When Zondervan published it in 1979, the book had the distinction of being the first major work of serious fiction to appear on the list since the publication of *Strettam* by Elva McAllaster in 1972.

One of the challenges for book publishers is to find and maintain the right mix and balance of new titles and "backlist" — books that have been in print for a year or more. Among Zondervan's ongoing strengths is the quality of its backlist; a stable publishing program requires much more than trendy subjects and million-copy bestsellers. But it is also true that high-volume popular books generate the capital needed to undertake major reference projects that often require the investment of considerable labor and money over a period of several years before the books are off the press. And it is also the nature of publishing that sometimes a book or series of books becomes a phenomenon that skews the picture and throws all the publishing aphorisms out the window. While *The Late Great Planet Earth* did that in the early seventies, even that was but a shadow of things to come — three decades later, in 2002.

The most significant reference work published in the seventies was *The Zondervan Pictorial Encyclopedia of the Bible*. In contrast to the instant book, this project took more than eleven years, nearly a million dollars, and the work of 240 scholars to complete. It was begun in 1963 under the guidance of Peter deVisser. Merrill C. Tenney served as general editor. By the time the first 15,000 sets were printed in February 1975 (on 170 tons of paper), the project had not only filled five volumes with nearly a million words each, but those words literally had filled a warehouse. The typesetting was begun before modern, computerized photocomposition became commonplace in religious book publishing, and the typesetting firm from Jackson, Michigan, had to rent a large warehouse just to store the miles of heavy lead type; not a line of the metal type for the five-volume set could be discarded or recycled until the project was ready for press.

The encyclopedia took its place alongside some great Zondervan projects of the past and some that have been completed since its publication: the *Jamieson, Fausset, and Brown Commentary*; the short-lived but significant *Expository Sermon Outlines on the Whole Bible* by Charles Simeon; the Amplified Bible and the Berkeley Version of the Bible; *Halley's Bible Handbook*; and more recently, the New International Version of the Bible (NIV), and the new *Book of Life*.

There were other developments in academic books in those years, some of which might have rivaled the encyclopedia project in typesetting complexity had it not been for the use of computer technology. The three-volume *New International Dictionary of New Testament Theology*, edited by Colin Brown, was a landmark work that was copublished with Paternoster Press in Great Britain; it received high acclaim in reviews and has gone into several printings since its completion in early 1979. The two-volume *Linguistic Key to the Greek New Testament*, translated from a German work and revised by Cleon L. Rogers Jr., offered a verse-by-verse grammatical analysis in an attractive form. Zondervan gradually helped to fill a void that existed in Hebrew aids to the Old Testament.

The New International Version of the Bible immediately stimulated the publication of numerous reference works and commentaries. One of the first such projects was the thirteen-volume *Expositor's Bible Commentary* which took nearly fifteen years to complete and involved the contributions of seventy-eight scholars under the direction of General Editor Frank E. Gaebelein.

During the seventies, Zondervan began to publish books for university classrooms for the first time in cooperation with Probe Ministries International of

Dallas, Texas. Probe was established in the late seventies to provide a forum in which to present the integration of Christian faith and academic studies by using a lecture-series technique. The highly effective "Christian Update Forum" was a blend of speaking and teaching sessions on a university campus over a four-day period. The "Christian Free University Curriculum Series" constituted the publishing arm of the Probe program. The first titles appeared in 1977, and the series eventually featured fifteen books in academic disciplines ranging from psychology to literature, from business to the arts, before being discontinued in 1987.

In the meantime, Zondervan's list of textbooks for Christian institutions continued to expand and by 1980 amounted to 275 titles. That year, academic sales accounted for about 17 percent of the books Zondervan sold, up from 12.6 percent in 1973. Some of the most significant titles were *The New International Dictionary of the Christian Church*, a work by 180 scholars directed by General Editor J. D. Douglas; *Basic Principles of Biblical Counseling* and *Effective Biblical Counseling* by Lawrence J. Crabb Jr.; *Common Roots* and *The Secular Saint* by Robert E. Webber; and *A Theology of Christian Education* by Lawrence O. Richards.

One of Zondervan's innovations at that time was a program so well liked that it was subsequently imitated by many other publishers. In 1978, President Peter Kladder had the idea to establish a way to give authors a voice in the publishing process that isn't tied to editorial or marketing. In Kladder's words, "I want someone who will talk with our authors, encourage them, answer their questions, take care of their problems, and do it without dollar signs in their eyes." Carol Holquist was asked to start the program, called Author Relations, that July. There were no guidelines, just the vision to do something that gave authors the sense of being cared for. Holquist says Kladder "reminded me often that my first responsibility was to find and solve problems related to our authors, and to make them think that Zondervan was the best place in the world to publish. He was very proud of the fact that other publishers copied what we were doing, and he told me in the later years of his life that it was one of his better ideas."

Another major development characterized Zondervan book publishing in the decade that produced *The Late Great Planet Earth, Joni,* and *The Zondervan Pictorial Encyclopedia of the Bible.* This was Zondervan's widening role as an international publisher. From the time Pat and Bernie undertook to publish the "Shilling Series" with Marshall, Morgan & Scott in 1934, there has been a lively exchange of titles between Zondervan and publishers in Great Britain—including Hodder & Stoughton, Pickering & Inglis, Paternoster Press, and Scripture Union, in addition to Marshall. Eventually many foreign distributors also established a relationship with Zondervan. Foremost among these are R. G. Mitchell Family Books (formerly Home Evangel) in Canada, S. John Bacon PTY in Australia, STL (Send the Light) Distributors in Great Britain, Word of Life Publisher in South Africa, and G. W. Moore in New Zealand. There were also distributors in Nigeria, Rhodesia, Kenya, Ghana, Hong Kong, the Philippines, Japan, Korea, Singapore, India, Norway, West Germany, Belgium, and Mexico.

The seventies, moreover, brought unprecedented activity in the number of foreign rights sold. In 1970 the rights to 36 titles were granted to overseas publishers, of which 21 were for West Germany and 10 were for Great Britain. The number jumped to 82 the following year and increased to 174 in 1974 as many more countries became involved. In 1980 the number was 98. West Germany and Great Britain accounted for a large share of these from year to year, but publishing in Spanish and Portuguese and various Chinese dialects was growing rapidly.

Evangelical firms in many Third World nations undertook ambitious publishing programs that were not economically feasible prior to the seventies. For example, Zondervan books appeared on the lists of eleven Chinese publishers based in Taiwan and Hong Kong. And in 1981 a Korean bookstore opened in San Francisco; in importing books from Korea, it created another market for translations of Zondervan books.

Eventually Zondervan and other religious publishers will likely be publishing manuscripts for the Third World that originate, not in Western culture, but in the Third World nations themselves.

As of 2006, *The Late Great Planet Earth* has been published in twenty-two languages, *Joni* in forty-four, and *A Shepherd Looks at Psalm 23* in twenty-two. Language and cultural differences still hinder the spread and impact of the gospel in many parts of the world. But *Joni* symbolically offers hope that this will change. A picture of Joni Eareckson usually adorns the cover of the various editions of her book, and the personal title seldom changes. Joni's charming smile and picturesque name know no language barriers.

12

Breaking New Ground

As dramatic changes were taking place in evangelical publishing in the early seventies, Zondervan itself was changing in far-reaching ways. Three months before the first copies of *The Late Great Planet Earth* came off the press in 1970, Peter Kladder Jr. was named corporation president and chief executive officer. Pat Zondervan became chairman of the board, and the executive committee named two new vice presidents, Robert G. Bolinder in sales and Robert K. DeVries in book publishing.

The next year the corporate structure expanded as Zondervan reorganized with several full-fledged divisions: Zondervan Publishing House; Family Bookstores; Singspiration; Singcord, the recording division; and the Zondervan Broadcasting Corporation, which operated radio stations WJBL AM and FM in Holland, Michigan, and WAUK AM and FM in Waukesha, Wisconsin.

The company had grown in size, diversity of product, and influence to a degree unimaginable to Pat and Bernie at the time they began their book business in Grandville in 1931.

After the death of Bernie Jr. on January 2, 1970, it became obvious that a large part of the executive leadership would have to be shared by persons outside the Zondervan family. Kladder was a natural choice to become president. As treasurer since 1956, he had helped to expedite numerous acquisitions, guide diversification, and cultivate a style of management that befitted the changing character of the company. He maintained a profile of quiet efficiency both within and beyond the corporation's walls.

His style of leadership was exemplified by his role on the General Editorial Committee of the book division. The committee acted by consensus on proposals introduced by the editorial members. Each vote bore equal weight except on the rare occasions when, in a complex decision involving a large financial commitment or corporation policy, the other members turned to Kladder for the final decision. His peremptory yes or no was accepted without further question as the wisest decision.

In 1973 Kladder developed Compudisc, an innovative sales program. This is a computerized plan in which individual discounts were determined by averaging a dealer's volume of business with Zondervan over the previous four quarters. The average was recomputed after each quarter. Thus dealers could increase their discount in any of the four product lines—books, Bibles, printed music, or recordings—by raising the average from one quarter to the next. Compudisc enabled small stores to achieve better discounts, thus narrowing the gap between them and large dealers.

Also in 1973, Fred Holtrop became treasurer of the firm, succeeding Marvin Veltkamp, who had filled the position briefly.

The responsibility fell to Kladder to guide the company through its decision to "go public," that is, to offer stock in the public marketplace for the first time in the company's history. From the start the board of directors felt that the stock would be sought primarily by people who appreciated Zondervan's Christian testimony and distinctively religious products. And there was a conviction that these people would be interested in the stock even if the market was in a downturn in the troubled economy of the seventies.

Kladder explained why the Zondervan Corporation chose to go public: "Basically, we were concerned with the perpetuation of the publishing house. The main purpose of the offering was not to accumulate cash or to get cash for capital growth, but to broaden the base of ownership. We felt that there were many people who were investment-minded, but who were also like-minded spiritually and would be eager to see their money working two ways: first, to grow in an investment situation, and second, to be supportive of a kingdom cause."

Once the decision was made, Kladder began to tell the Zondervan story to underwriting companies. The board selected William Blair Company of Chicago. The plans were to issue 200,000 shares, of which 165,000 would be sold by shareholders. It was anticipated that the stock would sell at about $12 per share. Then the Mideast oil embargo put the nation's economy in turmoil in the winter of 1973–74, and the public offering was delayed.

It was October 1976 before the issue could be revived, and this time the Ohio Company of Columbus was the underwriter. The Ohio Company went to the open market with 305,879 shares of stock, of which all but 100,000 were from selling stockholders. A five-year warrant accompanied each share, meaning that the purchaser could buy another share for $9.25, the opening price, at any time before 1981. The response was even better than expected.

"We believed that, over the long term, the majority of our stock will be in the hands of people who can relate to us personally," Kladder said. "We were quite amazed at the investment market Zondervan has been able to attract, and I believe this has been basically because of our unique product line." Kladder's words about the nature of the stockholders would come back to haunt him and the company some ten years later.

Two other developments in the corporation directly benefited the employees. One was a profit-sharing plan introduced in 1969. The other was a quarterly bonus pool program initiated in 1974; employees received shares of the bonus pool according to their longevity with the company and their basic wages.

■　■　■

The corporation broke ground for a new production and warehousing plant in the Grand Rapids suburb of Kentwood on November 1, 1973. The 80,000-square-foot facility at Broadmoor Avenue and Fifty-second Street SE was the first ever built by the company. It boasted one of the most innovative warehouse systems in the publishing industry. The installation included a floor-to-ceiling warehouse with shelves 195 feet long rising to a height of 45 feet. Lifts, called "Racker-Stackers," in eight aisles stored books in shelf spaces assigned by an onboard computer. The same number of books that previously had to be stored in 65,000 square feet of floor area could then be stored in 13,000 square feet. The automated lifts could store books at heights that humans could not reach unaided. By the operator's use of two computer cards, a Racker-Stacker could store and retrieve books in one operation, always "remembering" in which cubicle the books had been placed.

Most of the books were not stored in cardboard cartons. Instead, they are stacked on cardboard pallets, then "shrink-wrapped" by machine with a clear plastic wrapping before storage. This results in both a cost saving and a reduction of dust.

The system had 87,000 storage cubicles in all. A title would be stored in more than one aisle so that if any of the eight Racker-Stackers broke down, there would be no problem filling demands for that title. The fastest-selling books are assigned to the lower-front sections nearest to the lift operator of each aisle.

The print shop, bindery, and production offices moved into the Kentwood plant in the fall of 1974, and the warehouse and shipping departments joined them in January 1975. The editorial department moved to Kentwood from Lake Drive in May 1976, and the Bible Department in 1980. Besides new presses and a computerized photocomposition typesetting system, the new equipment included a wastepaper recycling system that collected up to five tons a week. Zondervan fulfilled most of its typesetting and printing needs on its own equipment, but cloth and spiral bindings and large print runs such as in Bibles are produced by outside manufacturers.

The total workforce of the corporation rose to more than five hundred in late 1973 and by 1981, at the fiftieth anniversary, numbered more than seven hundred. The increase was spurred by the rapid growth of the Family Bookstores Division and the acquisition of the John Rudin Company. Both enterprises were involved in spreading the gospel message through selling books but used different means to do it.

There were twelve company-owned retail stores when Bill Zondervan was appointed general manager of the Family Bookstores in 1969. The number of stores doubled in four years under Bill's leadership and redoubled in the following five years. In September 1973 the twenty-fifth store was opened, in Northridge, California; there were thirty-five by June 1974 and forty a year later. The Family Bookstore offices moved from quarters on Louis Street in downtown Grand Rapids to the third floor of the Lake Drive building in 1975.

Bill Zondervan retired in 1980; during his eleven years as general manager, the stores had increased in number from twelve to fifty-six. He was succeeded as general manager by G. Larry Branscombe, who had joined Family Bookstores five years earlier and had most recently been the national training manager.

In late 1980, the retail chain opened a discount store, called the Factory Outlet, in the Grand Rapids suburb of Wyoming. The store is the first of its kind for Zondervan, offering remaindered stock, slightly damaged goods, and other titles from many publishers at reduced prices.

Seven stores were added to the Family Bookstores chain in 1981 to bring the total to sixty-four in twenty states. At that point, Zondervan made it a policy to open stores only in established shopping malls, a move that caused some people to criticize the company, for it would sometimes open stores in a community where a Christian bookstore already existed. To this Pat responded, "We have developed the strong sense that in many areas one Christian bookstore cannot meet all the needs. It is important to note that we have established our Family Bookstores in shopping centers; most of the other Christian bookstores are unable to move into these centers because it requires $100,000 or more to place a store in a mall. We have come to the conclusion that if we are going to serve the public, that's the place where we will do it."

And Family Bookstores had indeed been reaching the public. It was estimated that 30 percent of the chain's customers were unchurched. The stores promoted the gospel message with the slogan "Just Good Books."

Regarding the powerful ministry that Christian bookstores could have, one manager of a Family Bookstore, Mario Romine of Euclid, Ohio, said: "Because of the Christian mall bookstore, I, my wife, and at least thirty friends and relatives are Christians today. My wife and I happened to be browsing in the bookstore, and we picked up a book that looked interesting. I read it, eventually became saved, and here I am today managing the bookstore myself!" Need it be added that the book was *The Late Great Planet Earth*?

These were the glory days of Zondervan's ownership of the Family Bookstore chain. The revenues from the fifty-seven Family Bookstores in operation in 1980 totaled $18,400,000, one-third of the corporation's total revenues of $54,500,000. This represented growth of more than 600 percent from the division's revenues of $3,000,000 only a decade earlier, when there were about one-fourth as many stores. About 18 percent of the stores' revenues in 1980 came from the sale of Zondervan publications. The explosive growth of Family Bookstores paralleled the growth in religious retailing as a whole in the United States. The industry's revenues nationwide were estimated at $770 million in 1980, an increase of 20 percent over the $644 million of 1978.

The opening of new stores and the implementation of new programs by Branscombe kept the Family Bookstores growing at an impressive rate up until Family Bookstore employees bought themselves away from Zondervan and HarperCollins in 1994. Branscombe appointed three regional managers who were responsible for recruiting and training personnel, investigating sites for additional stores, and improving merchandising techniques. The managers are Al VanderVeen, North; Tom Mockabee, South-Central; and Volney James, western region.

Hand in hand with this regionalization was the introduction of computerized cash registers in each store. The registers served as computer terminals linked with a central computer in the Grand Rapids headquarters. These allowed a daily accounting of books and other products sold and promoted better marketing and inventory control.

■ ■ ■

Another Zondervan retail operation was the former John Rudin Company, which Zondervan purchased in 1972 and made its Book of Life Division.

John Rudin founded his company in Chicago in 1923 to sell a home reading program comprising an eleven-volume set of books sold door to door. This set was arranged for family reading with maps and illustrations, footnotes, and stories to dramatize and clarify the meaning of the Bible text for children. More than three-quarters of a million copies of this set, called *The Book of Life*, were sold.

When Zondervan purchased the company, it laid plans to develop a completely new set of *The Book of Life*. Gilbert V. Beers, an educator and children's author from Elgin, Illinois, was hired as the creative director to work under the guidance of Rex Jones, who had been associated with the Rudin company for fifteen years and was then Zondervan's divisional vice president.

While this massive project was getting under way, Zondervan celebrated the fiftieth anniversary of *The Book of Life* in 1973 by issuing the old set in a new gold binding. Then in October 1977 the Book of Life offices moved from Chicago to Grand Rapids. Along with Jones, some other key members of the organization made the move, including John Rock, general sales manager;

Carlyle Paul, office manager; Carol Mikal, order fulfillment; Larry Galmish, assistant sales manager; and Kathryn Frey, regional sales manager.

Kathryn Frey surpassed even Pat Zondervan in employment longevity. She went to work for the John Rudin Company in 1925 and retired in 1981 after fifty-six years with the company. Even though she was already past the age when most people think of retirement, she readily came to Grand Rapids in 1977, leaving behind in Chicago many relatives and a favorite pastime: attending the Chicago Cubs home opener each April at Wrigley Field.

The sales people themselves numbered about 2,000, of whom about three-fourths were part-time representatives who supplemented other incomes by selling The Book of Life. Many stories were told to the office staff regarding incidents in which The Book of Life proved to be the means of introducing the gospel message to people who had not heard it before.

The new Book of Life was published and introduced in October 1980 after seven years of work and an investment of more than $2 million. It was virtually a Bible encyclopedia for the family. It had twenty-two volumes of narrative, a volume that provided a guidebook and an index, and another volume that contained the complete text of the Bible in large print. The Bible volumes were available in both the King James Version and the New International Version.

The basic text narrative gave a careful paraphrase of Scripture. The material was divided into about five hundred reading units, and each unit was arranged into the following four parts:

- An introduction with important background information and a unit theme
- The narrative, relating the events of the Bible in easy-to-read language
- "The Bible for Daily Living," which gave suggestions for applying the Scripture reading to everyday living
- A concluding feature, called "The Bible Comes Alive," which explained and illustrated interesting facts about Bible life and times

The set was lavishly illustrated with more than six thousand photographs, paintings, and illustrations and more than two hundred maps, charts, and diagrams.

Because of its encyclopedic content, The Book of Life appealed to ministers and teachers apart from family use. A Gallup poll on the subject of Bible reading at that time indicated that as many as 37 million adults who identified themselves as Christians had never read the Bible. For many of them, *The Book of Life* provided the means by which they could begin to read the Bible and discover other Zondervan publications as well.

A third retail operation, Retail Marketing Services, was formed in 1977 to provide for greater use of direct mail in sales and promotion. Among the services it provides were the *Church Library Newsletter,* issued bimonthly, and a Book-a-Matic club plan for church libraries.

◾ ◾ ◾

Other acquisitions by Zondervan during the seventies served to expand one of the existing divisions of the corporation—music publishing—in contrast to the purchase that created a whole new division in Book of Life. Yet acquisitions comprised only part of the significant developments on the music scene. The most far-reaching of these was John W. Peterson's decision to leave Singspiration and Zondervan.

From the time Peterson had met Pat and Bernie, a friendship had developed that transcended their business relationship. When Peterson became president of Singspiration in 1957, he looked especially to Pat for encouragement and inspiration. Peterson wrote:

> Though not a musician himself, Pat's enthusiasm for my compositions never flagged. He loved music and had the remarkable ability of sending a word of cheer just when I needed it most. Like the time he wrote me from London where he had attended a meeting during Billy Graham's London Crusade: "Cliff [Barrows] is using 'Surely Goodness and Mercy' each night. He says he gets notes sent up to the platform if he doesn't use it early in the service."
>
> The Zondervans' teamwork was almost uncanny, though they were unique individuals: Pat, the man of action and decisiveness, the trailblazer; Bernie, a bit more quiet, with a somewhat visionary spiritual quality. True to their word, they never tried to call the tune when it came to artistic policy.... They made valuable suggestions, but basically the creative and production sides of Singspiration were in my hands.
>
> I had been warned not to move to Grand Rapids—warned that I'd get caught up in a business routine and my creative juices would dry up. If anything, the opposite happened. Pat, especially, had the "go get 'em" quality that

a person of my temperament needed to push me ahead. He and Bernie also had wisdom on another count. They knew that if I were to create, I had to have a certain amount of isolation.[15]

Nevertheless, as pressures of managing steadily increased for Peterson, an allergic and asthmatic condition worsened, and his interests outside Zondervan grew. With the reorganization of the Zondervan Corporation, Peterson decided it was time to bow out and find a means of devoting more time to creative work in a more healthful climate than Michigan afforded. On February 2, 1971, Peterson resigned as president of Singspiration, sold his share of the company to Zondervan, took the position of executive composer—and moved to sunny Arizona.

Peterson knowingly left behind him a staff that had the ability to create musical works commensurate with the standards he had set for himself. Norman Johnson and Harold DeCou had been his top assistants. Chuck Van Horn was still office manager. John Rasley had joined the staff as an editor. And in 1970, Don Wyrtzen, son of the famous evangelist Jack Wyrtzen of "Word of Life," became youth editor.

Influenced by the folk-music trend of the sixties, Wyrtzen introduced some new ideas and styles to Singspiration. Ralph Carmichael had pioneered the Christian folk musical with the successful *Tell It Like It Is* put out by another publisher. But the theological ambiguity of that work and a fear that Christian folk music could become trapped in superficiality made Singspiration cautious about developing the new style. Nonetheless, the instinctive need to be progressive prevailed, and the *Folk Hymnal*, a compilation by Peterson and Johnson, was published in late 1970. It was a breakthrough. It succeeded in being both conservative in its theological content and progressive in its musical taste.

In the meantime, Pat Zondervan provided leadership as the new president of Singspiration, but the managerial structure did not really crystallize until 1976. The division was strengthened by the creation of a sales staff for Singspiration and Singcord products separate from the book and Bible sales. Four sales representatives were appointed in 1972, among them James L. Williams, who became sales manager in 1975.

Zondervan was making acquisitions in the music field at that time. One company it purchased was Fiesta Music of Hollywood, California, a small publisher that held the copyright to the well-known song "Down from His Glory." At about the same time Zondervan purchased the larger Stamps-Baxter Music Company.

Stamps-Baxter had grown out of a music company founded in Dallas, Texas, in the late twenties by Virgil O. Stamps. Some time later he invited J. R. Baxter Jr. of Chattanooga, Tennessee, to form a partnership with him. Part of the company's ministry was conducting singing conventions and "all-night sings" throughout the southern United States. They produced songbooks for these conventions and offered them through the mail on the popular radio program that featured the Stamps Quartet. Much of the music was published in the "shape-note" tradition; in this style, the note for each line or space in a clef has a distinctive shape that enables people to discern a melody even if they don't "read music."

Stamps died of a heart attack in 1940, and when Baxter died in 1960, Baxter's widow carried on the business.

Pat Zondervan had long had a penchant for southern gospel music. And as the history of Zondervan demonstrates, Pat often found that his being in a certain place at a certain time was clearly by the leading of God. Pat was preaching in the Dallas suburb of Duncanville in 1974 when he heard that Mrs. Baxter had died. Upon going to the funeral home, he was told by family friends that the Baxters had been childless and the future of the company was uncertain. In her will Mrs. Baxter left the company to four employees, but three of them were ready to retire and the fourth had other interests and was no longer living near Dallas. All four were interested in selling their shares, and the purchase of the company by Zondervan was completed in July 1974.

Pat assumed the leadership of Stamps-Baxter for a while, even though he was already greatly involved in Singspiration and Singcord and was theoretically semi-retired. He divided his time between Grand Rapids and Dallas until the printing operations for Stamps-Baxter were moved to Michigan. Zondervan continued to produce shape-note books and recordings, holding the copyright to such well-known Stamps-Baxter songs as "Where Could I Go But to the Lord?" until it sold all its interests in music publishing in 1992.

Pat served as a vice president of the Gospel Music Association, a tribute to his great love for a kind of music that often expresses the same qualities he possessed — warmth, enthusiasm, and sincerity.

All of Zondervan's music enterprises were merged under one umbrella division in the Zondervan Corporation in 1976, and John Helder became the divisional executive vice president. Helder had served for a year as vice president of marketing for Book of Life and prior to that had spent two years as general manager of radio station WAUK and eight years as sales manager of WJBL. Zondervan had determined in the early seventies that the broadcast medium did not fulfill the company's historical objectives in publishing, and in 1975 it sold both stations and dissolved the Zondervan Broadcasting Corporation.

When Helder became vice president of the new Singspiration division, Don Wyrtzen was appointed the director of music publications. Several of Wyrtzen's songs enjoyed wide popularity, including "Yesterday, Today, and Tomorrow," "Love Was When," and "Worthy Is the Lamb." In 1975 he collaborated with John W. Peterson on the musical *I Love America*; this was the first time Peterson had worked with another composer on a major work. Wyrtzen's church musical *Home for Christmas* was premiered at Zondervan's Christmas dinner for employees in December 1980. Earlier that year he was honored as the Alumnus of the Year by King's College in Briarcliff Manor, New York. Wyrtzen also held a Th.M. degree from Dallas Theological Seminary.

Singspiration continued to publish a variety of choral and solo material for church use. In 1979 it published *Praise: Our Songs and Hymns*, the latest in a line of hymnals that included *Inspiring Hymns*, released in 1951, and *Great Hymns of the Faith* in 1968. All these hymnals emphasized music of post-Reformation times and American origin. But *Praise* was distinct from its predecessors in its bold juxtaposition of traditional hymns and contemporary popular songs, many of which were not originally created for congregational use. Thus, on consecutive pages one finds two compositions from 1971 — "Through It All" by Andrae Crouch and "Something Beautiful" by William J. Gaither — positioned between two nineteenth-century pieces — "Jesus Loves Even Me" by Philipp Bliss and "He Lifted Me" by Charles H. Gabriel. *Praise*, a large hymnal of 572 songs, also contains forty pages of worship resources that are available in either the King James Version or the New International Version of the Bible.

There were two other achievements for Zondervan during the seventies that are major innovations in the gospel-music field. One was a program of music conferences and choral clinics, and the other was the "VIP" subscription music program.

Singspiration held its first music conference at Boca Raton, Florida, in 1970. The conferences and accompanying choral clinics enjoyed tremendous popularity and success. The conference was a four-day regional program intended to assist and instruct church musicians, especially choir directors and accompanists. Prominent composers and creative artists joined with Singspiration staff members in a program of performances and workshops. Several were held each year in key cities in the United States and Canada.

The VIP Club was formed in the late seventies and was in part an outgrowth of the Singspiration innovation of providing demonstration records and tapes for musicals and cantatas. Three times a year subscribers received a package of materials that included new Singspiration music, octavo arrangements with listening cassettes, musicals and cantatas in book-and-record combinations, and other benefits. This program met with a good response from choir directors and other church musicians.

Thus Zondervan's music publishing changed in many ways during the seventies. But one even more dramatic story of Zondervan publishing in that decade remains to be told.

■　■　■

Nothing in print equals in its beauty, importance, and value the New International Version of the Bible. It was the culmination of great traditions and continues to have a lasting influence on religious publishing and the Christian church. The NIV eventually replaced the King James Version as the best-expressed, bestselling, and best-loved English version of the Bible. And it gained preeminence after nearly a century of vigorous Bible translation activity that produced an array of versions too numerous to mention.

In the preparation of those two translations, there are some striking parallels between the King James Version and the NIV — parallels that make such bold claims credible. The King James culminated a century of Bible translation and publishing in the English language that had begun with Tyndale's Bible in 1525, which was itself indebted to the first English edition, the Wycliffe Bible of 1382. Tyndale was burned at the stake in 1536 for translating God's Word into the language of the people. But a movement had already been set into motion that eventually brought forth Coverdale's Bible in 1535; the

"Great Bible" in 1539; the popular and trustworthy Geneva Bible in 1560, which also introduced modern versification; the "Bishops' Bible," authorized by the Church of England, in 1568; and several other versions.

King James I of England authorized the formation of a translation committee in 1604. The work was entrusted to three panels of scholars, who numbered forty-seven in all—the largest translation team ever assembled to that time. The King James Version was published in 1611. F. F. Bruce explains the other circumstances that caused this version to gain predominance in its own time and maintain that authority for three hundred and fifty years.

> The translators drew on the work of all their predecessors and on versions in other languages, with constant reference to the original text. Annotations relating to theological or ecclesiastical controversies were excluded; this greatly facilitated the widespread acceptance of the version. The translators' feeling for prose rhythm made their work admirably suited for reading aloud.[16]

The next Protestant Bible to enjoy widespread use was the Revised Version, a revision of the King James Version produced by a group of eighty-three English and American scholars in 1885. An American edition, the American Standard Version, was published in 1901, and this in turn formed the basis for the Revised Standard Version, completed in 1952. Between 1901 and 1952 a number of new versions appeared, especially of the New Testament, but none attained lasting popularity. Rather, in the past thirty years there has poured forth a wide variety of translations and versions that enjoy extensive use today. Some are team efforts, and some are paraphrases by individuals; some are formal, and others are highly idiomatic. But the New International Version is the only contemporary translation that matches the King James Version in its breadth of scholarship, reliance on the original languages, and emphasis on the aesthetic qualities of the English language. This is how the NIV came into being:

First, some members of the Christian Reformed Church thought it was desirable to have a new and accurate translation of the Bible in contemporary language, prepared by scholars who were committed to the inerrancy of Scripture. Later they shared their idea with the National Association of Evangelicals. These two groups called together a number of scholars in 1965 to discuss the proposal, and this led, the following year, to the creation of the

Committee on Bible Translation, a self-governing body of fifteen persons from various denominations. In 1967 the New York International Bible Society committed itself to underwriting the project financially, enabling the committee to enlist many distinguished scholars from the United States, Canada, Great Britain, Australia, and New Zealand. One hundred scholars in all had a part in the translation.

The Committee on Bible Translation appointed as its executive secretary Edwin H. Palmer, then pastor of the Grandville Avenue Christian Reformed Church in Grand Rapids. Palmer had been recommended to the committee at the suggestion of Gert TerKeurst, Pat Zondervan's secretary.

The work began in earnest. The translation of each book of the Bible was assigned to a team of scholars. Then an Intermediate Editorial Committee checked and revised the initial translation; their work was then reviewed and revised by the General Editorial Committee; and finally the revision was reviewed by the Committee on Bible Translation. In each of these revisions, the translation was examined for its faithfulness to the original languages and for style. Experts in English writing and style were members of the review committees. The result of this time-consuming process is that probably no other translation has been so thoroughly reviewed and revised from committee to committee as the New International Version.

Another feature is that the Committee on Bible Translation hired one of America's leading book designers, Ernst Reichl, to design the typography. *Publishers Weekly* later commented that the NIV "represents new directions in Bible design and production as well as in translation."

The magnitude of the project in time and cost was far greater than the Committee originally imagined. The New York Bible Society's investment eventually exceeded $2.5 million. In 1971 Zondervan was selected as the publisher and contributed financially by advancing royalty payments to the society. Zondervan continued to pay royalties throughout the thirty-year life of the original publishing contract.

The Gospel of John, published by Zondervan in August 1973, provided the public's first look at the New International Version. Then the entire New Testament came off the press in October that same year. It was promoted as "a major new modern English translation for people who take their Bible seriously," and it won instant acclaim from evangelical leaders and periodicals throughout the country. The gold-stamped brown cover and the sandy-colored paper with wide single-column type was recognizable everywhere. In the years that followed, other editions were developed by Zondervan's Bible Division, including an innovative children's edition with Memory Margin, in which selected verses were enlarged and placed in the margins for easy recognition and memorization.

▪ ▪ ▪

As the NIV New Testament began to win a permanent place in homes, churches, and classrooms, the Committee on Bible Translation pressed forward with the translation of the Old Testament.

The typesetting for both the NIV New Testament and the entire Bible was done by Auto-Graphics, a leading company for computerized photocomposition located in Monterey Park, California. This is the same firm that scored a landmark achievement in computer programming in *The Layman's Parallel Bible,* which Zondervan published in November 1973, just a month after the NIV New Testament was released. The *Parallel Bible* places four versions side by side on each two-page spread. Some very sophisticated programming was required to produce the type so that each spread had the same verses for each version, regardless of how many lines of type they filled, and also include the appropriate footnotes for each version.

The New International Version of the entire Bible was published in October 1978. The first printing was for 1.2 million copies, of which all but 75,000 were sold by the publication date. The printing was done in three large plants in the eastern United States, and it required 3.5 million pounds of paper, or seventy-eight train carloads. A remarkable aspect of this first printing is that seven editions were issued simultaneously, an achievement unprecedented in Bible publishing. The "standard" edition had a single-column format that attractively displays poetry—which constituted about 40 percent of the Old Testament. This edition comprised 1,635 pages. There were two double-column editions, one of which was a compact size well-suited to church pew racks. All of these editions were published in both cloth and leather bindings. The seventh was a clothbound children's edition, complete with four-color illustrations and a large section of original Bible helps.

The release of the NIV Bible was promoted in a thirteen-city campaign of pastors' breakfasts and press conferences featuring three men who had assisted the Committee on Bible Translation toward its memorable goal: Edwin H.

Palmer; Youngve Kindberg, president of the New York International Bible Society; and Ronald N. Haynes, executive vice president of Zondervan's Bible Division.

The truly international quality of the NIV applies not so much to the breadth of its sales and distribution as to the nature of its use of English. It is a translation that in its clarity and vocabulary is highly suitable for persons who use English as a second language. This is illustrated by the experience of one missions organization. A team of linguists had worked for several years to provide a new Bengali translation of the Bible to replace the one produced in the early nineteenth century by the great missionary William Carey. The team in Bangladesh had recently completed and published the New Testament, but the Old Testament loomed as an endless task. Nevertheless, as they had done with the New Testament, the linguists began to prepare a "basic English" version that could be used alongside the biblical-language texts for producing the Bengali translation. They discovered that their sample chapters were so similar to the reading of the newly published NIV Old Testament that they decided to adopt the NIV as their basic text, saving themselves many hours of labor and advancing the schedule for the actual translation into Bengali by many months.

In the *Times Union and Journal* of Jacksonville, Florida, on January 20, 1979, staff writer Barbara White wrote,

> P. J. Zondervan caresses a Bible as he holds it. It is an old friend. He has helped place Bibles in thousands of hotel and motel rooms since 1938 when he became a member of the Gideons Society, and he is cofounder of the publishing house which recently published the fastest-selling hardbound translation of the Bible ever produced....
>
> "People are hungry for a readable translation of the Bible in the language of today, by men who know it is the inerrant Word of God," Zondervan said.

And the fact that the first printing of the NIV was the largest for a cloth book in the history of publishing demonstrates that the New International Version fulfills that desire. The next decade will reveal whether it also fulfills its promise to "replace" the King James Version as the most popular translation of the Bible in use in the English language.

13

> Be Thou my Vision, O Lord of my heart —
> Naught be all else to me, save that Thou art;...
> Be Thou my Wisdom, and Thou my true Word —
> I ever with Thee and Thou with me, Lord.
> TRANSLATED BY MARY K. BYRNE,
> THE BOOK OF THE GAEL

Golden Opportunities

The wavy locks were white and the gait was a little slower, but P. J. Zondervan radiated a golden healthfulness at Innisbrook Golf and Country Club in Tarpon Springs, Florida, on his seventy-second birthday, April 2, 1981. He was semi-retired from business at the time but maintained a daily schedule as busy and varied as ever. He bore responsibilities as chairman of the board of the Zondervan Corporation and served on the boards of several Christian outreach organizations. He had an active speaking schedule for Gideons International. And he still liked to arise at a predawn hour to get a certain amount of work done in quiet solitude before the phone started ringing.

It ran contrary to his Dutch temperament to consider passive retirement. He was, after all, only two years and two months older than Ronald Reagan, then President of the United States.

Pat Zondervan was happy. He had always enjoyed life and work. And now he had a blessed privilege that few men experience: celebrating the fiftieth anniversary of the firm he helped to found.

Many honors had been heaped upon Pat. He was a member of the International Gutenberg Society, Who's Who in America, the United Airlines Million Miler Club, and the Professional Hall of Fame, to name a few.

One of the most heart-warming honors he received was the proclamation of "P. J. (Pat) Zondervan Day" in Grand Rapids on Tuesday, December 4, 1973. The occasion paid tribute to his fifty years in publishing communications, for he began to work for the William B. Eerdmans Publishing Company in 1924. The proclamation by Mayor Lyman S. Parks also praised his efforts as an important benefit to his community and expressed appreciation for his contribution in helping to make Grand Rapids an important center for religious publishing.

The celebration climaxed with a ceremony that evening at the Civic Auditorium. There John W. Peterson led a choir and orchestra in the premiere of his new cantata, *King of Kings,* in Pat's honor, and City Commission Chairman Patrick Barr presented Pat with a key to the city. Vice President Gerald R. Ford sent a telegram of congratulations to his friend:

> ... You have provided the residents of our community with a unique service which is badly needed during these changing and challenging times, and for that we are all grateful. Best wishes in your future efforts to keep the spiritual message alive and available to all of us.

Another kind of honor had a special poignancy. Pat never graduated from high school. But the fruits of his life devoted to Christian publishing enabled countless others to learn and to grow intellectually and spiritually in college and seminary classrooms around the world. On May 24, 1969, John Brown University of Siloam Springs, Arkansas, conferred on Pat the honorary degree of doctor of literature. Lee College in Cleveland, Tennessee, conferred an honorary doctor of letters on May 14, 1972. These are fitting tributes to a man who had never been far from a book, whether it was a Gideon New Testament, a dusty classic plucked from a minister's library for reprinting, or the newest release from the high-speed presses.

Pat Zondervan and Wilma Zondervan Teggelaar were honored at the corporation's Christmas dinner for employees at the Marriott Inn on December 1, 1980. More than five hundred persons attended. Among the special awards presented to Pat was an etched rock crystal bearing the inscription:

THE ZONDERVAN CORPORATION

50 YEARS

PAT ZONDERVAN

FOUNDER AND CHAIRMAN

1981

"A FAITHFUL MAN SHALL ABOUND

WITH BLESSINGS . . ."

PROV. 28:20A

A similar crystal was presented to Wilma. On it were inscribed these words:

THE ZONDERVAN CORPORATION

50 YEARS

IN MEMORIAM

BERNARD ZONDERVAN, SR.

1981

". . . A RIGHTEOUS MAN WILL BE

REMEMBERED FOREVER."

PS. 112:6B

Pat's career in publishing spanned the administrations of eleven U.S. presidents. The company that began on a farm and had sales of $1,800 one month in 1931 had grown to become a multifaceted corporation that did $54,500,000 worth of business in 1980. Yet the vision and dedication that led Pat and his brother Bernie to start Zondervan Publishing House in the depths of the Depression never waned. Every book, Bible, record, and song had been produced with the desire to bring glory to God and to spread the message of the gospel.

The Zondervan Corporation remained committed to these goals as it marked its fiftieth anniversary.

■　■　■

Zondervan was propelled into the decade of the eighties with a momentum that contrasts with the calm and disciplined demeanor of the company's offices and production centers. The seventies saw books finding new markets and coming off the press in unprecedented numbers. The music divisions used electronic and printed media in exciting combinations to serve church choirs in new ways. The path to ministry began to lead up driveways and sidewalks in selling *The Book of Life*. And the Bible went forth in a wide array of versions and styles to suit every taste and meet every spiritual need.

Part of the story Zondervan wrote in the eighties was an extension of ministries already begun. Another part, however, was completely new.

One of the new enterprises at that time was the New Benson Company. In August 1980 Zondervan acquired the John T. Benson Publishing Company of Nashville, Tennessee, a leading producer and distributor of religious recordings, tapes, and printed music, and a holder of many music copyrights. At the same time, Zondervan reached an agreement with Paragon Associates, Inc., also of Nashville, and out of these two companies formed the New Benson Company, of which Zondervan owned 51 percent. Robert Mackenzie, an executive of Benson, became president of the new company.

The merger put fourteen individual recording labels under the Benson publication rights with eighty recording artists. Included among the gospel singers whose works New Benson was recording were Pat and Debbie Boone, on the Lamb & Lion label; Dallas Holm, Greentree; Doug Oldham, Impact; James Ward; the Rambos; and Andrus-Blackwood. New Benson also took over distribution of the Singspiration artist albums featuring vocalists such as Christine Wyrtzen.

New Benson had unique production and distribution capabilities that would greatly enlarge Zondervan's share of the Christian music market that by that time had grown to become a $100 million industry. The facilities in Nashville included more than 3,000 square feet of studios, 21,400 square feet of modern offices, and 27,000 square feet of warehouse. The company's impact was felt quickly in that New Benson did $4.8 million in sales in its first four months.

The acquisition of the Benson Company also added the line of Impact Books to Zondervan's book publishing, a line that included titles by such well-known authors as Elton Trueblood and Ann Kiemel.

Some of the "extensions" of established Zondervan ministries in the eighties involved the New International Version of the Bible. In 1981 came *The NIV Pictorial Bible*, a 1,256-page edition with special-feature sections and more than 500 four-color illustrations. This was a remarkable achievement for those pre-computer days in that Zondervan obtained the color and design plates from a British publisher, but inserted the NIV in place of the version used in Great Britain—and made it fit into the space allowed. Not like an ordinary book, where you could ask the author to cut a little bit here or add a little bit there.

In 1983, Zondervan published the *NIV Thompson Chain Reference Bible*, which combined a time-honored format with the contemporary version that was on its way to becoming North America's most popular English translation.

The phenomenally successful youth edition, *The Student Bible*, was prepared under the guidance of bestselling author Philip Yancey, then executive editor of Campus Life Books, in early 1982. There is an interesting story behind it. Bruce Ryskamp, who was at that time the head of the Bible division, tells it this way: "The *Insight New Testament* was *The Student Bible's* forerunner, and we sold 30,000 copies and got 31,000 unsold copies back from stores and still decided to do the whole Bible. In fact, it was my total ignorance of Bible publishing that allowed Philip to convince me to say yes to doing the whole Bible after the dismal failure of the New Testament." It turned out to be a wise decision.

Several of Zondervan's significant reference works in the eighties were biblical language books that were also by-products of the New International Version. These included the four-volume *NIV Interlinear Hebrew-English Old Testament*, edited by John R. Kohlenberger III; the four-volume *Reader's Hebrew-English Lexicon of the Old Testament* by Terry A. Armstrong, Douglas L. Busby, and Cyril F. Carr; and the rather esoteric *NIV Triglot Old Testament*, which put the NIV side by side with the Hebrew text and the Septuagint Greek text.

■   ■   ■

Because of the close relationship between the New International Version and so many of the company's books, Zondervan merged the Book Division and the Bible Division in January 1980. Robert K. DeVries was then executive vice president of the combined division; Paul M. Hillman, formerly managing editor of textbooks, became director of publications. Stanley N. Gundry, formerly a professor at Moody Bible Institute, oversaw the NIV-related products as part of his duties as the managing editor of academic books. David Hill managed the Bible Department.

Not all significant Zondervan titles in the eighties were connected with the New International Version of the Bible — not by a long shot. Among successful titles released in the early eighties were the groundbreaking *Fearfully and Wonderfully Made* by Dr. Paul Brand and Philip Yancey, which was still selling 12,000 copies a month even eight months after its release; *Love Life for Every Married Couple* by Ed Wheat; *Lonely, But Never Alone* by Nicky Cruz with Madelene Harris; *Heirs Together: Mutual Submission in Marriage* by Patricia Gundry; *The Hurting Parent* by Margie Lewis with her son, Gregg Lewis; and *Encounter With Terminal Illness* by oncologist Ruth Lewshenia Kopp with Stephen Sorenson.

In 1981 Zondervan also published the first two volumes of *The Bible Student's Commentary*. These volumes on Genesis are the first to be translated from a highly acclaimed Dutch commentary called *Korte Verklaring*, "the Short Commentary." Short is a relative term, since each volume runs to more than three hundred pages.

Along with changes in the editorial department, two executives were hired for marketing and promotion, paving the way for some creative new efforts that affect all divisions of the corporation. Philip Wolf, who served Hewlett-Packard for nineteen years in sales and marketing, became director of corporate market planning in late 1979. At about the same time Robert Schwalb was named director of advertising and sales promotion; Schwalb was formerly president of the Boblin Agency on Long Island.

Zondervan's most ambitious marketing effort was the launching of a campaign to open new general-trade markets in the fall of 1980. The book that spearheaded the drive was a novel, *Esther: The Star and the Sceptre*, by a Zondervan author well-known for nonfiction, Gini Andrews. Six other titles were part of the campaign, which focused largely on New York City: *Encounter With Terminal Illness; David: Shepherd and King* by Charles Gulston; *The Art of Getting Along With People* by the bestselling writer Cecil G. Osborne; *A Step Further* by Joni Eareckson and Steve Estes; *Uganda Holocaust*, a journalistic account of the terrorist regime of dictator Idi Amin and its aftermath, by Dan Wooding and Ray Barnett; and *Armageddon, Oil and the Middle East Crisis* by John F. and John E. Walvoord—a book that was oddly prophetic in light of the two Persian Gulf wars that came later.

The reasoning behind the campaign struck a keynote for Zondervan's hopes for the decade. The announcement of the campaign by Zondervan President Peter Kladder Jr. (which today might be seen as prophetic), was reported this way by *Publishers Weekly*:

> Kladder explains that since *Esther* is a novel with wide appeal to Jewish readers as well as Christians and others, the book was chosen as "the point

of a wedge of seven Zondervan books intended to open an ongoing channel into the general book market." ... Zondervan's reason for entering the secular bookstore market is that it's "where large numbers of people who seek helping books like ours do their buying," notes Kladder. "I'm convinced that a significant share of our potential market never enters a Christian bookstore.

"We believe that the 1980s will be turbulent and stressful times for businesses as well as for individuals," Kladder notes. "The firm must change in some ways if we are to survive, let alone grow, during the turbulent times that are already upon us." He stressed, however, that efforts in secular bookstores are "in addition" to Zondervan's traditional commitment to the Christian bookstores market.[17]

In the annual report to shareholders, Kladder reported that "although the effort did not reap as great a sales success as hoped for, it did establish criteria to open new markets. And there was strong evidence of a correlation between promotional efforts and sales."

The challenge to confront change and to grow in meeting the challenge was a common theme sounded by Kladder and the Zondervan Corporation. In a guest editorial in *The Bookstore Journal*, the publication of the Christian Booksellers Association, Kladder wrote:

> Without the challenge of change, we have a tendency to be easygoing, to live by tradition rather than by results. There will be very little the same in our industry in 1990 that was present in 1980.... The eighties are certain to be a period of high technological impact and true innovation, and one of the major impacts is going to be in communications.[18]

As the company entered its sixth decade, there was a pervasive spirit of optimism that the path that led from *Women of the Old Testament* to *The Late Great Planet Earth*, from a $4.95 Bible commentary reprint to the New International Version, from *Favorites No. 1* to the New Benson Company, would lead to new achievements and new ministries in that fast-changing world.

Within just a couple of years, however, that optimism would fade as Zondervan entered the darkest period in its history. A writer in *Publishers Weekly* would later call it Zondervan's "decade of travail."[19]

14

Comeback

Zondervan grew rapidly in the early eighties. In 1982 it became publisher of Chosen Books, an inspirational imprint based in Lincoln, Virginia, and purchased the Tapley-Rutter Company, a Bible and specialty book bindery in Moonatchie, New Jersey. Those events were followed in 1983 with the acquisition of the Fleming H. Revell Co. of Old Tappan, New Jersey; the acquisition of Marshall Pickering, a publishing company in the United Kingdom; and the completion of the purchase of the Benson Company, the music and recording company in which Zondervan had first gained an interest in 1980.

In the book division, the evolution toward separate editorial departments came to fruition in 1981 with the establishment of General Trade Books under the direction of Cheryl Forbes and Academic and Professional Books guided by Stan Gundry. That year also marked a step forward in the application of computer technology to biblical scholarship with the release of the *NIV Complete Concordance*, edited by Edward W. Goodrick and John R. Kohlenberger III—a harbinger of electronic wonders to come. After a year of planning was put into the project, it was turned over to a computer, which made 4 quadrillion (1 million times 4 billion) decisions in 240 hours—a task that would have taken many thousands of hours for individual humans to accomplish. The concordance was patterned after the two-hundred-year-old *Cruden's Complete Concordance* — a work that required many years of labor and caused such mental anguish that Alexander Cruden was confined three times in an asylum.

"Celebrity" books of the stature and "crossover" appeal to secular markets of *Man in Black,* the autobiography of Johnny Cash published in 1976, were largely absent from the Zondervan list in the early eighties. Yet the publishing house remained a major communications company that reached a wide spectrum within the evangelical community.

A leading trade book for 1983 was *Loving God* by former White House aide Charles W. Colson, which received the Gold Medallion Award from the Evangelical Christian Publishers Association. (Colson received another Gold Medallion in 1987 for *Kingdoms in Conflict.*) Another Gold Medallion winner in the growing Christian fiction category was *MacIntosh Mountain* by Victor J. Kelly (1984). Academic books receiving Gold Medallions through 1985 included *Eternal Word and Changing Worlds* by Harvie Conn, *General Revelation* by Bruce Demarest, volume 12 of the *Expositor's Bible Commentary* (encompassing Hebrews through Revelation), and *From Jerusalem to Irian Jaya* by Ruth A. Tucker (which served as a reminder to the publishing house that not every book needs a catchy title to find its readers). Tucker subsequently added several outstanding books to Zondervan's list, including another Gold Medallion winner in *First Ladies of the Parish.*

The Bible department continued to grow; its crowning achievement being the publication in 1985 of *The NIV Study Bible.* This work, long in the making by several members of the original NIV translation committee, had been dealt a temporary setback when Edwin H. Palmer, its general editor, died of a heart attack in September 1980. But his position was ably filled by Kenneth L. Barker, professor of Old Testament at Dallas Theological Seminary. This study Bible became a bestseller and eventually had 2 million copies in print. A revised edition was published in 2002.

Among Benson's achievements was the bestselling Easter musical, *The Day He Wore My Crown,* released in 1981. Recording artist Sandi Patti was Christian music's top-selling vocalist; her career crowned in 1985 with the gold album *More Than Wonderful* on Benson's Impact label. In 1982 Benson released the Master-Trax accompaniment music track series, an innovation in the gospel music industry. (Benson improved on that in 1987 by introducing Hi-Lo Trax accompaniment featuring a high key and a low key on one tape.)

▪ ▪ ▪

In the meantime, the growing corporation looked toward the future with a carefully planned transition of leadership. Pat Zondervan retired as chairman of the board, Peter Kladder moved from president to chairman, and James G. Buick was brought in as the new president and chief executive officer.

Buick had most recently been division president and corporate vice president and controller with Brunswick Corporation, a bowling and marine company, and had been responsible for turning around the Recreation Center Division (250 bowling centers around the world). He also had evangelical credentials that fit with Zondervan's identity: a graduate of Greenville College in Illinois and a member of the board of trustees of Spring Arbor College in Michigan, both institutions supported by the Free Methodist Church. The combination of a good strong corporate background and an unflagging Christian faith would serve him well in the difficult times that lay ahead.

Buick took the reins amid feelings of optimism and confidence for the future.

Then the bubble burst. Buick quickly discerned that things were not all as they appeared. After seeking advice inside and outside the company, he contacted the Securities and Exchange Commission because Zondervan was then still a publicly held corporation. In December 1984 the SEC began an investigation, in which it determined that investors had been misled about Zondervan's financial condition and discrepancies had been hidden from the company's independent auditing firm. The SEC said that annual and quarterly financial reports had overstated the "work-in-progress" inventory and understated the accounts payable. By the time the investigation was completed in mid-1985, Zondervan had taken "writedowns" of $13 million. There were also various personnel changes at upper executive levels in several divisions of the corporation in addition to the retirement of Peter Kladder.[20]

The company's weakened financial condition led to a series of takeover attempts during 1986 and 1987. The stock fluctuated during this time from a low of $7.00 a share to a high above $30.00. Most noteworthy was an attempted takeover by Christopher J. Moran, a British financier, whose overtures spread alarm among the employees, most of whom were participating in an employee stock purchasing program and most of whom, as evangelical Christians, empathized heartily with Zondervan's publishing mission. To the employees, nothing typified the threat to Zondervan's evangelical mission more than Moran's suggestion that the retail division, Family Bookstores, should start opening its doors on Sunday.

The tension mounted as the holdings of Moran and his associates grew to about 43 percent of the Zondervan stock. Special prayer meetings were held in addition to the customary weekly chapel services.

Then righteousness prevailed. Moran suddenly dumped his stock in May 1987. Other speculators bailed out, the stock plummeted, and the crisis temporarily eased. (The SEC later accused Moran of acting on insider trading information.)[21]

Zondervan remained up for sale, however, and many changes were still occurring in the corporation's leadership and organization in an effort to cope with the uncertainties looming in the future. For example, the company shut down its printing plant and bindery in 1987, laying off more than forty people.

Making a Better Workplace

One result of Jim Buick's strong corporation background was the upgrading of the Human Resources (personnel) Department, which had been instituted at Zondervan in the late seventies. HRD came to play an increasingly active role in everyday life for Zondervan employees. These are some of the developments from 1985 to 1993:

- Each position was assigned a job description, a job level, and a pay range, based on careful studies, with pay ranges revised periodically for inflation
- Fringe benefits were improved (and enhanced still further under HarperCollins)
- In-house training and educational programs of many kinds were begun, fondly referred to as "BBU"—Brown Bag University
- Blood drives, which had been discontinued in the early eighties, were resumed

(The two foremen involved promptly formed their own printery, bought much of Zondervan's equipment, and hired a number of the laid-off employees.) At the end of the year, Zondervan Corporation became three divisions—Bibles, books, and electronics—under the umbrella title of Zondervan Publishing House, directed by Vice President Bruce Ryskamp.

The trade department experienced some instability, changing publishers twice in less than three years—Cheryl Forbes being followed by Joseph Allison and then Stan Gundry. For several years Gundry served as publisher of both the academic and trade book departments. The only celebrity book to grace the list during the mid-eighties was *DeLorean*, the autobiography of automobile executive John Z. DeLorean, in 1985.

The Bible department (*The NIV Student Bible*) and academic books, with a strong backlist, remained solid. Established authors, both trade and academic, such as Joni Eareckson (now Tada), Philip Yancey, and Larry Crabb, continued to bring new books to the list. In 1987 Zondervan started an electronic publishing division (later named New Media) and became the first

Buick instituted monthly employee informational meetings featuring financial reports, departmental presentations, and question-and-answer sessions. He also introduced "CVR," an opinion and evaluation survey commissioned with an outside firm, Corporate Values Research, which enabled employees to voice their concerns all the way up to the operating committee.

Zondervan also increased its community involvement by sponsoring events such as an Elder Care Fair and a Day Care Fair for both employees and the public.

In 1991 the Women's Resource Center of Grand Rapids honored Zondervan with its Women in the Workplace Award. This award recognized progress on issues such as sexual harassment policies, day-care services, progressive benefit packages, and training programs. Especially cited was the promotion of Anne L. Sherman to vice president and chief financial officer, the first woman to serve on the company's operating committee.

Christian publisher to sell its intellectual property in a software format. The next year the company produced its first "audio pages," books read on cassette tape. It also inaugurated National Religious Books Week, now sponsored by the ECPA. And Benson released *Carman Live . . . Radically Saved!*—that popular artist's first Gold Record.

■ ■ ■

The crisis finally passed when the Zondervan Corporation was acquired in September 1988 by the venerable old publishing company, Harper & Row. The purchase price was $56.7 million, or $13.50 per share. Zondervan was once again a privately owned company.

Harper was founded in New York City in 1817 by four Harper brothers, the oldest of whom, James, later served as the mayor of the city for a year. The firm has an illustrious history. In the nineteenth century Harper & Brothers was publisher for many of Great Britain's greatest novelists and thinkers, such as Sir Walter Scott, Charles Dickens, William Makepeace Thackeray, Wilkie Collins, Thomas Carlyle, Disraeli, and John Stuart Mill. Harper was a pioneer in producing sets of books with uniform bindings and uniform prices in 1843—a commonplace today, but not then. In the late 1800s, long before paperback publishing became common during the Great Depression, Harper issued the Library of Select Novels in paperbacks at twenty-five cents apiece.[22]

The company's author list still reads like a who's who in literature and contemporary thought. Harper also became a leading publisher of textbooks for elementary and secondary schools and colleges. Its diversified publishing program and its history of innovation and stability held promise of a successful marriage with Zondervan's own multifaceted enterprise.

Harper & Row had a religious publishing division in San Francisco, one with a much broader range of titles than Zondervan's carefully tended evangelical Christian list. When Harper purchased Zondervan, both sides tacitly understood that the marriage would be blissful only if two conditions prevailed: Zondervan's book editorial departments would remain free and independent to exercise their evangelical philosophy, and Zondervan's operations would not be moved from Grand Rapids to San Francisco.

And those conditions did prevail. Moreover, both firms reaped immediate benefits. On one side, Harper gained access to a market it did not have, namely, the thousands of stores comprising the Christian Booksellers Association. In exchange, Zondervan achieved financial stability and the opportunity to reassert its place of leadership in publishing, music, and communications in the evangelical community.

Zondervan adopted a mission statement that reflected its dual identity:

We are a communications company seeking to glorify God and serve Jesus Christ—

- Through excellence in the publication and distribution of the Bible and Scripture-based products.
- Through responsible stewardship for the company's owners.

Not Doing Things by the Book

Telephone rings and computer clicks and beeps are common sounds at Zondervan. But not wedding bells. Therein lies a story, best told through excerpts from a mock news release written by one of the editors to commemorate the event, which took place on March 5, 1990, in the Kentwood plant.

> The Zondervan Corporation, which has published many books on love and marriage, didn't go by the book last Friday. An editorial office became a chapel and the lunch hour a reception for the wedding of Gina Shepard, an editorial assistant, and Richard Doorn, a production supervisor at nearby Steelcase, an office furniture manufacturer.
>
> The ceremony, using the traditional form of matrimony of the United Methodist Church, was performed by an editor, the Rev. Robert D. Wood, as seven colleagues in the academic and professional books division looked on....
>
> Most of the several hundred other Zondervan employees were unaware of the event until after the ceremony.... The recessional to the department's coffee area was accompanied by a taped rendering of the traditional wedding march from *Lohengrin* and followed by the popping of corks from bottles of sparkling grape juice and the cutting of a cake decorated with the message "Congratulations, Rich and Gina."

Reversing the tide of expansion, Harper soon sold off the Book of Life and the Tapley-Rutter Company. Revell and Chosen Books had already been sold in 1986.

More change was coming. Rupert Murdoch, who presided over a worldwide communications empire that included book publishing, newspapers, and television holdings, had earlier purchased Harper and then bought William Collins, a publisher in the United Kingdom that had a literary heritage much like Harper's. The new enterprise was called HarperCollins, of which Zondervan became a part. The familiar "Z" logo that had represented Zondervan since the mid-seventies gave way to a new red-and-blue international logo combining the fire of Harper & Row's venerated torch symbol with water from Collins' logo.

There is perhaps a cultural irony in this. In North America, as throughout the rest of Western culture, a secularizing tide was increasingly pushing organized religion out of public life and expression. Yet now, through HarperCollins, Zondervan had access to secular media, such as bestseller lists and network television, that were largely closed to it in the past (see the story of *The Late Great Planet Earth* in the chapter "The Late Great Seventies"). And three Zondervan titles were featured on the front cover of *Publishers Weekly* on October 5, 1990.

■   ■   ■

The publishing and music milestones of 1989 signaled Zondervan's new lease on life. Twenty-six Zondervan titles were among the hundred top-selling Christian reference works that year. Nine books and seven Bible editions were on Christian bestselling lists simultaneously. The New International Version achieved number one for the first time on the *Bookstore Journal*'s Bible bestseller list, a spot it has not relinquished to this time. Zondervan introduced the *NIVpc*, Bible study software linking the Greek New Testament and the NIV Bible for IBM-compatible computers. In music, Sandi Patti received a Platinum Record, symbolizing one million copies sold, for her album *Hymns Just for You*. Benson artist Larnelle Harris won his fifth Grammy Award.

The successes of 1989 continued into 1990. Bookstore dealers chose Zondervan as "Supplier of the Year" for outstanding service in order fulfillment. Sales representatives began using state-of-the-art laptop computers. Among the outstanding publications and releases were *The NIV Exhaustive*

Concordance, another electronic achievement produced by Goodrick and Kohlenberger; *The New Revised Standard Version; macBible* and *ScriptureFonts* for on-screen Bible study; and *Revival in the Land*, a music video by Carman that became an instant Gold title on the day it was released.

Zondervan also added to its collection of Gold Medallion book awards, Dove music awards, and other honors too numerous to list. Moreover, Zondervan placed five titles on the list of the bestselling books in Christian publishing in the 1980s.

With war clouds gathering over the Persian Gulf, Zondervan prepared a new edition of John F. Walvoord's book *Armageddon, Oil and the Middle East*, which had first been published in the mid-seventies. The book was released in January 1991—just in time for Operation Desert Storm, the United Nations-supported assault on Iraq in retaliation for its invasion of Kuwait a few months earlier. *Armageddon* soon had 1.5 million copies in print. The Gulf War was over in a matter of weeks, and interest in the book waned soon thereafter, but not before it reached sixth place on the *New York Times* trade paperback list.

Two books released in 1990, however, illustrate the impact of HarperCollins's ownership and the new, greater role copublishing would play at Zondervan.

Tom Landry is the autobiography (written with Gregg Lewis) of the long-time coach of the Dallas Cowboys in the National Football League. His Christian testimony gave him credibility in the CBA stores, and America's passion for football ensured the book's popularity in the ABA (American Booksellers Association) market. *Tom Landry* spent a number of weeks on major bestseller lists and on one day, September 19, 1990, was positioned as follows:

#3 New York Times

#5 Publishers Weekly

#8 Washington Post

#10 Baker and Taylor, Ingram, and Waldenbooks

#19 B. Dalton

That success was soon followed with the publication of *Comeback* by Dave Dravecky with Tim Stafford. Dravecky, like Landry a Christian in professional sports, was an ace lefthander for the San Francisco Giants of the National League when his career was cut short by cancer in his pitching arm. After surgery and rehabilitation, Dravecky made a remarkable comeback that inspired sports fans across the nation. But the comeback was short-lived, for he broke that arm while pitching in his second game. Eventually the arm was amputated to stop the spread of the cancer. As with Landry's book, *Comeback* achieved high ratings on bestseller lists and was awarded a Gold Medallion. In 1992 Zondervan and Harper copublished a sequel, *When You Can't Come Back*, and released a feature-length film on the Dave Dravecky story.

Tom Landry and *Comeback* would be difficult for any publisher to exceed. But for sheer drama, notoriety, and *chutzpah*, nothing could match *Under Fire: An American Story*, the memoirs story of retired Marine Lt. Col. Oliver North, which Zondervan copublished with HarperCollins New York in October 1991.

■   ■   ■

No personality aroused more controversy during the eighties than "Ollie," who had served on the staff of the National Security Council during the presidency of Ronald Reagan. In that role he became the central figure in what was known as the Iran-Contra affair. The Reagan administration was accused of covertly selling arms to the anti-American government in Iran (allegedly in an attempt to gain the release of Americans held hostage in the Middle East by Islamic terrorist groups) and then illegally diverting the funds to help the Contras, a rebel army in Nicaragua.

The affair unfolded as a classic confrontation between political liberals and conservatives overlaid with the conflicting emotions that always surfaced where the "Religious Right" was concerned. These emotions were heightened by North's testimony telecast live before congressional interrogators and by his running feud with the special prosecutor in the case, Lawrence Walsh. In 1989 North was convicted on three of sixteen felony charges, but they were overturned later that year. Nevertheless, it was the threat of having Walsh bring additional charges that led to the unusual way the book came into being. *Under Fire* was itself a covert operation from start to finish — a cloak-and-dagger story of the highest order.

The project was carried out in secret, with only a handful of people having knowledge of it at either publishing house.[23] It began in early 1989 when Jim Buick was called to Washington, D.C., to meet with North, HarperCollins CEO George Craig, a few lawyers, and some other people. North and his representatives were approaching HarperCollins because, since it was expected that all parties would have to keep this project secret for a while, they did not feel they had the option of auctioning the book on the open market. And HarperCollins was their first choice in part because North wanted access to the evangelical market through Zondervan.

After that meeting, several more Zondervan people were brought into the loop, including Bruce Ryskamp and Stan Gundry and, later on, Scott Bolinder, Zondervan's new trade publisher. (Scott, by the way, was none other than the son of Robert G. "Bob" Bolinder, who had worked at Zondervan from 1969 to 1977 as sales manager and, later, senior vice president.) Talks continued behind closed doors, and a full year passed before the deal was sealed at the end of a full day of discussion and negotiations on January 5, 1990. And this came only after Zondervan had the assurance that the book would fit its mission. As Gundry describes it in his personal journal, "None of us [including HarperCollins] wanted a book that would essentially be a whitewash. We were hoping that he would be at least reasonably candid and that there would be a real story here. From the Zondervan side, I was also looking for those elements that would determine whether or not the book would be appropriate for the CBA. I was empowered by Bruce and Jim to give either a go or a no-go answer on behalf of Zondervan should matters proceed to that point."

The project probably set a record for the number of nondisclosure statements accumulated. The man and the book were never openly discussed, but only alluded to, and then only when absolutely necessary, in veiled references to "Mr. Smith" (North) and "Mr. Smith Goes to Washington" (the book).

The book was written with William Novak, the biographer of several distinguished people, including auto executive Lee Iacocca, First Lady Nancy Reagan, Speaker of the House Tip O'Neill, and Sydney Biddle Barrows, the "Mayflower Madam." Buick, Ryskamp, Gundry, and Bolinder were able to see the manuscript and proofs at every crucial stage, including the final set of proofs.

It seems almost incredible that although the operation spanned two-and-a-half years from the date of the first negotiations to the book's publication and release, it remained secret until the very end. Gundry wrote,

> There had been rumors circulating earlier that appeared one place or another in the media, but no one really picked up on the story or blew the cover. It was

only at the last minute that this story really broke into print.... Early in the week of October 14, reporters from the *New York Times* began smelling out the story somehow and began poking their noses around HarperCollins, New York. So contingency plans were made to break the story earlier if necessary. The story did in fact appear in the October 16 issue of the *New York Times*, and that turned out to be the day of announcement and press releases — in other words, one day earlier than had been originally anticipated.

The media had a field day with both the contents of the book and the undercover way in which it was created.[24] But not everyone was happy with the sensational release. Books from the first printing of 450,000 copies were already being shipped without warning to both secular and religious bookstores, in quantities determined by the publishers. HarperCollins supposedly based its shipments to some bookstore chains on the number of copies ordered for *When You Look Like Your Passport Photo, It's Time to Go Home* by humorist Erma Bombeck.[25] Christian booksellers, accustomed to exercising their faith "decently and in order," were even less prepared than their secular counterparts to handle the surprise.

Some of the employees of the publishing houses were not happy either. Some editors were concerned that, while North's memoirs were newsworthy and it was right that his story be told, they wished Zondervan had not been involved. Because North was the darling of the Religious Right, the editors feared the book would only fuel public perceptions that evangelical publishers like Zondervan were captive to political conservatives and fundamentalist activists. The publishers defended the project.

"Mr. North," said Stan Gundry, "did want his own spiritual journey through the years to be a natural and integral part of the book. He has many admirers within the Christian community. He felt it was a natural partnership." Scott Bolinder stated, "Oliver North is a colorful and controversial person. More than that, though, we have come to know him as a deeply committed Christian."[26]

Under Fire reached #1 on the *New York Times* nonfiction bestseller list, #3 in *Publishers Weekly*, and #4 in the *Los Angeles Times*.

In the end, the book probably changed few minds about either North or the Iran-Contra affair. How one felt about the book depended mainly on how one felt about Lt. Col. Oliver North to begin with.

There have been undercover operations in book publishing before *Under Fire*, but the way the book got into print, with all its controversial dimensions, is surely one of the most remarkable events in the long and storied history of book publishing.

Under Fire was also a spectacular way for Zondervan to close out its sixth decade. It had had to overcome many obstacles during the eighties and survive a crisis that threatened its very existence, but it emerged stronger than ever and eager to make an ever-increasing impact on the church and society. It was building for the future—literally. Just over the horizon was a new headquarters that would bring all of Zondervan's Grand Rapids operations under one roof for the first time in more than forty years.

15

> *I suggest that the only books that influenced us are those*
> *for which we are ready, and which have gone a little farther down*
> *our particular path than we have yet gone ourselves.*
> E. M. FORSTER
>
> *When you reread a classic you do not see more in the book than you did before;*
> *you see more in you than was there before.*
> CLIFTON FADIMAN

A Purpose Driven® Company

It was with a great sense of anticipation that Zondervan employees began moving into the new company headquarters in Cascade Township in January 1992. The two-story, $13 million building that faces the intersection of Patterson Avenue SE and 52nd Street caddy-corner is impressive both inside and outside. It is framed by 16,000 square feet of reflective insulated glass. At the time it was built, its 350,000 square feet were meted out in three connected rectangular "pods"—one for offices, cafeteria, and conference rooms, the other two for the distribution center.

Beyond the reception desk at the main entrance is a lobby two stories high topped by skylights, its centerpiece a life-sized bronze sculpture of Jesus washing the disciple Peter's feet. The half-ton art piece, titled "Divine Servant," was created by Max Greiner Jr., owner of the Greiner Art Galley in Kerrville, Texas. It was commissioned by then-President and CEO Jim Buick "to remind us all of Zondervan's overriding mission to follow Christ's example of serving others."

The open feel continues past the lobby into a large, two-story atrium that serves as dining room and auditorium, with two walls consisting mainly of windows and with a winding staircase coming down near the center. The office areas of the building have high ceilings and modular partition walls. (If there is one flaw in the building, it is having the staircase projecting into the middle of the atrium—the only "auditorium"—which is awkward for speakers and inhibits a sense of solidarity.)

The headquarters, an anchor for Meadowbrooke Business Park, replaced Zondervan's three buildings that totaled 500,000 square feet—much more than Zondervan needed at that time. Just as important, the three buildings had been miles apart from each other. So as people came together under one roof for the first time since 1954, the whole company anticipated a new sense of community and integration. Some benefits were immediately obvious: for the first time, Zondervan had a cafeteria. Yet probably few employees realized how much the work culture would change. It was not just a matter of being

A Taxing Decision

When Zondervan was looking at potential building sites in 1990, it caused a stir in the local press by pushing for tax breaks from the municipalities involved. At one point Buick said the company would move to Indiana if no breaks were offered. That prompted an editorial cartoon in the *Grand Rapids Business Journal* in June showing two babies (Cascade Township and Grand Rapids) crying with empty popsicle sticks in hand because the double popsicle (resembling a business building) was lying on the ground and melting into a pool called Indiana. The cartoon was titled "Ground Zero," with the Z fashioned to look like the first letter in Zondervan's company logo. That same month, John Douglas, an iconoclastic columnist for the *Grand Rapids Press*, wrote a critical piece, headlined "Bible Tells Zondervan to Pay Taxes," in which he took the company to task for snubbing Jesus' statements about taxes in the gospel of Matthew. Eventually Zondervan did receive a twelve-year tax break from Cascade Township and thus decided to build there.

together in one building. The events of the next two and a half years also had a great impact.

Unfortunately, the euphoria of the move vanished temporarily when a down-sizing, or "restructuring," was announced in late February—even before the building was fully occupied. Fifty-seven positions (about 3 percent of the workforce) were eliminated; forty-eight people lost their jobs, while other spots remained unfilled. But the even more dramatic structural changes on the horizon would ultimately benefit the work culture.

■　■　■

Not long after the downsizing, President Buick made an unsuccessful effort to negotiate a buyout from HarperCollins. Then the music part of the business took the spotlight. The Christian music industry was growing and changing rapidly. Increasing consolidation was giving the message that you had to become a bigger player or get out of the business. First, try bigger. In September 1992, Zondervan lost out to publishing archrival Thomas Nelson in a bid to purchase Word, the book and music publisher, from Capital Cities/ ABC Inc. Second, get out. In November, Zondervan, which had been in the music business since World War II, did just that. It sold Nashville-based Benson Music Group, which at that time was one of the largest Christian music companies.

That meant Zondervan now had two divisions: book publishing and the retail stores. In September 1993 it was announced that those divisions would become two distinct business units, Zondervan Publishing House and Family Bookstores, each reporting directly to HarperCollins Publishers. Buick would retire at the end of the year, and the divisions' vice presidents, Bruce Ryskamp and Les Dietzman, would become president and CEO of their respective companies. As Buick put it to the employees, in selling Benson and paving the way for a logical restructuring, "I worked myself out of job." About twenty jobs were eliminated. A synergy remained between ZPH and FBS, which was Zondervan's biggest customer. For the first time since its founding, Zondervan was out of the retail business.

Another effect of the restructuring was the merger of Zondervan's two book departments, trade and academic, formed in the early 1980s, into one department. Scott Bolinder, who came to Zondervan in 1989 to head up the trade department, now became vice president, just as his father, Bob Bolinder had been more than a decade earlier, and publisher. Stan Gundry, who had been the general manager of book publishing, remained vice president and became editor-in-chief. The staff structure changed also, with some editors designated for acquisitions (under Scott's supervision) and others (under Stan's supervision) designated for "development"—managing books through the process from line editing to press.

But that was only one change. Ryskamp's elevation to CEO set in motion a positive sea change in the working culture at Zondervan. The tone was set by Bruce himself. First, he fostered a team approach to problem solving. The newly formed Leadership Team set the example, with the various department heads meeting on Tuesday mornings to make decisions collectively. Soon departmental and cross-departmental committees and task forces, including managers and regular employees, became common as a means to solve problems and bring innovation. Second, Bruce connected well with the employees. He treated everyone alike regardless of what kind of job they had or where they fell in the chain of command. (Early on, he held group breakfasts in the cafeteria with eight or ten employees at a time from different departments.) He established and led monthly employee meetings that did everything from reviewing the financial status (ahead or behind on budget and profits?) to introducing new employees and giving service awards to having various task forces or departments report on their progress and special achievements to reading letters received from people around the world that told how a Zondervan book or Bible or other product had changed their lives.

When the company was purchased by HarperCollins, Zondervan developed a "statement of purpose," reflecting its dual identity as a steward of the Christian faith and the Bible and a steward of financial and material resources for a parent company. That statement was replaced when the Leadership Team gathered in a retreat and, starting with a blank sheet, drafted a mission statement together with a list of commitments and a Scripture verse of assurance. Afterward, employee teams gave input and helped refine them. Later on, the Leadership Team also developed a set of "shared values." All this set the tone for Zondervan as a purpose-driven company.

The net result of Bruce's leadership and the company's being under one roof brought many developments. The human resources department blossomed, adding many new employee perks to the traditional weekly chapel service, semiannual blood drives, and annual summer picnic and Christmas

Our Mission

To be the leading Christian communications company meeting the needs of people with resources that glorify Jesus Christ and promote biblical principles.

Our Commitments

- Provide an environment that encourages employees to thrive.
- Build innovative and mutually beneficial relationships with authors, customers, suppliers, and each other.
- Listen to those who attend church to understand the evolving needs of people.
- Create excellent communication resources consistent with biblical principles in a timely and profitable manner.
- Develop all cost-effective distribution channels to expand global impact.
- Serve our local community and care for the environment.
- Operate our business with integrity and meet our financial objectives.

Our Assurance

"May the God who gives endurance and encouragement give you a spirit of unity among yourselves as you follow Christ Jesus, so that with one heart and mouth you may glorify the God and Father of our Lord Jesus Christ."

—ROMANS 15:5–6

party. Eventually there was a humor committee (offering unusual monthly events), a wellness committee (with a well-equipped fitness room off the atrium), and community projects (such as the United Way and the ACS Relay for Life). Zondervan adopted Bring Your Child to Work Day and held craft sales and BBUs (lunchtime Brown Bag Universities). Employee training programs abounded, in computer training, shared values, management skills, and other areas. The dress code changed also, with casual dress becoming the norm on Fridays.

Bruce Ryskamp also had a passion to raise the company's profile and level of participation in the greater Grand Rapids community. This began with greater support of the United Way, but much more followed. Each year, based on an employee survey, a committee would choose several area nonprofit organizations—both religious and nonreligious—to support financially. Employees were encouraged to spend one paid workday a year volunteering for a worthy cause. The company sponsored programs on the local public television station (such as the epic series *Baseball* by Ken Burns in 1994) and the summer outdoor Picnic Pops concerts of the Grand Rapids Symphony at the Cannonsburg Ski Resort.

And Zondervan extended charity beyond West Michigan. The company has teamed up with various organizations for such causes as promoting literacy, spreading God's Word, and fighting the AIDS epidemic in Africa. For example, in 1999 Zondervan and the International Bible Society arranged with World Vision to provide Bibles to needy families in developing countries. The goal of the Share the Light program was to give away up to a million Bibles in dozens of languages in twenty-two countries. For each Zondervan or Zonderkidz Bible sold at full price in the United States from October through December, World Vision would give out a free Bible.

Some programs aided social causes accompanied by promotional marketing. In 2003 Zondervan partnered with the Christian rock group the Newsboys to promote literacy. During their "THRIVE—It's All in the Word" world tour, the Newsboys gave onstage endorsement to the bestselling *NIV Student Bible*, gave away 43,000 samples of the book of Romans, and promoted an Internet Bible-reading plan. The eight-month tour covered forty cities in twenty-two states, Mexico, and Puerto Rico.

It was probably not surprising to most employees when Zondervan in 2003 was named one of the "forty best Christian places to work" in the whole United States in a polling created by the Best Christian Workplaces Institute and *Christianity Today*. A cover story in the April 2003 issue of the magazine rated the company second only to Group Publishing in Colorado in the large media category. The results were based largely on the results of surveys given to employees at the firms that participated. (Zondervan attained number one in the category in 2005.)

It seemed a little anticlimactic, but significant nonetheless, when, just a month later, the Michigan Business and Professional Association selected

Zondervan as one of West Michigan's fifty-one Best and Brightest Companies. The qualities on which the awards were based were diversity and multiculturalism, work-life balance, employee communications and recognition, compensation and benefits, employee education and development, recruitment and retention, employee motivation and enthusiasm, community initiatives, strategic planning and integration.

But we're getting ahead of our story. There was one more structural change to come after ZPH and FBS became separate companies. In November 1994, some executives of Family Bookstores, including Les Dietzman, along with George Craig, then president of HarperCollins, and Bruce Ryskamp bought Family Bookstores from its parent company. It became an independent firm, and it was a friendly separation. The headquarters of the retail chain, which changed its name to Family Christian Stores, did not move. They stayed in the building, continuing to share with Zondervan the common areas such as the atrium, cafeteria, restrooms, the fitness-locker rooms, and many conference rooms.

It would have been easy during those rigorous times to fail to notice the passing of two of the founding members of the publishing house. Pat Zondervan died on May 6, 1993, at age eighty-four at a retirement home in Boca Raton, Florida. He had suffered two strokes in preceding years. Pat was active in the company until 1984, when he retired as chairman of the board. Then, on Sunday, November 27, 1994, Wilma Zondervan Teggelaar, Bernie's widow, died while singing in a church service. She was eighty-two. At the time of their deaths, only one family member—Bernie and Wilma's grandson, Bernard "Bud" Zondervan—was working for the company. Bud worked at Zondervan for twenty-four years before leaving in 2000 to take a management position at HarperCollins's distribution facility in Scranton, Pennsylvania. As of this spring, Pat's wife, Mary, was still living in a retirement community in Boca Raton. (Bill Zondervan, who retired as head of the Zondervan bookstores in 1980, died in California on August 9, 2002, at age eighty-three.)

Meanwhile, realizing that there are more English-speaking people outside the United States than in it, Zondervan took a step in the early 1980s to become a truly global publisher. Relations between British and American publishers have always been plentiful and strong. But in 1983 Zondervan bought Marshall Pickering (a company itself formed from the merger of two

Shared Values

Initiative: **We are willing and empowered to proactively contribute to the success of the company, its customers, and other employees.**

> "Whatever your hand finds to do, do it with all your might."
> —Ecclesiastes 9:10

- Participating actively in fully empowered teams
- Going the extra mile to meet customer needs
- Taking responsibility for identifying, developing, and strengthening skills
- Exploring better ways to achieve our goals and those of the company

Accountability: **We are responsible for our own actions and answerable to others.**

> "Each one should test his own actions."
> —Galatians 6:4

- Taking responsibility to follow through on tasks and projects in a timely manner
- Communicating information and concerns in a clear and timely manner
- Sharing knowledge necessary for others to succeed and grow
- Being good stewards of time and resources

Excellence: **We give our personal best.**

> "In everything set them an example by doing what is good."
> —Titus 2:7

- Striving for quality in service and products
- Pursuing personal and professional growth
- Balancing work and personal time to ensure long-term success
- Thinking globally

Respect: **We have as much consideration for the personal and professional worth and dignity of others as we do for ourselves.**

> "Do to others as you would have them do to you."
> —Luke 6:31

- Building relationships on trust and reliability
- Communicating with kindness, openness, and honesty
- Expecting the best from one another
- Honoring one another's unique personal qualities and professional expertise

Integrity: **We maintain high ethical and moral standards in speech and in personal and professional conduct.**

> "Simply let your 'Yes' be 'Yes,' and your 'No,' 'No.'"
> —Matthew 5:37

- Respecting confidentiality
- Keeping commitments and admitting mistakes
- Dealing with issues and conflicts face to face with the appropriate people
- Upholding biblical ethics and honest business practices

Innovation: **We seek out new possibilities in every area and embrace groundbreaking change that adds value.**

> "See, I am doing a new thing!
> Now it springs up; do you not perceive it?
> I am making a way in the desert
> and streams in the wasteland."
> —Isaiah 43:19

- Inspiring individuals and collaborative teams to dynamically share imaginative, new ideas
- Cultivating a willingness to experiment, fail, evaluate, and try again
- Welcoming obstacles as opportunities for positive change
- Understanding that doing business in inventive ways requires intelligent risk-taking

companies Zondervan had long dealt with: Marshall, Morgan & Scott and Pickering and Inglis). The new relationship lasted until 1989, when Marshall Pickering was merged into HarperCollins UK.

Then, in 2001 Marshall Pickering was returned to Zondervan, not as a British partner, but as part of Zondervan itself. Not Zondervan UK, just Zondervan—a name not widely known among Christian retailers or consumers in Great Britain. Zondervan had generally worked through various distributors, especially Send the Light. In October 2000 Zondervan's leadership team began drafting a plan, and President Ryskamp presented it to HarperCollins just three months later. A public announcement was made in April 2001, and the operation officially began with the fiscal year beginning July 1. While Zondervan was a new name to many Britons, the company quickly made itself known. After Ryskamp and Bolinder hosted a dinner in England for about thirty key British authors in October 2002, they came to recognize and embrace Zondervan as a commercial publisher committed to core values.

Another move that enlarged Zondervan's global role was acquiring Editorial Vida from the Division of Foreign Missions of the Assemblies of God denomination in 1995. Vida, founded in 1946, was publishing in three languages: Portuguese (with operations in Sao Paulo, Brazil), French (Toulouse, France), and Spanish (Miami). When Zondervan purchased it, Vida had 900 titles in print and was working at completing the translation of the NIV into Spanish. That translation, the *Nueva Version Internacional* (NVI), was published in 1997. Zondervan sold Editions Vida France, the smallest of the three operations, in 2000. Editorial Vida has won numerous ECPA awards as a part of Zondervan. At the time of Zondervan's purchase, 30 percent of Vida's sales were in the United States; today that number is 70 percent.

"Vida" is a good name for a publisher because it means "life." People read books to enrich or improve their lives, whether they are looking for spiritual truth, studying to pass an exam, relaxing with a novel, grieving over the loss of a loved one, preparing a sermon, seeking counsel to fix a damaged relationship, or meditating with God. Books can be one means God uses to help us on days when life seems to be falling apart—or when the world itself seems out of control.

One such day was September 11, 2001, when terrorists hijacked planes and crashed them into the World Trade Center towers in Manhattan and the Pentagon in Washington, D.C., claiming more than 3000 lives and scarring America's psyche. The country and, indeed, the world changed that day and would never be quite the same—just as it felt when the Japanese attacked Pearl Harbor on December 7, 1941, and President John F. Kennedy was assassinated on November 22, 1963.

In the immediate turmoil and aftermath of 9/11, publishers expected to feel some pressure from authors to issue quick books. Zondervan right away resolved that it would not act hastily. But when Jim Cymbala—bestselling author of several books, including *Fresh Wind, Fresh Fire*—proposed a book, Zondervan gave it the go-ahead. After all, the Brooklyn Tabernacle, where Cymbala is pastor, is not that far from the World Trade Center; several members of its congregation had died in the disaster, and some others had been rescued from it.

The decision was made on September 18 with the hope of releasing the book within just two months. The timetable was extraordinary, requiring the best teamwork possible from the author and Zondervan's editorial, marketing, sales, and production departments. Cymbala, assisted by veteran writer Stephen Sorenson, delivered the manuscript on Wednesday, October 10. The editing was completed by the next Monday morning. The book went to the printer one week later, on October 18, as a 128-page softcover book entitled *God's Grace from Ground Zero*. The first copies arrived from the printer on November 15. The book sold more than 100,000 copies.

(This was Zondervan's first "instant" book—to use the publishing industry's term—since 1976, when it published *When Free Men Shall Stand* by United States Senator Jesse Helms.)

An additional project spurred by 9/11 was the quick release of a special edition of Philip Yancey's landmark 1976 book *Where Is God When It Hurts?* with a first printing of 700,000 copies. All of Zondervan's profits and Yancey's royalties were donated to the American Red Cross.

Zondervan's special products division, Inspirio, reissued a small gift book called *God Bless America*, which was written by Sue Johnson, a Zondervan employee, and was originally published several years earlier. More than 500,000 copies of the new edition were sold.

The spirit that drove these actions in the wake of 9/11 also led Zondervan to help U.S. troops in Iraq after the invasion of that country in spring 2003. Major Effson C. Bryant Jr., a senior Protestant chaplain serving at Prince Sultan Air Base in Saudi Arabia, contacted Zondervan, saying he would really like some software to complement the twelve Bible study groups he conducted each week. (Libraries at the larger military bases usually had computers.) He got his wish — and more. Zondervan donated copies of its new *Leader's Edition Bible Study Software*, not only to Major Bryant, but to more than one hundred other military chaplains stationed in the Persian Gulf region.

Two novels by Karen Kingsbury also emerged from 9/11: *One Tuesday Morning* and *Beyond Tuesday Morning*.

One wonders whether the emotional discomfort and the spiritual introspection that followed 9/11 were a significant factor in making a book published by Zondervan a year later a phenomenal bestseller. Perhaps. One thing is certain: it was not an instant book.

■   ■   ■

The *Grand Rapids Press* said it coyly in a feature article in September 2003: "Rick Warren needed seven years to write *The Purpose Driven Life*. It didn't take Zondervan that long to sell it."[27] It was in fact the fastest-selling book in the company's history and a phenomenon proclaimed by news media as being unequaled in the world's six centuries of book publishing.

The story begins in the early nineties when Bruce Ryskamp heard Rick speak at a conference on the future of the church. Rick was the pastor of Saddleback Valley Community Church in Southern California (at that time located in Mission Viejo but later next door in Lake Forest). After the conference, Bruce observed that so many pastors gravitated to Rick wherever he was that it was "like disciples sitting at Jesus' feet." Bruce suggested to Stan Gundry that he try to sign Rick to write a book for Zondervan, but Stan took his time, thinking that this was just another pastor who would write another lackluster book that would not sell. Yet Bruce kept coming back to Stan, and finally Stan began investigating who this guy Warren was and what he had to offer. Soon Stan led an acquisition team that attended one of the early Purpose Driven Church seminars for pastors and church leaders. At the seminar the team got all of forty-five seconds or so with Rick, but came away convinced he was a leader with great promise as an author. After several months of emails and phone calls, Rick agreed to a face-to-face meeting. The result is that both sides felt that they had a good alignment of values and that the chemistry was right. The rest, as they say, is history.

Zondervan published Warren's book *The Purpose Driven® Church* in 1995. Being a book directed toward a specific audience — pastors — it surprised everyone by selling more than 100,000 copies within a year (well above the hoped-for 35,000). Warren intended to follow that with a book for Christians in general — titled *The Purpose Driven® Life* — the next year. But the demands of the expanding ministry of Saddleback Church and Warren's national exposure put the book on a back burner.

One of the projects that occupied the innovative Warren was a website called *www.pastors.com*. In 2001 he launched a global electronic newsletter designed to mentor pastors, missionaries, and others in ministry. The very first issue of the free newsletter, called *Rick Warren's Ministry Toolbox*, began circulating among 50,000 pastors in one hundred countries. Through seminars at Saddleback, Warren had already connected with almost 200,000 pastors.

The stage was set. In early 2002 Warren was ready to write the book. The catch was that he had a different concept for it from what he and Zondervan had originally planned. Building on the platform provided through *pastors.com*, he had designed a six-week campaign, called "40 Days of Purpose," for church small groups. It was to begin in October, and he already had hundreds of churches signed up. He designed the book around it: forty short chapters developing five themes of purpose responding to the question raised in the subtitle, *What on Earth Am I Here For?*

Zondervan wondered, will it work? Will the book be so oriented to Warren's network that it won't appeal to Christians in the mainstream who are not within his reach? Can the manuscript be completed early enough for the book to get published on time? A lot was obviously at stake.

Warren did his part. Following the old injunction "You don't find time to write, you make time," Warren quarantined himself to write for the next few months in some place he called the "Bat Cave." Even so, the manuscript arrived later than intended, but Zondervan was geared up and had its teams in place to get the book to the printer on time. Once the editing was completed, it took only twenty-eight working days for the book to get to the printer. That was a record for a Zondervan hardcover book — and one that was more than three hundred pages long and had an intricate interior design to boot.

Warren had predicted that the book would create a lot of "buzz" and end up selling 10 million copies worldwide. He had told a Zondervan sales conference that summer that the "Purpose Driven" effort would be among the four largest movements in present-day Christendom. (He did not identify the other three.) Zondervan thought he was daydreaming. Who could have imagined, then, that even Warren's prediction fell short!

The book released on time in September. Small groups in more than 1,500 churches in all fifty states and nine other countries devoured it that fall (accounting for 475,000 copies), and more churches were signing up to use it the next spring. The book also sold well in stores. By January 2003, sales had reached a million copies and premiered at number 14 on the *New York Times* Hardcover Advice Best-Seller list. The next month it was on all kinds of lists: CBA, *Christian Retailing* magazine, and the *Wall Street Journal* Nonfiction, all #1; *Publishers Weekly* Religion, #1, and General Nonfiction, #7; the *New York*

The Most Ever

The question arises, is *The Purpose Driven Life* Zondervan's bestselling book ever (Bibles excluded)? *The Late Great Planet Earth* by Hal Lindsey sold somewhere between 30 and 35 million copies, according to various published sources, in the thirty years after it was released in 1970. But some 8 to 10 million of those were the Bantam paperback edition (since Zondervan at that time didn't have access to the general book market the way it did when *PDL* was published), and there were various other editions, including overseas, that added to the total. The total sales of all Zondervan editions stood at around 15 million in 2004. So *The Purpose Driven Life* does hold the record for total sales for a book bearing the Zondervan logo. And if it hasn't already passed Lindsey's book in total sales worldwide, it's only a matter of time until it does, even though we may never know precisely when the mark is reached.

Times, #2; and *USA Today*, for all books in print, #25. By May, sales were at 3 million; by November, six months later, 10 million. And by that time it had been on the *New York Times* list for forty-three consecutive weeks, including first place five times. It was the first book to sell a million copies through the Sam's Club discount outlet chain (eventually reaching 3 million), even outselling the sensational Harry Potter novels that were topping general fiction lists worldwide at that time. In September it had reached #8 in sales at *Amazon.com*, the top book-selling website. The book was named the ECPA's Charles "Kip" Jordon Book of the Year in 2003 and again in 2004.

There were also an audiobook from New Media and spinoff books and items from Inspirio, such as *The Purpose Driven Journal*, that became outstanding bestsellers.

In fifteen months the sales of *PDL* had reached more than 15 million copies (and the audiobook a noteworthy 230,000), and the number was approaching 20 million by mid-2004. (*PDL* represented about 7 percent of total book sales at Christian stores from March 2003 to February 2004, according to *CBA Marketplace*, [May 2004: 17]. Total sales of *PDL* for 2004 were even greater than for 2003.) No Christian book or other kind of nonfiction book had ever sold so many copies so fast. Not *The Prayer of Jabez* by Bruce Wilkinson (published by Multnomah), which reached 4 million in eleven months (by March 2001) and sold 8.5 million copies in 2001. Not even the first book in the popular "Left Behind" end-times fiction series (authored by Tim LaHaye and Jerry Jenkins and published by Tyndale).[28]

Total sales for *PDL* in its lifetime were approaching 30 million copies in late 2005. The book had stayed on *Publishers Weekly*'s list of Hardcover Bestsellers/Nonfiction titles for 144 weeks until it finally dropped off the top fifteen at the end of November 2005 (but returned to it at #12 on January 2). Also, in 2005 both *TIME* magazine and *U.S. News & World Report* called *PDL* "the bestselling hardcover book of all time" (not counting the Bible). Moreover, the latter also featured Warren as one of "America's Best Leaders" and had an article about him, "Preacher with a Purpose," in its issue of October 31, 2005.

Not to be lost amid all the excitement over *PDL* was the fact that sometime during 2004 the total sales of *The Purpose Driven Church* reached 1 million copies. The book was also judged one of the "hundred most influential books of the twentieth century."[29] In *Forbes* magazine, publisher Rich Karlgaard wrote a column entitled "Purpose Driven." In it he said,

> Most business books are big fat bores, except for those that are skinny bores.... Much better learning tools are novels, history books and biographies.... With that said, I give you the best book on entrepreneurship, business and investment that I've read in some time. It's not new and it's not a business book. It was written in 1995 and comes from the field of religion. It's titled *The Purpose Driven Church* and was penned by Rick Warren.... Were it a business, Saddleback would be compared with Dell, Google or Starbucks.

Karlgaard then listed some of the principles for effective churches gleaned from *PDC* that he felt would produce effective businesses as well, concluding with "Nothing should precede the purpose of your business. 'Plans, programs and personalities don't last,' says Warren. Only purpose lasts. It can heal your business, too."[30]

A question in many minds, including Zondervan's executives, was, when does the book lose its momentum and sales start slowing down? Some bookstores almost seemed to be tiring of having to feature *PDL* while many new titles were getting overlooked. But momentum still showed no signs of waning in mid-2004. (In September 2004, Lyn Cryderman, vice president and publisher of the book group, told the editorial staff that *PDL* sales were tapering off. Stan Gundry cracked that this meant the book was selling only 55,000 copies a week!) Many churches had enlisted for a new 40 Days of Purpose campaign in the fall. And stores began to realize that *PDL's* endurance was a blessing in that it had helped greatly in carrying them through the national economic slump the United States was only partway through when the book was released in 2002.

Zondervan has received many letters from readers telling how *PDL* has changed their lives. The news and broadcast media also have had many stories to tell. The Associated Press reported that a 40 Days of Purpose program conducted at a medium-security prison in Jamestown, California, had greatly reduced inmate violence. About a third of the prisoners participated in April 2003. In the year before the program, there had been five riots, 103 violent incidents, four staff assaults, 1,200 inmate disciplinary reports, and five lockdowns. In the year that followed, violent incidents dropped by a third, disciplinary reports declined 12 percent, and there was just one riot and lockdown.[31]

* * *

Still, no *PDL* story got more attention than an incident in Georgia that in fact led to another Zondervan book. In March 2005, a young widow and mother named Ashley Smith was held hostage in her apartment overnight by a man who was fleeing murder charges connected with the shooting of four people

Instant Success

Besides *Unlikely Angel*, Zondervan published several other books on a very fast track between 2004 and 2006. One was *Experiencing the Passion of Jesus* by Lee Strobel and Garry Poole. This book is a study guide geared to Mel Gibson's film *The Passion of the Christ*, which released to theaters in February 2004. The 96-page book went from manuscript to press in just two weeks. It was honored that summer with the ECPA's Jordon Book of the Year Award (the third year in a row Zondervan won the award). Another "instant" book was *Rick Warren's Bible Study Methods*, a new edition of a book that Warren had published with a different publisher early in his ministry, in 1981. This 272-page book was edited last December and went to the printer in early February.

Then, two years after writing *Experiencing the Passion of Jesus*, Strobel and Poole met another excellent opportunity to address popular culture. This time it was Ron Howard's film *The Da Vinci Code*, based on the bestselling novel by Dan Brown. Poole journeyed to London and Paris to shoot footage at sites mentioned in Brown's book, then wrote a group discussion guide (*Discussing the Da Vinci Code*), and a seeker-targeted book (*Exploring the Da Vinci Code*), and interviewed experts for a DVD curriculum — all aimed at tackling the key misconceptions about Christianity that *The Da Vinci Code* raises. Writing, editing, and filming were completed in less than three months this year, all to ensure that product would be available in advance of the film's theater release in May.

in an Atlanta courtroom. Keeping her cool, Ashley was able to talk frankly with Brian Nichols and gain his trust. At one point she read to him the first part of chapter 33 of *PDL*, and as the two of them talked about what she had read, he decided to turn himself in. He surrendered peacefully.

Within weeks of the incident, HarperCollins and Zondervan worked out a book deal with Ashley. They teamed her with writer Stacy Mattingly, who produced a moving account of Ashley's story, using interior dialogue mode, in just six weeks. The manuscript arrived at Zondervan just before the Fourth of July with the goal of having the book ready for press by the end of the month. (The book was copublished by Zondervan and Harper's William Morrow imprint, but Zondervan oversaw the editorial process and jacket design.) The book, entitled *Unlikely Angel: The Untold Story of the Atlanta Hostage Hero*, was released in September the same day that Ashley appeared on the television show *Oprah*. Unknown to Ashley, Oprah Winfrey had also invited Rick Warren, and the two met for the first time on TV. They also were interviewed together on ABC's *Good Morning America* program the next day. (*Unlikely Angel* debuted at number sixteen on the *New York Times* Nonfiction Best Seller list, behind — no surprise — *PDL* at number two.)

The book's release was carefully timed for *Oprah*, but the course of nature gave the event a different setting than expected. In late August, Hurricane Katrina devastated the Gulf Coast and the city of New Orleans in the worst natural disaster in U.S. history. People were preoccupied with and focused on relief efforts and saving lives. Yet the book in its own way offered a weary nation a different kind of relief — a message of hope and renewal in the midst of suffering and distress.

■ ■ ■

One last story is in order regarding the phenomenon of *The Purpose Driven Life*. While the book was gaining national attention, Rick and his wife, Kay, who had made several trips to Africa, became impassioned to confront poverty, the AIDS epidemic, and their tragic consequences on the continent. In 2003 they founded a nonprofit organization called PEACE (an acronym for "Plant and partner with churches, Equip leaders, Assist the poor, Care for the sick, Educate the next generation"). This ministry is centered on Rwanda but reaches into other countries as well. Rick and Kay are not doing this on their own; they have recruited other churches, as in Philadelphia, where they conducted a Stand for Africa Crusade in November 2005 following a citywide 40 Days of Purpose campaign.

PEACE drew attention and praise from national media, one example being *New York Times* columnist David Brooks, a Jew, who sees in the Warrens and other evangelicals like them a welcome resurgence of social responsibility accompanying their evangelism.[32] The initiative was also the cover story for the October 2005 issue of *Christianity Today*: "Purpose Driven in Rwanda: Rick Warren Has a Sweeping Plan to Defeat Poverty" by Timothy Morgan. And although it has not heretofore been mentioned in public, Zondervan, with the support of HarperCollins, contributed $2 million of its profits in 2003 to help PEACE get started. It was a poignant expression of both the company's mission and the striking opening line of *The Purpose Driven Life*: "It's not about you."

... *too different from other juveniles*
on the market to warrant its selling.
PUBLISHER'S LETTER REJECTING
AND TO THINK THAT I SAW IT ON MULBERRY STREET
BY DR. SEUSS, 1937

16

New Horizons

Zondervan has always been about books—but never just books. There used to be stores and music and radio stations. Bibles came in 1958 and, like books, have been an anchor for the publisher ever since. Today Zondervan also produces electronic media (CD-ROMs, audiobooks, videos and DVDs, multimedia curriculum) and gifts (including Bible covers, wall plaques, and cuddly teddy bears). And vegetables—well, sort of.

Larry the Cucumber and Bob the Tomato, the heroes of Phil Vischer's VeggieTales®, may well be the Christian equivalent of Mickey Mouse and Bugs Bunny. And while this sounds like kid stuff, Zondervan's relation to them characterizes some of the initiatives that have spawned new product groups and changed existing ones—initiatives such as promoting innovation, building partnerships, and entering the general marketplace.

One of the newer groups is Zonderkidz, the children's group founded in 1998. Like many other Christian publishers, Zondervan until then did just a smattering of children's books and Bibles (such as the very popular *Adventure Bible*) without a specific focus or imprint. Zonderkidz established itself in CBA quickly with *The Beginner's Bible* and the book *The Legend of the Candy Cane* (written by Lori Walburg, at the time an editor in the book

197

group) and launched a "Legends" series. In 1999 Zonderkidz acquired the Gold 'n' Honey imprint from Multnomah Press. In 2001 Zonderkidz teamed up with Vischer's Big Ideas Productions, a partnership that produces book tie-ins with the VeggieTales videos and *Jonah—A VeggieTales Movie*. (A million VeggieTales books were sold in the first eight months.) In 2003 Willow Creek Association became a partner with its Promiseland curriculum; it includes six different kits, aimed at different age groups and different times of year. A more recent partnership is the Faithgirlz!™ series by Nancy Rue, with the characters Lily and Sophie.

In forming Zonderkidz, the company was actually joining a trend. There occurred what Bruce Nuffer, associate publisher and executive editor of Zonderkidz, calls a "land rush," as various publishers established children's imprints and enlarged their editorial and marketing staffs. The result was that within five years the stores were overburdened, their children's shelves filled, mainly with picture books. Zonderkidz was looking to break out of the mold, both in the kinds of books it published and the markets they went into. One objective is to get books into the general marketplace—books that reflect biblical content and a Christian worldview, becoming dynamic but less didactic. Nuffer also notes that there are children's authors in the general marketplace who have not been able to be open about their Christian faith. Zondervan's initiatives and partnerships may change that. Still another goal is to publish for older kids, into the early teens. Both *The Edge Devotional Bible*, published in 2003 for "tweens" (ages eight to twelve), and the Illustrated Bible series have broken ground in that field.

A big moment for Zonderkidz came when Disney Productions announced it would release the motion picture *The Chronicles of Narnia: The Lion, the Witch and the Wardrobe* in December 2005. Because HarperCollins (general market) and Zondervan (CBA) hold the publishing rights for many of C. S. Lewis's works, including the Narnia series, it was only natural that they would be producing movie tie-ins, including the new editions of the Chronicles themselves, auxiliary books, study guides, and toys. The sense of anticipation was captured in the headline of a feature article in the *Grand Rapids Press*: "Narnia Is Nirvana for Zondervan."[33] The media were comparing the Narnia film and its side effects to the three Lord of the Rings motion pictures released from 2001 to 2003. The Lord of the Rings books by J. R. R. Tolkien were selling about a million copies a year before the movies came out; afterward, it was

20 million a year. It was expected the movie could boost the Narnia books to 60 million a year from its pre-movie 6 million a year. (When Zondervan began selling the Narnia books in Christian stores after HarperCollins obtained the publishing rights in 1999, their sales in those stores increased 300 percent, according to Kathy Needham, vice president of marketing for Inspirio.) And Disney has the movie rights for all seven Narnia books.

Some Zonderkidz ventures go beyond publishing. In 2001 and 2002 Zonderkidz joined with Project Angel Tree, a Christmastime campaign started by Prison Fellowship; together they provided gifts for nearly 70,000 children of prison inmates. In January 2004 Bob and Larry joined Donald Duck and some real-life celebrities—such as actress Whoopi Goldberg and First Lady (and former librarian) Laura Bush—to promote reading and literacy in a nationwide campaign called "Get Caught Reading." (About that same time, Big Idea declared bankruptcy and was sold to Classic Media, but Zonderkidz is able to continue publishing the VeggieTales books.)

Another fairly new product group is Inspirio. Several times in its history Zondervan has attempted to produce gift and specialty items. For instance, in the mid-eighties Zondervan Family Bookstores tried an unsuccessful venture named Harper's Fare. But it wasn't until 1992 that Zondervan found a way that worked. The idea that year was born in President Ryskamp. For some time Zondervan had been licensing rights to other companies to produce items such as Bible covers and devotional calendars. Ryskamp wondered why the company couldn't start making those things itself. Given that many of the products would be related to Bibles, Zondervan formed a Specialty Products Division within the Bible department, spearheaded by Doris Rikkers in the Bible department and Vice President of Production Caroline Blauwkamp. They spent a year gearing things up and then launched the first line of merchandise, about thirty products, in fall 1993. These included Bible covers, personal planners, perpetual calendars, miniature books, and block calendars.

The next year the specialty enterprise became a separate department, and at the beginning of 2001 it adopted the name "Inspirio," creating its own identity distinct from the book and Bible and software publishing. Its vision was to maximize Zondervan's assets and expand the reach of its authors through creative product development, often spun off from Zondervan books. A key factor was doing the right research to discover what people wanted and what they didn't. This selective process succeeded, as witnessed by the array of

Love Bears, Bible covers, home decor products, and inspirational booklets that have sold well, and continues to grow. In early 2006 Inspirio added a line of garden products that received a good reception. Inspirio products sell well not only in CBA stores, but in general outlets such as Wal-Mart, Kmart, and Sam's Club.

When Blauwkamp retired in August 2005 (having worked for no other company but Zondervan throughout her life), Valerie Buick (daughter-in-law of Zondervan's former president Jim Buick) became vice president of Inspirio. This year the gift book segment of Inspirio was moved to the Book Group.

■ ■ ■

As for partnerships, some of the most prolific for books, Bibles, and curriculum are the Willow Creek Association, Saddleback Church, the Christian Medical Society, and MOPS (Mothers of Preschoolers); for software there is Pradis. But the grandfather is Youth Specialties, whose partnership with Zondervan goes back thirty-six years, to 1970. This enterprise has spawned books and teaching tools for youth leaders and older teens and temporarily the *emergent* book imprint (which is now separate from YS). For five years Zondervan and YS also cosponsored the annual National Pastors Conference (originally begun by YS), which Zondervan now sponsors with the Leadership organization and InterVarsity Press. In April of 2006 the partners got married: Zondervan purchased Youth Specialties.

Other initiatives have changed how Zondervan gets its products into the hands of the people who read and use them. Today the products are sold in places that just a couple of decades ago, the company could only dream of. The brief honeymoon for "crossover" books in the seventies had long since faded. As Scott Bolinder, executive vice president and publisher, puts it, for a long time Christian publishing was virtually a "cottage industry," filling a vacuum in the Christian community. But that hole eventually was filling up. The challenge became to sell books and Bibles where they weren't sold before and to reach a broader spectrum of readers.

When HarperCollins purchased the company in 1988, everyone figured Zondervan's books would begin showing up in general bookstores in good numbers. It didn't happen. Harper's sales reps had their own books to sell, and for many of them, evangelical books were an unfamiliar genre. (The reverse was true also; Zondervan sales reps were not selling Harper books into CBA stores, even from its religious division, HarperSanFrancisco.) It was frustrating. Then, shortly after Ryskamp became CEO of Zondervan, the Leadership Team, at a retreat, decided it was time for Zondervan to assert itself and develop a strategy beyond "preaching to the choir." Despite many doubts, HarperCollins let Zondervan enter on its own the general stores affiliated with the American Booksellers Association. But the company didn't stop there. Led by Cris Doornbos, vice president of sales, Zondervan also moved into three more channels besides CBA and ABA. One was general merchandisers such as Sam's Club, Wal-Mart, and Cosco. The second was international sales, which had all been handled through Harper's branches—Harper Canada, Harper UK, Harper Australia, and Harper New Zealand. The third was what is today called Enhanced Publishing—providing customized editions of existing products for churches, parachurch ministries, or retail outlets such as Family Christian Stores or Sam's Club.

The idea was for Zondervan products to go where people shop. And the timing was perfect. Sales in CBA stores began leveling off in the early 1990s. At that time there were about 3,300 CBA stores; today there are about 2,200. In a changing culture, the monopoly that CBA once seemed to hold for evangelical book buyers had vanished. At this time, only 56 percent of Christian books and other materials are sold in Christian stores in the United States.[34] There is also less reliance on wholesale distributors such as Spring Arbor that had played a major role in the publisher-to-consumer process for several decades.

Sales Vice President Verne Kenney was a key figure in making Doornbos's idea work with general merchandisers. The initiative raised challenges internally because the general merchandisers wanted things done differently, such as different box sizes and different carton counts (that is, the number of books in a carton) from what the ABA and CBA stores required. But Zondervan came through. (When Doornbos left Zondervan in 2005 to become CEO at Cook Communications in Colorado Springs, Kenney was promoted to take his place.)

There is also a global challenge. The international Christian community is growing rapidly, and publishers must help the church outgrow American provincialism. Zondervan is meeting the challenge through international sales, working with English-speaking retailers in other countries and granting subrights to its Vida division and to many indigenous publishers overseas who translate products into their own languages.

By contrast, some new programs have been directed toward CBA retailers. One is the Core Inventory Initiative. Zondervan was the first in the industry to use technology to identify the key backlist titles not currently in stores and getting them back in. The core inventory is putting into one list the titles that account for 90 percent of Zondervan's unit sales and 90 percent of its revenue. This list has about 1,000 items out of the more than 3,000 currently in print. Along with that is the Core Replenishment Plan, a purchasing plan that offers stores various discount levels and other benefits depending on how well they maintain set in-stock rates on Zondervan titles. Retailers sign a one-year renewable contract with their Zondervan sales representative for this program.

■ ■ ■

Still other initiatives have had the effect that while people are buying more books than ever, fewer of them are being bought in bookstores. This holds true not just for Zondervan but for book publishing in general. A writer for the *New York Times* lamented that "the good news is that millions of consumers bought books last month. The bad news is that a lot of them skipped a trip to the bookstore, where they may have bought even more books."[35] In part this is because outlets like Wal-Mart can sell them cheaper; in part it is because communications technology has brought new ways for publishers to connect directly with the readers and to better understand them.

In 2005 Zondervan established the Office of the Consumer, headed by Tom Betts, to enhance this direct connection. This department absorbed existing programs such as Zondervan ChurchSource (direct marketing to church leaders and pastors), AuthorTracker, and Breakfast Club (an Internet-based reading club) and will include a major new web update when it is completed by the end of 2006. By the way, last year the Internet was expected to account for 20 percent of all book sales in the United States.[36] (Yet communications technology also helps bookstores. In 2001 Zondervan launched zBusiness, a full-service web catalog, an ordering and inventory management portal designed to serve retailers every hour of every day. The program hit a milestone in February 2004 when it produced $1 million in revenue within one month for the first time.)

On the other end of the publishing spectrum, Zondervan continues to serve its authors through its landmark initiative originally called Author Relations. When Carol Holquist left Zondervan to join another publisher in 1984, she was replaced by Joyce Ondersma, who later was joined by an assistant, Jackie Aldridge. The department today is called Author Care.

How does the wider market affect what Zondervan publishes? According to Bolinder, the big challenge today is having the courage to engage a broader vacuum, to confront an increasingly secular and pluralistic culture while staying true to the company's mission. Publishing that is not done by a nonprofit organization has to be viewed as a business opportunity, not just ministry. It takes discernment to manage the balance between ministry, integrity, and commercial success. And how is that done? By softening or manipulating the Christian message to make it more palatable — or by presenting well-argued, well-written books and other products that seek to transform people who are not imbedded in a Christian subculture? For Bolinder and Zondervan it is the latter, as represented, for example, in the engaging nonfiction by Philip Yancey (*What's So Amazing About Grace?*) and fiction by Walter Wangerin Jr. (*Jesus: The Novel*).

Moreover, a new vocabulary was developing in the late twentieth century. The term *postmodern*, which had been in academia and the general culture for several decades, finally made it into the Christian lexicon. With it came *emergent* — a new concept of the church trying to connect with the unchurched in new ways with the rest of the world. And *Generation X* — the young people in society. Zondervan has its share of books representing these cultural shifts, some of the most significant being *The Emerging Church* by Dan Kimball (2003), *A Generous Orthodoxy* by Brian McLaren (2004),[37] and *Velvet Elvis* by Rob Bell. A distinctive product is NOOMA®, a series of ten-to-fourteen minute DVDs that feature Rob Bell and that, like biblical parables, use experiences of life to teach spiritual truths and values for living.

Ironically, while *emergent* books and publications aimed at Generation X have drawn their share of attention and criticism (even in other Zondervan books), it was, in fact, a Zondervan Bible that stirred a national controversy.

■　■　■

New translations have been known to stir heated debate among evangelicals, but how often does it begin before a word of it is in print? This was the case with the TNIV—Today's New International Version. The furor began with a cover story in the March 29, 1997, issue of *World* magazine. The article, entitled "The Stealth Bible" (alternately entitled "The Feminist Seduction of the Evangelical Church: Femme Fatale") took Zondervan, the International Bible Society (IBS), and the latter's Committee for Bible Translation (CBT) to task for planning what *World* called a "gender-neutral" Bible. *World* saw this as a further sign of deterioration of evangelical integrity. And Zondervan, in *World's* view, had already shown its colors a year earlier by publishing a children's "gender-neutral" Bible, the New International Reader's Version (NIrV).

The firestorm led to a summit meeting in Colorado Springs—home of both IBS and some of the proposed translation's most vocal opponents. The meeting did not end the controversy, though it did soften the rhetoric a bit. The outcome? *World*, claiming victory, announced in its June 14 issue that Zondervan and IBS had abandoned their plans for the new translation. The problem was, they hadn't. Rather, they had declared that they would not replace the NIV; the NIV would remain, regardless of any new translation. And that had always been an option.

There are some great ironies here. One is that other translations from respected evangelical publishers (such as Tyndale House's New Living Translation) reflected the same approach to gender without arousing controversy. In fact, twelve of the twenty bestselling versions of the Bible were already gender neutral. Another is that some of the most outspoken opponents of the TNIV preferred the Revised Standard Version—a translation that evoked an outcry from many evangelicals when it appeared back in the 1950s. Also, the Evangelical Press Association rebuked *World* for using unethical journalistic practices in its reporting about the translation.

The whole idea of the TNIV is reflective of the history and motivation of the CBT from its beginning. From the time the NIV was introduced, the committee has met annually to review the translation, new scholarship, and archaeological findings. A major revision of the NIV came in 1984, and during the next two years there were many innovative editions, including an *NIV Thompson Chain Reference Bible*, *The NIV Study Bible*, and *The Student Bible*. Moreover, from the start, Zondervan published supportive academic books, including commentaries and concordances. About 1995, it became clear to the CBT that a major change in the translation was inevitable. Expressing gender was a big factor; the CBT saw that the translation must reflect the intention of the biblical writers and be inclusive where they were inclusive. Some church youth leaders and organizations found the NIV was outdated on that score and no longer wanted to use it. Teenagers had written many letters to Zondervan and the IBC about the NIV, asking, "Why does God care more for boys than for girls?" Many pastors were retranslating the NIV on the fly in their sermons to achieve gender accuracy. And the problem was not confined to North America; it also affected people who learned English as a second language. Indeed, the New International Version has always been truly "international," in both the makeup of the CBT and the diversity of the Bible's readers. And the English language was changing. The *Merriam-Webster's Collegiate Dictionary, Eleventh Edition*, published in 2003, contained 10,000 new words and had 100,000 changes in definitions compared with the tenth edition published ten years earlier.

The TNIV has been called "gender neutral," but the appropriate term is "gender accurate." Some languages, including Greek and Hebrew, are structured differently from English and do not handle gender vocabulary the same way. The original Scripture manuscripts use words that may appear on the surface to be masculine, but in meaning are more accurately translated to include both sexes. Moreover, the TNIV, like the NIV, continues to use male pronouns to refer to God in all three Persons — Father, Son, and Holy Spirit. It also seeks to maintain historical accuracy — for example, acknowledging that all the elders in the early church were men.

Zondervan introduced the TNIV New Testament in early 2002. By the time the complete Bible was released three years later, the controversy had died down. While in 2002 Zondervan had been receiving hundreds of negative emails a week, by 2005 there was an average of one a week. Moreover, Zondervan had a strategy for the launch that was unprecedented in Bible publishing. There were nine different editions, each aimed at eighteen- to thirty-four-year-olds, and including hardcover and leather bindings, men's and women's devotional editions, audio and electronic editions, and even a chronologically arranged edition called *The Story*. There were endorsements from leading evangelical figures, which defused much of the expected negative publicity. And many scholars quickly adopted the new version, uninfluenced by media reports of controversy.

In the end, it was an unexpected wrangle from a different segment of society that provided national marketing and media attention for the TNIV on a scale that Zondervan could have only dreamed of, even with its innovative marketing plan. For the launch, the Bible marketing team planned advertisements in media that connected with the young generation — places like *Modern Bride* magazine, MTV's website, AOL.com. The ads took a "soft" approach compared with many of the ads Zondervan had used over the years in promoting the NIV. Among the publications was *Rolling Stone* magazine, the icon of American society's counterculture. When the time came, however, the magazine refused to run the ad on the grounds that it was too "religious" for its market. This upset a Jewish reporter for the national daily newspaper *USA Today*, who promptly wrote a headline story about it. Being put in the spotlight, *Rolling Stone* began to feel pressure from both the left and the right, and in the end the magazine relented and published the ad. Paul Caminiti, vice president and publisher of Bibles, figures that Zondervan reaped a good $3 million worth of free publicity from the brouhaha. And probably to the

A Hip New Bible

An article by Laura Berman in the *Detroit News* on June 26, entitled "Zondervan Puts New Spin on an Old Favorite, the Bible," sums up the TNIV launch well: "At Zondervan, where the sacred and the salable meet in a way that's as old as the ancient hills — the drive is on to overcome the Bible's deficits. . . . The publishing house also illustrates the progressive face of modern Christian conservatism — the packaging is updated and contemporary, even if the message retains its eternal ring. Its hip new Bible, titled 'The Story,' is formatted to look more like a Tolkien epic than a traditional Bible, and organized to read more like a modern epic than an ancient religious text. . . . the size of a novel, printed with faux-gothic chapter headings and graphics, including maps of Israel designed to resemble maps of Middle-earth in 'The Hobbit.' . . . We may look East and West to see where American culture is going. But Zondervan's success . . . suggests the pulse is beating strong in the heartland too."

chagrin of the magazine's editors, it was not unusual in the weeks that followed for some young person to go into a store and ask for the "*Rolling Stone Bible.*"

Maybe *Rolling Stone* would have been more tolerant of *the street bible* by Rob Lacey. Published by Zondervan in the United Kingdom, this is a paraphrase of the Scriptures in a dialect that would probably make George Bernard Shaw apoplectic. Take, for example, the beginning of Matthew 5, a passage generally known as the Beatitudes. Lacey calls it "Who's Laughing?"

> Jesus sees how the troupe of groupies is growing, so he goes up the nearest hill and lets them follow. They listen in as he teaches his team:
>
> "I'll tell you who'll laugh last: the people who don't think too much of themselves, who *know* they're a mess — their ticket to heaven's already in the post (first class)."

Yet the book won the Christian Book of the Year Award at the Christian Booksellers Convention Ltd. in England in March 2004. It was afterward published in the United States as *The Word on the Street.*

Because the NIV is still the version most loved by millions of people, Zondervan's newest specialty Bible uses that instead of the TNIV. This is the *NIV Archaeological Study Bible*, one of the company's most ambitious projects for many years. Released in March 2006, this Bible has about 500 four-color photographs, many charts and maps, and 520 articles that deal with archaeological sites, cultural and historical insights, the reliability of biblical manuscripts, and more. It includes a CD-ROM containing the NIV text and all the photos, maps, and charts.

■ ■ ■

Producing four-color books such as that Bible had been, until recently, a sparse and sporadic enterprise for Zondervan. Many four-color books on the company's list were obtained from other publishers such as Lion Publishing in the United Kingdom. Today, however, technology and a changing world make manageable what once seemed almost impossible. In 2003 Zondervan published its first four-color college textbook, *A Survey of the New Testament*, *4th Edition*, by Robert H. Gundry. Two-color textbooks are also now part of the list, such as *Church History Volume One: From Christ to Pre-Reformation* by Everett Ferguson, published in 2005.

Textbooks, reference works, and Bible commentaries have been a mainstay at Zondervan almost from its beginning, but over the past two decades it has become the major publisher of Greek and Hebrew biblical language aids. For more than a half-century—starting in 1927, just a few years before Zondervan began—J. Gresham Machen's *New Testament Greek for Beginners* was the standard for people who wanted to learn New Testament Greek. Then, in 1993 Zondervan published *Basics of Biblical Greek* by William D. Mounce, a young college professor. Within three years it virtually displaced Machen's book and within ten years was selling 10,000 copies a year. Several things helped make this first-year Greek grammar so popular. It came with a workbook that got students into the Greek New Testament right from the very first lesson. Mounce was also at the front end of the software market by giving out free floppy disks that contained various Greek study aids. Moreover, the course was field-tested in various schools before it went into print. The course itself has some innovative ways to make it easier to master the Greek language.

In 2001 Zondervan published a corresponding course in biblical Hebrew by Gary D. Pratico and Miles V. Van Pelt, entitled *Basics of Biblical Hebrew*. It too came with a workbook, software study aids, field-testing, and innovative ways to approach the language. Along with these two beginning courses, Zondervan has continued to publish numerous other study materials for both biblical languages—second-year Greek and Hebrew courses, intermediate grammars, and various vocabulary building aids—under the guidance of Senior Editor-at-Large Verlyn Verbrugge.

A classic reference work, prized not so much by scholars and academicians as by the people in the pew, took on a new look in 2000 with the publication of the first revision of *Halley's Bible Handbook* in thirty-five years. With the approval and guidance of Henry H. Halley's great-granddaughter, Patricia Wicker, this twenty-fifth edition was revised by former Zondervan editor Ed van der Maas, includes new maps and photos, and uses the NIV instead of the King James Version. Yet the book also intentionally retains some of its original flavor both in its compact trim size and the interior design and type fonts. The older KJV edition remains in print. Moreover, a four-color edition is under way for publication in 2007. *Halley's* will very likely endure for many more generations to come.

■   ■   ▦

Still, the reality of publishing is that eventually even many good books will die. What happens when, say, the sales of a textbook taper off over the years so that while there is some demand, it's hardly enough to keep the book in print? Once again, technology has come to the rescue, creating "print on demand." With things digitized and computerized, it is now economically possible to publish books in quantities of as little as fifty or hundred copies and thus meet a special demand when a title might otherwise go OP—out of print.

Handling inventory is always a challenge for book publishers. How many copies do you keep in stock of a fast-selling title? When do you go back to press? Today a book can go back on press more quickly than ever before, and smaller print runs are more economical than they once were. If the aim, as Vice President Al Kerkstra, head of the distribution center, puts it, is to "engage the consumer," Zondervan is doing things right. The company declares titles OP with less frequency than before. Yet, even though the number of titles in print is greater than ever, they take up no more warehouse space than when there were fewer titles.

Interestingly, even with much better inventory control, Zondervan was running out of space in its distribution center, due to an increasing number of products from both old and new product groups. Several years ago Family Christian Stores gave back the space they were using and moved its warehousing offsite. And in 2004 Zondervan added a new "pod" (wing) to the building, providing 33,000 more square feet of warehouse space. This growth is understandable in light of the fact that in 1993 Zondervan sold 8 million units of product; in 1998 that figure doubled to 16 million; and in 2003 (with a big boost from *The Purpose Driven Life*), the number doubled again, to 32 million units.

The company is meeting its customers' demands. In 2005, CBA named Zondervan Supplier of the Year for the third consecutive year.

So Zondervan is meeting the challenges brought by more diverse markets and a more diverse audience. Publishing has changed. Yet there is a sense in which publishing is still the same, because, as Scott Bolinder puts it, "Content is everything. Publishing still consists of helping passionate authors relate their stories and ideas in such a way that readers are compelled to pick up a book and pass it on." What sustains a book after its initial release are the reader's feelings about it and his or her desire to tell others.

As Zondervan enters the fourth quarter of its first century, it expects to view even more new horizons. Some will result from a restructuring of the book and Bible publishing that occurred in the fall of 2005. These operations are now divided into Category Leadership Teams, each led by a triumvirate from editorial, marketing, and sales. These teams create interdepartmental dialogue and decision making farther front in the publishing process. The book teams, supervised by Lyn Cryderman, are Christian Living; Fiction/Inspirational; Children/Youth (Zonderkidz); Church, Academic, and Reference Resources; and Curriculum/Learning. The Bible teams, led by Paul Caminiti, serve different age groups: zero to fifteen, sixteen to thirty-four, and thirty-five and older.

Zondervan will also face these new horizons with new leadership at the top. On May 25, 2005, Bruce Ryskamp announced that he was stepping

Ahead of the Pack

When the Teamsters union threatened a strike against the United Parcel Service in August 1997, many companies began to panic, including book publishers. UPS is the largest package carrier apart from the U.S. Postal Service. Companies began to line up smaller carriers, most of whom were not equipped to handle the multiplied volume. Backups and delays were inevitable. HarperCollins turned toward smaller carriers and ordered Zondervan to do so. But Al Kerkstra had other ideas. He figured the strike would not last that long—UPS was too big a company to stay idle. So he suggested to President Ryskamp that Zondervan have the UPS management workers, who were not on strike, bring their trucks to Zondervan, fill them with book orders, and park them at the UPS warehouse. That way Zondervan's goods would be the first to get on the road when the strike was over. Ryskamp was skeptical, but liked the logic. He persuaded HarperCollins that this was a better course for Zondervan than approaching a smaller carrier. The strategy worked. The strike ended after sixteen days, and instead getting caught in the mammoth surge of backlog, Zondervan's products got into the stores as much as three weeks before other publishers' products.

down as president and had appointed Doug Lockhart, senior vice president of marketing, to fill the position. Ryskamp remained CEO until he retired at the end of September, when he turned those reins over to Lockhart as well. (Ryskamp continues to work with Zondervan and its parent company, serving as a special advisor to Jane Friedman, president and CEO of HarperCollins Publishers.)

As the head of all publishing marketing—books, Bibles, and Zonderkidz—Lockhart had already been a member of Zondervan's Leadership Team. Prior to coming to Zondervan in 2002 as vice president of marketing for Bibles, Lockhart was vice president of marketing for the children's division of McGraw-Hill Publishers; before that, he held various sales and marketing positions with Johnson & Johnson, a major pharmaceutical company. On becoming CEO, Lockhart stated, "Bruce's impact on this company and the industry will be felt for many years. I have big shoes to fill and will work every day to carry on the tradition of excellent leadership, vision, wisdom, and compassion Bruce embodies."

Lockhart and the Leadership Team held several meetings to discuss how Zondervan can best continue to achieve its mission and vision in the years ahead. In January he announced that he and the Leadership Team had identified six strategic growth initiatives:

- Maximize the current core business
- Focus on the consumer
- Expand global initiatives
- Build a vital events business
- Explore and secure acquisitions
- Expand online services

They also realigned some departments—"grouping together complementary disciplines"—to help achieve these goals and follow up on the founding of the Office of the Consumer and the Category Leadership Teams. Among the changes, New Media and Vida Miami Editorial were placed under Bolinder's supervision in Zondervan Editorial.

Zondervan will also view those new horizons with a new name. It sounds like an old name, but officially it is new. Pat and Bernie founded their company as Zondervan Publishing House. In the seventies, as a publicly owned company, it was known as The Zondervan Corporation. Under HarperCollins, it was once again Zondervan Publishing House.

After Bible sales leveled off in the late 1990s, Zondervan executives conducted what proved to be a landmark study. The study sought to learn what the name "Zondervan" means to people — its employees, its CBA customers, its authors and partners, and ultimately the end consumers who purchase their books, Bibles, and other products. What became evident is that Zondervan has a company culture and identity that surpasses many others in the industry. This is due in large part to the employees' embracing the company's mission and shared values. (The study showed that 30 percent of the employees can quote the mission statement exactly, and 66 percent of the rest come close.) This in turn led to the company's launching a new logo and "branding" initiative, highlighted by all the employees gathering at the Grand Center in downtown Grand Rapids in June 2001. Its parent company supported the initiative and gave Zondervan the opportunity to produce its own logo, a departure from years past when all its products featured the fire-water logo of HarperCollins. In developing a more focused identity, as then – Vice President of Corporate Communications Mark Rice put it, Zondervan seeks to be a "trustmark" to its retailers; that in turn will draw consumers. Rather than trying to be everything to everybody, the focus is on doing well what the company does best.

It does this as "Zondervan." Not Zondervan Publishing House or The Zondervan Corporation. The name is Zondervan. The name and the logo have changed, but the mission remains the same: "To be the leading Christian communications company, meeting the needs of people with resources that glorify Jesus Christ and promote biblical principles."

Afterword

As I looked out over the people facing me as I spoke during one of our monthly employee meetings, the thought struck me that more than half of those present had been with the company less than eight years. This meant that most of the employees had only a small glimpse of our company's rich history.

I decided then to prepare a historical overview of Zondervan and present it in a series of employee meetings. Little did I know that I would be the one who learned the most and discovered in new and fresh ways just how actively God had been involved every step of the way. Sometimes, during Zondervan's most difficult days, God seemed far away and silent, but now, as I studied the long history of Zondervan, I could see that God was not only present but actually carrying us through those valleys.

Zondervan's history enlightened me in another way: I could see that God chose, almost exclusively, ordinary people to accomplish extraordinary things. Zondervan moved forward and accomplished its mission only because people who were passionate and committed to the company's goals worked together.

As I looked over the list of names in that history, it became obvious that God knew our needs before we did and brought the right people to the organization at the right time.

During the past seventy-five years, the extended Zondervan family has grown from two people (Bernie and Pat Zondervan) to over four hundred; from a spare bedroom in a farmhouse to a modern facility of more than 380,000 square feet; from publishing one book a year to producing over five hundred new products every year; from being the smallest Christian publisher in the world to being one of the largest.

We will never know how many people are now in heaven because of a Zondervan book, Bible, piece of music, or inspirational gift product — at least not until we join Pat and Bernie and the hundreds of Zondervan employees who have gone before us. But if the customer letters we have received through the years are any indication, there will be thousands upon thousands of people praising God along with us — all of us touched by the work that the Zondervan brothers started seventy-five years ago.

It is my prayer that God will continue to use the people of Zondervan in even more powerful ways in the future as we work together to "meet the needs of people with resources that glorify Jesus Christ and promote biblical principles."

Praise God from whom all blessings flow.

BRUCE RYSKAMP
Former President
and CEO
Zondervan

Acknowledgments

This book has required the assistance and contributions of many people, including company executives and current and retired employees of Zondervan. Many have willingly offered their time and memorabilia to make this history as meaningful and informative as possible.

Since much of this book is a revision of the first edition, published in 1981, it is appropriate to recognize today some special people who made that book possible. Among them were the late Pat Zondervan and Wilma Zondervan Teggelaar, who knew the Zondervan story in a unique way and offered patient and invaluable help in this effort to tell it; Ted W. Engstrom, who as a former editor offered helpful research and assistance; and the late Gerard Terpstra, who as editor of the first edition proved the maxim that editor-friends who dare to write books definitely need editing.

For the Seventy-fifth Anniversary Edition of this book, I would like to thank Bob Hudson, friend and colleague and senior editor-at-large, who edited this book with the honing skills and gifted insight that have endeared him to so many of Zondervan's most valued authors; his work was indispensable in helping to make this book what it was intended to be. Thanks to Beth Shagene for her work in designing the book and laying out the elegant photo insert. I also thank Jean Graham, Melissa Monk, Elaina Morey, and especially Jackie Aldridge for their assistance in performing research that was essential to the completion of this book. I am grateful to Stan Gundry for sharing with me his personal journal regarding the book *Under Fire*. And I thank Bruce Ryskamp for his encouragement and confidence in inviting me to bring the Zondervan story up to date.

JAMES E. RUARK

Notes

1. *The Story of Grand Rapids*, edited by Z. Z. Lydens for the Grand Rapids Historical Commission (Grand Rapids, Mich.: Kregel, 1966), 7.

2. William C. Fletcher, *The Moderns: Molders of Contemporary Theology* (Grand Rapids, Mich.: Zondervan, 1962), 128.

3. John W. Peterson. *The Miracle Goes On* (Grand Rapids, Mich.: Zondervan, 1976), 73–75.

4. Ibid., 166.

5. Alice K. Montin, "Translator After Sixty-five," in *The Mature Years*, a magazine published by the Methodist Publishing House, 1964.

6. Jim Bishop, King Features Syndicate (August 1973).

7. J. D. Douglas, gen. ed., *The New International Dictionary of the Christian Church* (Grand Rapids, Mich.: Zondervan, 1974), 462.

8. William F. McDermott, "Book of a Lifetime," in *Christian Life* magazine (September 1960).

9. Dave Meade, "It's First Million for Rev. Halley," in the *Chicago Daily News* (May 20, 1960).

10. Peterson, *The Miracle Goes On*, 167.

11. Ibid., 170.

12. Paul E. Kauffman, *China Tomorrow* (Hong Kong: Asian Outreach, 1977).

13. "A Decade of Hardcover Bestsellers," in *Publishers Weekly* (February 22, 1980): 42.

14. Ray Walters, "Ten Years of Best Sellers," in the *New York Times Book Review* (December 30, 1979), 11.

15. Peterson, *The Miracle Goes On*, 193–94.

16. Douglas, *The New International Dictionary of the Christian Church*, 128.

17. *Publishers Weekly* (September 12, 1980).

18. "Our Response to the Pressures and Opportunities of the Eighties," guest editorial, *The Bookstore Journal* (September 1980): 33.

19. Connie Goddard, "Zondervan: Looking Ahead at 60," *Publishers Weekly* (15 March 1991): 33.

20. The *Grand Rapids Press* carried ongoing reports of these events, but this summary is largely based on an article by Jim Harger, business editor, published July 25, 1987.

21. "Zondervan Stockholder Accused of Insider Trading," *Grand Rapids Press* (2 October 1991).

22. Based on "A Brief History of the House of Harper," a special 1988 supplement to a company newsletter called *The House of Harper: A Bulletin of News and Information.*

23. Many of the details and quotes in this account come from the personal journal kept by Stan Gundry, which he generously made available to the author of *The House of Zondervan.*

24. The *New York Times* uncharacteristically marred its reputation for exactitude in journalism when, writing about the marketing strategies for *Under Fire,* it repeatedly referred to "Xondervan" (6 November 1991).

25. "What Do Ollie and Bombeck Have in Common?" *Publishers Weekly* (1 November 1991).

26. "Zondervan Teams Up to Tell North's Version of Iran-Contra Story," *Grand Rapids Press* (17 October 1991).

27. Rob Kirkbride, "Selling 'Purpose': Zondervan Relies on Churches to Help Promote Its Best-Seller," *Grand Rapids Press* (14 September 2003): E1.

28. Ibid. ECPA noted in its *Footprints Monday Rush Newsletter* of January 2, 2002, that the quickest-selling book before *Jabez* was *In the Kitchen with Rosie* by Rosie Dailey, who was at that time Oprah Winfrey's personal chef; the book sold 5.4 million copies in 1994. More trivia: The *New York Times* reported on July 18, 2005, that "Scholastic Inc. said yesterday that an estimated 6.9 million copies of *Harry Potter and the Half-Blood Prince* were sold in the United States in the first 24 hours the book was on sale, smashing the one-day sales record of 5 million set two years ago by the previous installment in the popular series" by J. K. Rowling (*www.nytimes.com/2005/07/18/books.html*).

29. See William J. Petersen and Randy Petersen, *100 Christian Books That Changed the Century* (Grand Rapids, Mich.: Revell, 2000).

30. Rich Karlgaard, "Purpose Driven," *Forbes* (16 February 2004).

31. Don Thompson, "Religious Study Cuts Prison Violence," Associated Press (13 May 2004).

32. David Brooks, "A Natural Alliance," *New York Times* (26 May 2005).

33. Rob Kirkbride, "Narnia Is Nirvana for Zondervan," *Grand Rapids Press*, Business Section (15 May 2005), E1.

34. Eric Grimm, "Changing Culture, Changing Stores?" *AspiringRetail*, the "Official Magazine of CBA" (January 2006).

35. David D. Kirkpatrick, "Book Buyers Stay Busy but Forsake Bookstores," *New York Times* (30 June 2003).

36. *Advertising Age* (11 July 2005): 6.

37. This book may have one of the longest subtitles since the eighteenth century, when unwieldy subtitles were fairly common on books published in America and Great Britain. McLaren's subtitle reads *Why I Am a Missional + Evangelical + Post/Protestant + Liberal/Conservative + Mystical/Poetic + Biblical + Charismatic/Contemplative + Fundamentalist/Calvinist + Anabaptist/Anglican + Methodist + Catholic + Green + Incarnational + Depressed-Yet-Hopeful + Emergent + Unfinished Christian.*

Index

A number followed by the letter *z* refers to a page in the photo section.

We want to hear from you. Please send your comments about this book to us in care of zreview@zondervan.com. Thank you.

ZONDERVAN®

GRAND RAPIDS, MICHIGAN 49530 USA

ZONDERVAN.COM/
AUTHORTRACKER